Power-Glide
Spanish Ultimate
Year 1

Power-Glide
FOREIGN LANGUAGE
COURSES

Power-Glide Spanish Ultimate Year 1
2005 Edition

Project Coordinator: James Blair

Development Manager: Dave Higginbotham

Editors: Heather Monson, C. Ray Graham, Richard Tice, Leticia Cabrera, Gustavo Cabrera

Editorial Assistants: Jocelyn Spencer Rhynard, Erik D. Holley, Julia Blair, Dell Blair, James Blair, Margaret Young, Ingrid Kellmer, Andy Bay, Ben Blair, Jennifer Rey, Raquel Lodeiro, Shauna Palmer, Gretchen Hilton, Emily Spackman

Translators: Robert Blair, Dell Blair, Raquel Decker

Voice Talent: Dell Blair, James Blair, Julia Blair, Robert Blair, Raquel Decker, Carlos Ramirez, Julio Salazar, Margaret Young

Layout & Design: Erik D. Holley

Illustrators: Heather Monson, Apryl Robertson

Story Writer: Heather Monson

Musicians: Paul Anderson, Marty Hughes, Scott Mills

Recording Engineers: Wade Chamberlain, Bruce Kirby, John Brady

© 1995-2003 Power-Glide. All rights reserved.
Printed in the United States of America
ISBN: 1-58204-247-0

Power-Glide Foreign Language Courses
1682 W 820 N, Provo, UT 84601

www.power-glide.com

Contents

Introduction 1

○ **Semester 1**   ○ **Module 1.1** **9**

    ○ **Section 1.1.1**   **Day One, 05:15 Hours** **11**
        ○ Activity 1   Mission to *Isla de Providencia* 14
        ○ Activity 2   Points, Lines, and Figures 17
        ○ Activity 3   More on Numbers 23
        ○ Activity 4   The Revolutionary DiglotWeave™ 26
        ○ Activity 5   DiglotWeave™: The Broken Window 29

    ○ **Section 1.1.2**   **Day One, 09:00 Hours** **37**
        ○ Activity 6   Getting Ready to Read Spanish 38
        ○ Activity 7   *El Alfabeto Romano* 40
        ○ Activity 8   Speed Learning: A Twenty Minute Workshop 42
        ○ Activity 9   Ditties 47
        ○ Activity 10   The Puzzle 50

    ○ **Section 1.1.3**   **Day One, 12:00 Hours** **63**
        ○ Activity 11   Reading the Puzzle Sentences 65
        ○ Activity 12   Stringing Together Your Own Narratives 67
        ○ Activity 13   Chatter at a Royal Ball 72
        ○ Activity 14   Toward Fluency 1 75
        ○ Activity 15   The Key to the Kingdom 79

○ **Module 1.2** **91**

    ○ **Section 1.2.1**   **Day One, 16:00 Hours** **93**
        ○ Activity 16   Self Quiz: Basic Expressions 95
        ○ Activity 17   More Points, Lines and Figures 98
        ○ Activity 18   Thinking *en Español* 104

    ○ **Section 1.2.2**   **Day Two, 08:00 Hours** **115**
        ○ Activity 19   Toward Fluency 2 116
        ○ Activity 20   More on Numbers 121
        ○ Activity 21   Demonstration Lecture 1 126

NOTE

To track your progress through the course, place a ✔ in the ○ after you complete a semester, module, section, or activity. As a general guide, semesters take approximately 3 1/2 months to complete, modules take approximately 1 month, and sections take approximately 1 week. These times are just estimates—you're welcome to learn at your own pace!

○   Activity 22   Stringing Together Your Own Narratives 127

○   **Section 1.2.3**   **Day Two, 14:00 Hours** **135**

○   Activity 23   Chatter at a Royal Ball 137

○   Activity 24   Observing Closely How Spanish Works 142

○   Activity 25   Focus on the Language 1-7 147

○   Activity 26   Questions in Spanish 153

○   **Module 1.3** **167**

○   **Section 1.3.1**   **Day Two, 18:00 Hours** **169**

○   Activity 27   Points, Lines, and Figures 171

○   Activity 28   Speed Learning: Five Mini-Dialogues 177

○   Activity 29   Body Parts 180

○   Activity 30   From Words to Discourse 183

○   Activity 31   A Lesson in Spanish 187

○   **Section 1.3.2**   **Day Three, 10:00 Hours** **193**

○   Activity 32   Chatter at a Royal Ball 194

○   Activity 33   Focus on the Language 8-10 199

○   Activity 34   Wrap-Up Activities 202

○   Activity 35   Toward Fluency 3 212

○   Activity 36   More on the Alphabet 217

○   Activity 37   A Geography Lesson 219

○   **Section 1.3.3**   **Day Three, 16:00 Hours** **225**

○   Activity 38   From Words to Discourse 227

○   Activity 39   Communication With Limited Means 231

○   Activity 40   Speed Learning and Self Quiz 235

○   Activity 41   Chatter at a Royal Ball 237

○   Activity 42   Observing Closely How Spanish Works 241

○   **Semester 2**   ○   **Module 2.1** **259**

○   **Section 2.1.1**   **Day Three, 23:30 Hours** **261**

○   Activity 43   DiglotWeave™: *Mi Primera Visita a México, Parte 1* 262

○   Activity 44   DiglotWeave™: *Mi Primera Visita a México, Parte 2* 264

○   Activity 45   Focus on the Language 11-12 269

○   Activity 46   Self Quiz 272

○   Activity 47   *Puntos, Líneas, y Figuras* 277

○   Activity 48   The Keys of Rome 283

○   **Section 2.1.2**   **Day Four, 10:00 Hours** **289**

○   Activity 49   *Una Lección de Geografía* 291

○   Activity 50   Spanish Ditties 293

○   Activity 51   *Una Lección de Español* 295

○   Activity 52   *A Continuación—Mi Primera Visita a México* 298

○   Activity 53   Culture, Adventure, and Numbers 304

○   Activity 54   A Joke in Spanish 307

○ **Module 2.2** **317**

   ○ **Section 2.2.1**   **Day Four, 14:00 Hours** **319**

      ○ Activity 55   Chatter at a Royal Ball 321

      ○ Activity 56   Focus on the Language 13-14 323

      ○ Activity 57   Wrap-Up Activities 325

      ○ Activity 58   Creating Your Own Mini-Story Plots 329

      ○ Activity 59   Focus on Action 335

      ○ Activity 60   A Mother Talks With Her Baby 340

      ○ Activity 61   Questions of a Child 343

   ○ **Section 2.2.2**   **Day Four, 19:00 Hours** **347**

      ○ Activity 62   About Verb Conjugation 350

      ○ Activity 63   Points, Lines, and Figures 353

      ○ Activity 64   A Spanish Lesson 358

      ○ Activity 65   Spanish Verbs 361

      ○ Activity 66   Familiar Words 364

      ○ Activity 67   Chatter at a Royal Ball 365

      ○ Activity 68   DiglotWeave™: An Incident in a Park, Part 1 ... 367

      ○ Activity 69   Chatter at a Royal Ball 369

      ○ Activity 70   A Geography Lesson 372

○ **Module 2.3** **383**

   ○ **Section 2.3.1**   **Day Five, 16:00 Hours** **385**

      ○ Activity 71   Retelling a DiglotWeave™: An Incident in a Park ... 388

      ○ Activity 72   Poems 393

      ○ Activity 73   Ditties 394

      ○ Activity 74   Focus on Action 396

      ○ Activity 75   A Spanish Lesson 400

      ○ Activity 76   A Mother Talks with Her Child 402

      ○ Activity 77   Irregular Verbs 405

   ○ **Section 2.3.2**   **Day Six, 11:30 Hours** **411**

      ○ Activity 78   A Spanish Lesson 413

      ○ Activity 79   Questions of a Child 416

      ○ Activity 80   Chatter at a Royal Ball 418

      ○ Activity 81   Verbs: *Saber* vs. *Conocer* 421

      ○ Activity 82   Wrap-Up Activities 423

      ○ Activity 83   A Surprising Discovery 427

      ○ Activity 84   What a Beautiful Sight! 429

      ○ Activity 85   Questions and Answers 431

   ○ **Section 2.3.3**   **Day Six, 17:00 Hours** **439**

Appendix A • Answers **451**

Appendix B • Scope and Sequence **467**

Appendix C • Index of Marginalia **475**

Introduction

Using This Course

Welcome to Power-Glide Foreign Language Courses! You hold in your hands a very powerful and effective language learning tool. Power-Glide courses are designed so that individual students working alone can use them just as well as students in traditional educational settings. However, before starting, we'd like to offer a few tips and explanations to help you get the most from your learning experience.

The course is divided into semesters, modules, sections, and activities. Each page has a tab denoting how it fits into the course structure, and students can use these tabs to navigate their way very precisely through the course.

Each semester has three modules. Each module has two or three sections, and each section begins with a page or two of adventure story, ends with a section quiz, and has several language activities in between.

Sections are followed by quizzes, and modules are followed by tests which we encourage students to use to solidify their mastery of the materials presented in the modules and sections. These quizzes and tests are very helpful for students seeking credit for their course work.

In this course, students will find a variety of different activities. These activities include DiglotWeave™ stories, counting and number activities, storytelling activities, activities designed to build conversational ability, audio-off activities for building reading comprehension, Spanish-only activities for building listening comprehension, and much more.

These different activity types accommodate different types of learning, and all are learner-tested and effective. Students will no doubt notice that each activity begins with a new picture. These pictures are drawn from Hispanic cultures and countries and are included for students' interest.

How to Use the Appendices

- Appendix A contains answers for different activities throughout the course. Answers to activity questions and exercises are provided for checking the student's own work. ***Answers to module tests and section quizzes are found on the last page of the book and are provided for grading purposes—the answer page may be removed if desired.***

- Appendix B contains the Scope and Sequence for this course. The Scope and Sequence document is particularly useful for students seeking credit, but it is a handy guide for everyone of what students can expect to learn from this course.

- Appendix C is an index of marginalia, or information found in the margins throughout the course. In an effort to squeeze even more fun, useful information into this course, we have included cultural information on different Spanish-speaking countries (one or two countries per module).

Students are encouraged to familiarize themselves with these appendices, as they can be valuable resources for finding information quickly.

Getting the Most Out of This Course

- Recognize the audio on and audio off symbols.
- Understand the text.
- Speak and write.

Audio Symbols

The audio-on and audio-off symbols, as mentioned previously, are highlighted bars like those below. Watch for them to know when to use your audio CDs.

When you see this bar, press play on your CD.

When you see this bar, press pause on your CD. Do not push stop. Pausing will allow you to continue the track where you left off, rather than at the beginning of the disc.

Understanding the Text

1. Look over the material and compare the Spanish to the English.

2. Listen to the audio tracks while following the written text.

3. Listen to the audio tracks a couple of times without looking at the written text.

4. Don't be shy. Use the pause button to stop the audio for a moment if you want more time to practice.

Speaking

1. Read the story or material out loud in chorus with the audio, and keep the meaning in mind.

2. Turn the audio off, read each sentence out loud in Spanish, and then look away and repeat the same sentence without looking. Think of the meaning.

3. Now cover up the spanish, look at the first English sentence, and try to say it in Spanish. Check to see if you did it right. Repeat this process for all the sentences in the activity.

4. Play the recording of the text, but pause the audio after each English sentence and say the Spanish yourself.

5. Using notes of key words only, try to say the Spanish sentences without using your activity book. It's okay to put the sentences into your own words, just keep them in Spanish as much as possible.

Writing

To write, just follow the same directions for speaking, but write your sentences instead of speaking them.

For additional information, activities, cultural information, and more, visit our website at <http://www.power-glide.com>.

Course Conventions

Objectives

Each activity has a shaded box letting learners know what they will learn during the activity.

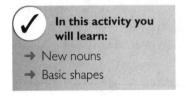

In this activity you will learn:
→ New nouns
→ Basic shapes

Sections also have objectives boxes. These section objectives are drawn from the activity objectives within the section. Appendix B contains a list of all the activity objectives for your convenience when reviewing for quizzes or tests.

Performance Challenges

Lesson suggestions and performance challenges help students, as well as parents or teachers, to fill out each lesson and reinforce its content. Performance challenges are a new feature designed to help students use and apply the words and concepts presented in different activities. Performance challenge boxes are located at the end of activities and look like this:

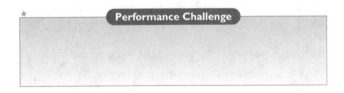

Performance Challenge

Not all activities have performance challenges, but students are encouraged to try the performance challenges that are included. All these features make this course enjoyable and accessible to everyone from brand-new students to experienced language learners.

Audio Indicators

Some portions of this course have corresponding audio. The shaded audio boxes at the beginning of sections and selected activities indicate which audio disc and track to use. The example audio box below indicates that disc 5, track 33 contains the audio for the given activity.

Disc **5**　Track **33**

Recall the audio symbols described earlier.

You will use these bars together with the shaded audio box.

Here is an example scenario for how to use all of the audio indicators:

- If an activity has audio, you will see the shaded audio box indicating which disc and track to use. In this example, we'll suppose that the audio box indicates disc 1, track 1.
- At the first audio-on bar you reach in the activity, insert audio disc 1 into you CD player and play track 1.
- When you reach the audio-off bar, press *pause*.
- The activity may or may not have more audio. If it does, you will see another audio-on bar. When you reach it, press *play*.
- When you reach another audio-off bar, press *pause* again.
- When you have finished your study session, press *stop* on your CD player.

Progression Tracking

The Table of Contents lists each semester, module, section, and activity in the course with a preceding checkmark circle. To track your progress through the course, place a ✓ in the ○ after you complete a semester, module, section, or activity. As a general guide, semesters take approximately 3 1/2 months to complete, modules take approximately 1 month, and sec-

tions take approximately 1 week. These times are just estimates—you're welcome to learn at your own pace!

How to Receive Credit

In order to provide as complete a foreign language experience as possible for our learners, Power-Glide enables learners to receive high school credit for their course work. For more information on how to receive credit, please visit our website at: <http://www.power-glide.com/credit>.

The Power-Glide Difference

Why Are Power-Glide Programs So Effective?

Power-Glide programs are effective because they are a blend of the best innovations based on up-to-date understanding of linguistics and learning psychology.

With few exceptions, language learning methods have not changed much in the past 50 years. What you typically find today are the old "listen-and-repeat" methods done with new technology: tapes, CDs, computers, etc., and packaged and worded to make them seem new. But they usually aren't new at all. They are the same old "uglies" of language learning repackaged to look new. The essence hasn't changed.

But occasionally a few creative geniuses have made breakthroughs in language learning. For example:

- Caleb Gattegno, 1960s, THE SILENT METHOD
- James Asher, 1960s, TOTAL PHYSICAL RESPONSE
- Dee Groberg, 1970s, MNEMONICS/ PHONETIC APPROXIMATION
- Tracy Terrell, 1980s, THE NATURAL APPROACH
- Robert Blair, 1990s, DIGLOTWEAVE™/ADVENTURES/ETC

Each breakthrough added something to language learning effectiveness, but each focused almost exclusively on its own approach. Then one linguist, Dr. Robert Blair, took the most revolutionary step of all.

He put the best of them together into a systematic learning process, added his own innovations, and tested and validated it with thousands of students. The result is now known as the POWER-GLIDE method.

Only once in a while do major breakthroughs in language learning occur. Power-Glide has made such a breakthrough. The creator of this methodology, Dr. Robert Blair, has studied virtually every type of language learning process around the world and has selected the very best ideas from among them. Thus Power-Glide programs do not limit themselves to one type of learning strategy but have the best of all worlds. Most developers of language training have one primary strategy that they use. It might be listening and repeating, or role playing, or mnemonics, or games, or DiglotWeave™ narratives, or any number of other approaches. While these methods might be good for certain situations, the Power-Glide programs use each strategy for its best application. Thus the overall learning is accelerated.

A Few of the Unique Features of Power-Glide

(And What They Mean To The Learner)

1. **Language specific.** Unlike most language training programs, Power-Glide courses are designed for speakers of specific languages, rather than the "one size fits all" approach. This takes advantage of what each language community knows and doesn't know, avoids wasted effort, and also allows special techniques to address language-specific problems.

2. **Based on up-to-date information/research on linguistics and learning methodology.** While the Power-Glide method is revolutionary, it is based on solid research and the most up-to-date information on the relevant disciplines.

3. **Involves learners in immediate use of the language in real situations.** Power-Glide courses avoid the drudgery of rote memorization of words and rules by immediately involving the learners in practical use of the language in real situations. This keeps interest, confidence, and motivation high.

4. **Uses adventure stories and activities.** From the beginning, the students are involved in an adventure story and activities that are like a fun game to them. Thus they enjoy their studies and are highly motivated to continue the learning.

5. **Uses multiple methods of learning: music, stories, activities, and more.** People have different learning styles. By using various methods, music, stories, etc., everyone's style will be included and interest and variety will be enhanced.

6. **Uses Diglot-Weave™.** Students start with familiar stories in their own language and gradually transition word by word, into the other language. The context provides the meaning and thus makes the learning an almost effortless, natural process.

7. **Takes learners from the known to the unknown along the easiest path.** While learning a foreign language can be challenging, it does not need to be brutal. The Power-Glide method guides the learners through the most productive and gentle paths.

8. **Uses memory devices and phonemic approximations.** Learning the right pronunciation and remembering the words and phrases of another language are greatly facilitated by using memory devises and acceptable approximations from the user's own language. This also reduces the "fear" of learning that many people experience.

9. **Starts with young children before their language "compartments" solidify.** While Power-Glide programs can be used by anyone at any age, it includes courses for young children whose minds are still open to learning a language as a native speaker. By doing so, the language will feel like skin rather than clothes.

10. **Doesn't require teachers.** One of the greatest advantages of Power-Glide courses is the fact that the teacher, parent, or facilitator doesn't need to know the language in order to assist the learner in the process. The one assisting also learns as an unexpected by-product of their helping.

11. **Uses tests and gives academic credit.** By working with school systems, many Power-Glide courses include academic tests which are recognized as, and can qualify for, school credit. This systematic testing also provides additional motivation and pacing.

12. **Many other innovative strategies.** Increases motivation, retention, joy of learning, and desire to use the target language.

What People Are Saying About Power-Glide

"Speaking and thinking spontaneously in a foreign language is challenging, but is an important goal that is hard to achieve with traditional programs. In Power-Glide courses, emphasis is not on mechanics and rote learning. This course aims to teach children in a manner that simulates natural language acquisition."
Stephanie Heese, reviewer, *The Review Corner*

"Thirty years ago, in Guatemala, I used Dr. Blair's materials and they were the best I had ever seen. Now that I could 'test' the materials with more than 40 students in various classes, I am even more convinced that they are the best language teaching materials in existence today."
Herbert Horne, linguist, former teacher for Wycliffe Bible Translators, and current homeschool co-op administrator.

"Most curriculum developers seem to have forgotten what it was like to sit endlessly in a classroom listening and pretending to be interested in boring subject material, but not Dr. Blair."
Susan Moore, reviewer, *Editor's Choice*

"As one who designs educational programs for individual students in our school, I must tell you how impressed I have been with the Power-Glide material. I was able to examine the second year course material for our community college. Your course is more comprehensive!"
Linda Rittner, Director, Pleasant Hill Academy

"Miles beyond the traditional text in creativity and interest level."
Cathy Duffy, author, *Christian Home Educators' Curriculum Manual*

"Power-Glide delivers what it promises. With this course you won't be intimidated to teach a foreign language. Every successful lesson learned will motivate you to move on to the next one."
Kathy von Duyke, editor, *KONOS Helps!*

"Unlike other higher-priced courses, the approach does not contain repetitive drills, is not strictly hearsay, and does not promise subliminal learning. It is fast-paced and takes full concentration. The use of the full-sized textbook included with the tapes makes it a more comprehensive course than others with twice the number of the tapes."
Anne Brodbeck, reviewer for Mary Pride's, *Practical Homeschooling*

"I really love the way that a concept is presented, used in various examples and then left for the student to take the next leap and apply key information in different ways. You can actually watch the light bulb flash brightly above your child's head! She gets it!"
Nancy Lande, author, *Homeschooling: A Patchwork of Days*

"I've been chipping away at Spanish for 20+ years and have purchased umpteen zillion programs. I was immediately impressed by how much conversational fluency I felt I gained in the two short hours of my flight home."
Cafi Cohen, author, *And What about College? How Homeschooling Leads to Admissions to the Best Colleges and Universities*

Semester I

QUEEN ELIZABETH ISLANDS
Greenland
(DENMARK)
Nuuk (Godthab)
Reykjavik
ICELAND
CANADA
ROCKY MOUNTAINS
UNITED STATES
Ottawa
Washington, D.C.
APPALACHIAN MOUNTAINS
NORTH ATLANTIC OCEAN
UNITED KINGDOM
Dublin
IRELAND
London
PORTUGAL
Lisbon
Madrid
SPAIN
Rabat
MOROCCO
Western Sahara
MAURITANIA
Nouakchott
MALI
Dakar
SENEGAL
Banjul
THE GAMBIA
Bissau
GUINEA-BISSAU
GUINEA
Conakry
Freetown
SIERRA LEONE
Monrovia
LIBERIA
Bamako
Ouagadougou
Accra
CAPE VERDE
Praia
Bermuda
THE BAHAMAS
Nassau
Havana
CUBA
MEXICO
Mexico
BELIZE
Belmopan
GUATEMALA
HONDURAS
Guatemala
San Salvador
EL SALVADOR
Tegucigalpa
NICARAGUA
Managua
San José
COSTA RICA
Panama
PANAMA
Clipperton Island
(FRANCE)
Kingston
Port-au-Prince
DOMINICAN REPUBLIC
Santo Domingo
Puerto Rico
Caracas
VENEZUELA
Georgetown
GUYANA
Paramaribo
SURINAME
Cayenne
French Guiana
(FRANCE)
Bogota
COLOMBIA
Quito
ECUADOR
ANDES
GALAPAGOS ISLANDS
(ECUADOR)
BRAZIL
PERU
Lima
La Paz
BOLIVIA
Brasília
PARAGUAY
Asunción
CHILE
Santiago
Buenos Aires
ARGENTINA
URUGUAY
Montevideo
SOUTH ATLANTIC OCEAN
St. Helena
(U.K.)
Falkland Islands
(Islas Malvinas)
(administered by U.K.,
claimed by ARGENTINA)
Stanley
South Georgia and the
South Sandwich Islands
(administered by U.K.,
claimed by ARGENTINA)
SOUTH ORKNEY ISLANDS
Equator

Module 1.1

Throughout this module we'll be learning about Spanish culture from all over the world.

Keep these tips in mind as you progress through this module:

1. Read instructions carefully.

2. Repeat aloud all the Spanish words you hear on the audio CDs.

3. Go at your own pace.

4. Have fun with the activities and practice your new language skills with others.

5. Record yourself speaking Spanish on tape so you can evaluate your own speaking progress.

Isla de
Providencia

Day One, 05:15 Hours

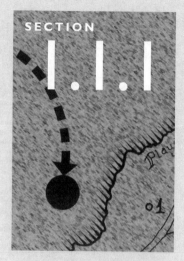

Ten Days to Rendezvous

It's just before dawn. You and your companion are intelligence officers assigned to parachute onto *Isla de Providencia*, a tiny island in the Western Caribbean. It has been seized by invaders from an unknown place of origin. Your mission is to discover why this tiny island was singled out for capture. What is there on the island that is of such value? A submarine is to pick you up in ten days at midnight at the north point of the island, where you will report to one Agent *Paloma*.

On *esta isla*, you are to be met by three agents, code-named *Chiquita*, *Rey*, and *Reina*. You were given the code name Rumplestiltskin, and your fellow officer the name Stumpelriltskin. The people of the island speak Spanish. You and your fellow officer, Stump, have never studied the language, but you know that English has taken hundreds of words from Spanish, like *amigo*, *macho*, *siesta*, *adiós*, and such. From just living in America, you've picked up phrases like *yo también* (me too), *más o menos* (more or less), *un poco* (a little), *(yo) no hablo español* (I don't speak Spanish), *¡perdón!* (pardon!), *sí señor* (yes sir), *no señora* (no ma'am), *¿qué pasó?* (what happened), *(yo) no comprendo* (I don't understand), *por favor* (please), *muchas gracias* (thanks a lot), *buenos días* (hello/good day), *hasta la vista* (so long).

You review these, working on saying them smoothly and rapidly: *yo también, más o menos, un poco, no hablo español, ¡perdón!, sí señor, no señora, ¿qué pasó?, no comprendo, por favor, muchas gracias, buenos días, hasta la vista.*

Just before departure you are given four new phrases and some pronunciation helps.

In this section you will:

→ Use words and phrases for introductions and greetings.

→ Use and say numbers 1-6.

→ Use geometrical shapes

→ Use and say numbers 10, 100, and 1000.

→ Learn what a Diglot-Weave™ is and how it works.

→ Read a DiglotWeave™ story.

 Disc 1   Track 1

English	Spanish	Pronunciation
1. You speak English?	*¿Usted habla inglés?*	*usted* avla inglace
2. What is this?	*¿Qué es esto?*	resembles "K. S. S-toe"

	English (cont.)	Spanish	Pronunciation
3.	I don't know.	*No sé.*	rhymes with *José*
4.	How does one say this?	*¿Cómo se dice esto?*	resembles *"Como say thee-say S-toe"*

You review these several times, working on saying them smoothly and rapidly: *¿Usted habla inglés? ¿Qué es esto? No sé. ¿Cómo se dice esto?* Remember, you can pause the audio as often as you like, to review.

You jump into the dark ahead of Stump and land just fifty yards off shore. You hide behind some rocks. Stump is nowhere to be seen. You wait for dawn, worried about him, hoping he landed nearby. As it begins to get light, you see a woman walking up the beach toward you. With her are two Russian wolfhounds. As she comes near, you take a chance. You step out of hiding and ask, «*Perdón, Señora, ¿Usted habla inglés?*» Startled, she hesitates but then answers, «*¿Inglés? No...español.... Yo hablo español y francés.*» Then she extends her hand and says, «*Buenos días, señor, yo soy la señora Quintana.*» Pointing to the dogs, she adds with a smile, «*Y éste es Rey...y ésa es Reina.*»

Recognizing the dogs' names as the code names *Rey* and *Reina*, you figure this lady is your contact. «*¿Chiquita?*» you ask. «*Sí, señor. Yo soy Chiquita. Y usted es el señor...*»

You give her your code name. She nods, then, looking up and down the beach, asks, «*¿Y el otro...Stumpelriltskin?*» You shake your head. She motions for you to follow: «*Por favor, señor, venga conmigo.*» You take it to mean, "Please, sir, come with me."

As you follow her up to her beach house, you reflect on her words *conmigo* "with me," *venga conmigo* "come with me," then on her words *yo hablo español* "I speak Spanish," contrasting it with *¿Usted habla español?* and *¿Usted habla inglés?* You deduce that "I speak English" would be *yo hablo inglés* and that "I am Spanish" would be *yo soy español*, but you're unsure how to pronounce *yo soy* American. You comment, «*Yo soy...American.*» She nods. «*Mmm, usted es americano. Sí, yo sé.*» Of course she knows.

You race through these expressions, playing with them, concentrating mainly on increasing fluency. You don't worry about memorizing the expressions; you just want to be familiar enough with them to say them easily.

- *Venga conmigo, señor.*
- *Por favor, venga conmigo.*
- *¿Usted es americano?*
- *Sí, yo soy americano.*
- *Yo no soy español.*
- *Yo hablo inglés.*
- *Yo no hablo español.*

- *Yo sé.*

- *Sí, yo sé.*

- *No, yo no sé.*

- *¿Usted habla inglés?*

- *No, yo no hablo inglés.*

- *Perdón, ¿Usted es Chiquita?*

- *Perdón, señor, no comprendo.*

- *¿Es usted Chiquita?*

- *O, sí, yo soy la señora Quintana, yo soy Chiquita Quintana.*

- *Y éste es Rey.*

- *Y ésa es Reina.*

- *Buenos días, señora Quintana.*

- *¿Habla usted inglés?*

- *Usted habla inglés un poco, ¿no?*

- *Rey y Reina, ¿qué pasó?*

As you finish practicing, you approach a small house whose whitewashed walls take on a pinkish glow in the light of the rising sun. To learn what adventure awaits you there, please proceed to Activity 1, "Mission to *Isla de Providencia.*"

ACTIVITY

In this activity you will:

→ Use words and phrases for introductions and greetings.

Disc **1**   Track **2**

Hispanic Culture Overview

Many Hispanic cultures share similar customs. In general, people in Hispanic cultures maintain less personal space than people in the United States. It is considered rude to eat while walking in public. Meals are family events and are not as rushed as they tend to be in the United States. People are generally considered more important than schedules, so punctuality is viewed differently in Hispanic cultures than it is in the United States. The Spanish language and the Roman Catholic religion are two of the oldest and most important cultural bonds in Hispanic cultures.

Mission to *Isla de Providencia*

Arriving at the door, *la señora Quintana* bids you enter: *«Por favor, pase.»* You bid her go ahead of you, saying, *«Señora, por favor, pase usted.»* She smiles and goes in, expressing thanks with *«Gracias, muchas gracias.»*

As you enter, you meet a gentleman who bids you welcome with *«Bienvenido.»*— sounds a bit like "B. M. B'Knee though"—and then introduces himself, *«Yo soy el señor Quintana, Gustavo Quintana.»* You ask him, *«Usted habla inglés?»* He replies, *«No, señor, pero usted habla español bien. Usted es americano, ¿no?»* Before you can respond, a girl comes in and speaks with the man and lady of the house. In a moment, they excuse themselves and leave. The girl introduces herself as *Mariela* and offers to help you. Together you work on pronunciation and spelling. You work on pronouncing fluently these new expressions. Again, you don't focus on memorization, just on listening and connecting the sounds with the right meanings.

English	Spanish
Yes, please.	*Sí, por favor.*
This is *Rey*; that is *Reina*.	*Este es Rey; ése es Reina.*
Go ahead.	*Pase. Pase usted.*
Thanks, sir.	*Gracias, señor.*
Welcome!	*¡Bienvenido!* ("B. M. B'Knee though")
Do you speak Spanish?	*¿Habla usted español?*
I am English.	*Yo soy inglés.* (or just: *Soy inglés.*)
I am not French.	*Yo no soy francés.*
You are American.	*Usted es americano.*
Are you American?	*¿Es usted americano?*
I am American.	*Yo soy americano.*
I speak English.	*Yo hablo inglés.* (or just: *Hablo inglés.*)

English *(cont.)*	Spanish
I am Spanish.	*Yo soy español.* (or just: *Soy español.*)
I speak English a little.	*Yo hablo un poco de inglés.*
Come with me.	*Venga conmigo.*
Mr. *Gustavo Quintana*	*El señor Gustavo Quintana*
And the other?	*¿Y el otro?*
I know.	*Yo sé.*
I don't know.	*Yo no sé.* (or just: *No sé.*)

Looking over your lists, you notice that when an accented letter is capitalized, the accent can be left off: for example, *éste / Este*.

You also review a list of your previously learned expressions.

English	Spanish
Me too.	*Yo también.*
more or less	*más o menos*
a bit, a little	*un poco*
Thanks much.	*Muchas gracias.*
I don't speak Spanish.	*No hablo español.*
Pardon.	*Perdón.*
Yes, sir.	*Sí, señor.*
How does one say…?	*¿Cómo se dice…?*
in English	*en inglés*
in Spanish	*en español*
What is this?	*¿Qué es esto?*
I don't understand.	*No entiendo.*
Good day.	*Buenos días.*
So long.	*Hasta la vista.*

Remember, you can turn off the audio and review as often as you need to. Now may be a good time to pause and review what you've learned so far. If you've been listening closely, you've probably mastered well over 30 Spanish words and expressions!

After practicing your pronunciation, cover the English column. How many of the Spanish words do you recognize? Don't get caught up trying to memorize the words. You will see them often throughout the course. As you see them used in different contexts, you will gradually acquire their meaning.

As you and Mariela sit, lacking words with which to communicate, you initiate some language exploration. Pointing to the door, you ask, *« ¿Qué es esto? »* She says what sounds like *« la puerta, »* and you relate it to the word port or sea port, a door to a country. She writes it, "the door = *la puerta*" and then asks, *« ¿Cómo se dice « la puerta » en inglés? »* You tell her. In a moment, you've each acquired several new words.

English	Spanish	
foot	*pie*	(sounds a bit like P.A.)
hand	*mano*	(related to manual, handbook)
head	*cabeza*	(not caboose-ah but cabase-ah)
mouth	*boca*	("Put a coca in your *boca*!")

While you're arranging these words into your memory storage, *la señora Quintana* comes in with a concerned look on her face. She looks at you and says something you don't understand about Stumpelriltskin. You guess she's made contact with him. She turns off the lights and points out the window, where you see figures carrying bright lights and shining them back and forth as they proceed slowly up the street.

It looks like the invaders are conducting an area search. You've had no time to explore the area or plan a defense. You need a place to hide. *Chiquita* shows you to a hidden room in the basement. She hands you a large notebook, a CD player, and several CDs. Then, motioning for you to keep still and keep quiet, she backs out of the room and closes the door behind her, leaving you alone in the darkness.

With nothing else to do but wait, you turn on your pocket flashlight and examine the notebook. It seems to be full of Spanish activities. You decide to try the first few while you wait for *Chiquita* to return. Remember to pause the audio any time you want to review!

Performance Challenge

How many greetings and introduction words can you say? Try to remember them without reading them out of the book.

Points, Lines, and Figures

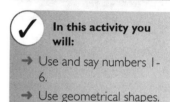

ACTIVITY

2

ACTIVITY 2

Puntos, Líneas, y Figuras

INSTRUCTIONS Listen and point to the words that correspond with the words you hear. Learn to comprehend, understand, and act on what is said.

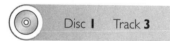

✓ **In this activity you will:**
→ Use and say numbers 1–6.
→ Use geometrical shapes.

◎ Disc **1** Track **3**

A. Scatter Chart

B. Look, Listen, and Read

INSTRUCTIONS Look at the figures in the left column, listen to the description, and read along in the right column.

Points, Lines, and Figures	Spanish
1. ●	*Un punto.*
2. ────	*Una línea.*
3. **1**	*Un número, el número uno.*
4. ●● ──	*Dos puntos y una línea.*

Facts and Figures on Spanish Speakers of the World

- There are over 340 million Spanish speakers in the world.
- In the United States, there are 14.5 million Spanish speakers.
- The greatest concentrations of Spanish speakers are found on the American continents.
- The Spanish language differs in different parts of the world. The Spanish spoken in Spain is called Castilian Spanish. That spoken in Latin America is known as American Spanish. In this course, we include pronunciations and vocabulary from both.

Points, Lines, and Figures (cont.)	Spanish
5. — — — ● ● 3	Tres líneas, dos puntos, y un número, el número tres.
6. 3 2 1 — —	Tres números; los números tres, dos, y uno; y dos líneas.
7. ● ● ● ● — — 2	Cuatro puntos, dos líneas, y un número, el número dos.
8. — — — 3 4	Tres líneas y dos números, los números tres y cuatro.
9. 1 2 3 4 5 ● ● ● ● ●	Cinco números; los números uno, dos, tres, cuatro, cinco; y cinco puntos.
10. ● ● ● ● ● — —	Cinco puntos y dos líneas.
11. — ● ● ● ● ● ●	Una línea y seis puntos.
12. 1 2 3 4 5 6	Seis números, los números uno, dos, tres, cuatro, cinco, y seis.

Study Spanish: Millions of Spanish Speakers

Spanish is the official language of Spain, Mexico, and several countries throughout Central America, South America, and the Caribbean. In addition, Spanish is the second most commonly spoken language in the United States. It is possible to find Spanish speakers in practically every country in the world. That adds up to a lot of people speaking Spanish!

C. Look and Listen

INSTRUCTIONS Look at the figures and listen to the descriptions.

Points, Lines, and Figures
1. ●
2. —
3. 1
4. ● ● —

Points, Lines, and Figures (cont.)

5. — — — ●●3

6. 321——

7. ●●●●——2

8. ———234

9. 12345●●●●●

10. ●●●●●——

11. —●●●●●●

12. 123456

D. Multiple-Choice Frames

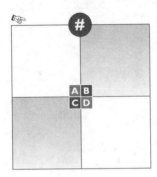

INSTRUCTIONS Following, you will see a series of frames, each with four sections. You'll hear the frame number and then a sentence referring to what is in one of the four sections. In the following pause, identify which section is referred to and listen for the answer. For each frame there will be three identification problems. Check the correct responses in Appendix A, on page 451.

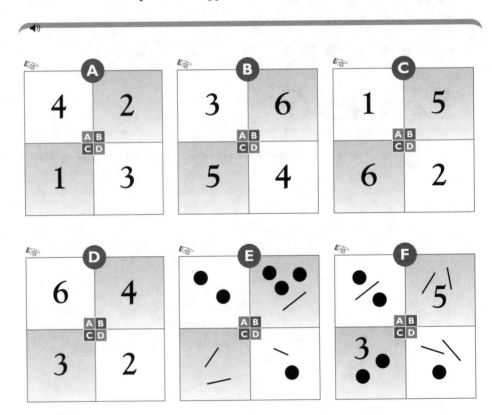

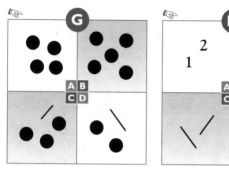

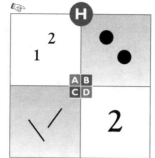

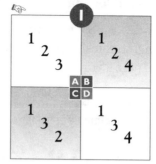

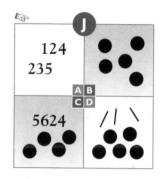

E. Listen and Draw

INSTRUCTIONS Listen and draw quickly what is described. Check your answers in Appendix A, on page 451.

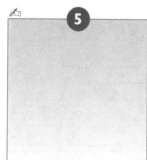

F. Read for Meaning

INSTRUCTIONS Read the Spanish phrases for comprehension. Then, write an English translation in the space provided. Check your answers in Appendix A, on page 451.

Spanish	English Translation
1. *Una línea y el número uno.*	....
2. *Un punto y el número cinco.*	....
3. *Dos números, los números tres y cuatro.*	....
4. *Seis puntos, tres líneas, y dos números; los números tres y uno.*	....

Performance Challenge

Use the numbers you have learned today to count different objects around your home.

More on Numbers

Más Acerca de los Números

INSTRUCTIONS   Listen to and read this exercise. With the help of memory aids, you will learn the pronunciation and usage of several Spanish numbers.

Ten / *Diez*

Using four letters—D, S, C, and N—you have the makings of the numbers ten and hundred. The Spanish word for 10, *diez* or *dec-* comes from Latin *dec* or *des-*, which we recognize in *dec*ade, *dec*imal, *dec*iliter, and other words having to do with the concept ten.

Listen to it: *diez*. One way to spell that would be the initials "D.S.," said rapidly. Repeat "D.S." Associate the meaning with ten. Say it as one syllable, accenting the "S": *diez*.

Hundred / *Cien*

The Spanish word for 100, *cien* or *cen-*, comes from the Latin *cent-*, which we recognize in *cen*tury, *cen*tennial, and other words having to do with the concept hundred.

Listen to it: *cien*. One way to spell that would be the initials "C.N." Repeat "C.N." (standing for *cen-*), associating it with the meaning hundred. So, with the four letters "D.S." and "C.N." (*diez* and *cien*), you have the pronunciation of *ten* and *hundred* in Spanish.

Thousand / *Mil*

Like *diez* and *cien*, the Spanish word for 1000 (*mil*) comes from Latin. We recognize it in words like *mil*l-levy, *mil*limeter, and *mil*lennium, all having to do with the concept *thousand*.

Listen to it: *mil*. It sounds more like *meal* than *mill*. You can associate it with its English sound-alike, as in corn*meal* (corn ground up into a thousand tiny grains). Repeat *mil*, associating it with its meaning *thousand*.

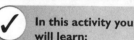

In this activity you will learn:
→ Use and say numbers 10, 100, and 1000.
→ Use geometrical shapes.

Disc 1   Track 4

Study Spanish: Traveling Throughout the World

Each Hispanic country holds fascinating history and culture just waiting to be discovered! You will be able to meet and become friends with people from other countries, an opportunity that is much more difficult without a common language.

Listen and repeat: 10; 100; 1000; 10,000; 100,000.

> **NOTE**
>
> Some English numbers change slightly in different combinations, for example, we say five but fifteen. The same happens with some Spanish numbers. In certain combinations the word for hundred is "C.N.-toe" (*ciento*). For example, 110 is not "C.N.D.S." (*cien-diez*), but "C.N.-toe D.S." (*ciento diez*), said rapidly in three syllables, not five.

Listen and repeat: 10; 1000; 110; 10,100; 10,010; 10,110; 100,000; 100,010; 100,100; 100,110; 110,110.

A short pause will be left for you to say each number before it is said on the CD. Ready? Say it: 1000; 100; 10; 110; 10,000; 100,000; 10,100; 10,110.

Review for production; the numbers: *seis, cinco, cuatro, tres, dos,* and *uno*.

You've already learned three of the seventeen elements of the Spanish numeric system: 10, 100, 1000. Say them.

Seis / Six

The Spanish word for 6 (*seis*), like our English word *six*, is related to Latin *seks* (as in *sextet*). Spanish dropped the "k" sound. Listen to it: *seis*. This independent form rhymes with *ace*, doesn't it? Listen: *seis*. Say *seis* a couple of times with the meaning in mind.

Cinco / Five

The Spanish word for 5 (*cinco*) and its alternate (*quin-*) is from Latin *quin-* (as in *quintuplets*). The first part of *cinco* reminds us of the English word *sink*. It will help you to see that a *sink* has *five* surfaces: four sides and a bottom! Listen: *cinco*. Say *cinco* a couple of times with the meaning in mind.

Now review in your mind these numbers: 6, 10, 5, 100, 6, 5, 10, 1000, 6, 5, 10.

Four / Cuatro

The Spanish word for 4 (*cuatro* or *cator-*, and also *cuar-*) is from Latin *quattuor*. English has it in *quart, quartet,* etc., all having to do with the concept *four*. The first part of *cuatro* rhymes with *squat*, as in "*squat* down on all fours." Listen: *cuatro*. Say *cuatro* a couple of times with the meaning in mind.

Review in your mind these numbers: 4, 5, 6, 10, 100, 1000.

Point to the number you hear: 4, 5, 10, 100, 1000, 6.

Two / Dos

The Spanish word for 2 is *dos*. It comes from Latin *duos*. It sounds much like a *dose* of medicine. *Two* spoonfuls make a *dose*. Listen: *dos*. Say *dos* a couple of times with its meaning in mind.

Three / Tres

The Spanish word for 3 is *tres*. It sounds much like *trace*, but rhymes more with *dress*. Think of *tracing* a number 3 on a *dress*. Listen: *tres*. Say *tres* a couple of times with its meaning in mind.

Point to the number you hear in cluster A, then in cluster B.

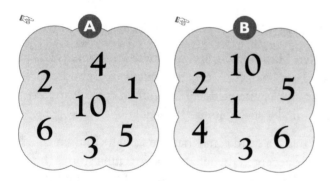

Review these numbers: 3, 6, 4, 2, 5, 1, 6, 3, 4, 10, 100, 1000.

ACTIVITY **4**

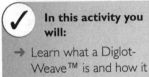

In this activity you will:

→ Learn what a Diglot-Weave™ is and how it works.

The Revolutionary DiglotWeave™

Study Spanish: A People Rich in Culture and Tradition

Remember that when you study a language, you also study the culture of those who speak it. You will find that traditions are very important in the Hispanic world. Many people still follow the traditions of their ancestors, whether they come from Spanish, Incan, Mayan, Aztec, or another descent. It is exciting to learn more about the food, clothing, music, literature, art, holidays, and many other cultural aspects of the Spanish-speaking people. You will be surprised about how much you can learn about your own native language and culture by studying another language and culture.

The DiglotWeave™ Explained

The DiglotWeave™, from the Greek *di*, meaning two, and *glot*, meaning language, is a breakthrough in language learning. This methodology smoothly weaves the new language into the learners' own, taking them from the familiar to the unfamiliar. Gradually moving from their own language to the target language quickly builds comprehension skills and increases confidence.

Story of DiglotWeave™ Narratives

Professor Rudy Lentulay of Bryn Mawr University was invited to teach a class in Russian for twenty minutes a day, two days a week, to kindergarten children. He hesitated to accept the invitation because he doubted children could learn any significant amount of language under such a limited schedule.

Professor Lentulay decided to make a word game that even small children could play out of learning Russian. He accepted the job. He made telling stories the focus of the course. Each week, he told a story with Russian words sprinkled sparsely, then more abundantly, each story using vocabulary employed in previous stories.

The children had to understand the words and their meanings through visual and verbal context. Once an expression started in circulation, the children were expected to use it in place of its English equivalent. The objective was to catch someone using an English word or phrase instead of the Russian equivalent. Before the end of the term, he was telling complete stories—even stories from Russian literature—entirely in Russian, and the six-year-old American children were understanding them.

Technology Behind The DiglotWeave™

You may recall stories written in a style that replaces words with pictures. A story written in this style is called a rebus. The Webster's Revised Unabridged Dictionary defines a rebus as "A mode of expressing words and phrases by pictures of objects whose names resemble those words, or the syllables of which they are composed." Rebus stories are effective for helping learners to think in the new language. DiglotWeave™ narratives build on the rebus methodology by introducing the actual foreign words into the story.

While it may seem at first to be simple random word replacement, the process is carefully and deliberately designed to lead the learner to an understanding of the foreign language. Power-Glide's development team may take hours or even days to compose a DiglotWeave™ that will effectively teach the learner how the language works naturally, in the same way you learned to speak English as a child.

Learners fit together unfamiliar words and phrases with those that are familiar like a puzzle. In this way, they begin to think in the foreign language by understanding the underlying rules for composing sentences. DiglotWeave™ narratives represent hours of meticulous crafting to bring foreign language learning to a more friendly level.

Philosophy of the DiglotWeave™

The concepts behind the DiglotWeave™ are simple, and we use them unknowingly in our own lives. Have you ever received an assignment at school that required you to learn new terminology? In this case, you learned a *foreign language* by trying to understand how the new terminology fit in with what you already knew. After time, you learned the new terminology and how to use it freely in communication.

As a child you learned to communicate with others by listening while they spoke their *foreign language*. You picked out some words you knew, but they were weaved-in with others you didn't know.

Perhaps you've observed that young children understand a great deal of what is said to them, but still struggle with some words. After time, however, children learn more and more how to speak—not just by repeating words but by creatively communicating. There's little more satisfying to a child than the exhilarating feeling of finally being understood.

When a child says, "I falled down," you understand right away that she needs milk, cookies, and a big hug. Her grammar may not have been perfect, but she was in fact communicating. Without expressly sitting down with her for a frank lecture about past, present, and future tense, she'll naturally learn through exposure to say "fell." A DiglotWeave™ is very much the same way; it teaches you the basics of communication in a very effective way.

DiglotWeave™ Example

INSTRUCTIONS   Read these three short sentences and try to interpret their meaning. Read them three times before continuing.

1. My *casa* has *dos ventanas*.

2. That's right.

3. My house *tiene* two windows.

What do the sentences say? Without formally explaining what *casa*, *dos*, *ventanas*, and *tiene* mean, you've been able to determine their meaning through putting the puzzle together yourself. This is the revolutionary effect of Power-Glide's DiglotWeave™.

DiglotWeave™: The Broken Window

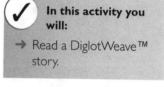

INSTRUCTIONS   Listen to and read the following story. You will acquire vocabulary through the story based in English that gradually adds Spanish words

✓ **In this activity you will:**

→ Read a DiglotWeave™ story.

Disc **I**   Track **5**

Study Spanish: Increase Your Opportunities

With so many different languages spoken throughout the world, speaking more than one language is increasingly important. The ability to speak Spanish will be a great asset as you seek different career opportunities, whether at home or abroad. Not only could you qualify as a translator or interpreter, but with so many Hispanics now living in the United States, Spanish speakers are needed in virtually every profession, from fast food to medicine.

The Broken Window—*La Ventana Rota*

A *Cuento* about a Smashed *Ventana*

Would you like me to tell you *un cuento*? Okay, let me tell you *un cuento* about some naughty *muchachos*—some *muchachos y* some *muchachas*— who were playing with a ball in *la calle* near *una casa*. In this *dibujo* you can see *la casa. Mi cuento* concerns *estos muchachos, la pelota* that they are playing with, *y una* glass *ventana* on *la segunda* story *de la casa.*

Besides being about some *muchachos* playing *pelota en la calle* near *una casa* with glass *ventanas*, this *cuento* is about *un hombre* who is *el* owner *de la casa*. This *hombre* is not out *en la calle* with *los muchachos*. No. He is *en* his *casa* when *el cuento* begins. I can tell you now, *el hombre en la casa* gets *muy enojado* at *los muchachos*.

Maybe I had better describe *el hombre* to you. You see, *el hombre es muy alto*. He is *tres* meters *alto* and weighs four hundred pounds. *El es un gigante, un gigante* like Goliath *en la Biblia*.

Here is *un dibujo* of *el gigante* who is *el* owner *de la casa*. Look at his *manos* and his *pies*, how *grandes* they are. Look at his *brazos* and his *piernas*, how *largos* they are. *Su cabeza* is as *grande* as a Texas watermelon. Look at *el gigante: su cara, su boca, su nariz*, how *grandes* they are.

In the beginning of *el cuento*, some little *muchachos* and *muchachas* are playing *pelota en la calle* near *esta casa*. Probably they shouldn't be playing *pelota en la calle* near *la casa*, but not all *muchachos* are aware of what can happen. As you might guess, one *de los muchachos* hits *la pelota*, and *la pelota* sails up high *en el aire*. *En este dibujo* you can see *la pelota* up in *el aire*. I think you know what's going to happen. But before continuing *mi cuento*, let me describe some of the features *de la casa*.

You can see them in *este dibujo*. *La casa tiene una puerta. Esta es la puerta*. Of course, almost every *casa tiene* at least *una puerta*. Have you ever seen *una casa* that didn't have *una puerta*? When you leave your *casa*, do you usually go out *la puerta*, or do you open *una ventana* and crawl out?

Back to some of the features *de la casa. La casa tiene un* roof, *un techo. Naturalmente el techo* is on top *de la casa. Este es el techo de la casa*. You might have *visto una casa* without *una puerta*, and you might have *visto una casa* without *una ventana*, but you *probablemente* haven't *visto una casa* without *un techo*.

What usually sticks up out of *un techo*? *Correcto, una chimenea*. Y, sure enough, sticking up out of *el techo de esta casa es una chimenea. Ésta es la chimenea*, and you see black *humo* billowing out of it. That's what *chimeneas* are for—to let *el humo* out into *el aire*. You wouldn't want your *casa* to fill up with *humo*, would you? The *humo* would *probablemente* choke you and would surely blacken the inside of *la casa*. Does *una chimenea* serve any other purpose than to let *el humo* out *de la casa* into *el aire*? Does it make *una casa* look pretty? Can you enter *una casa* through *la chimenea*?

What other things does *la casa tiene* besides *puertas, un techo, y una chimenea* sticking out of *el techo*? Well of course, *la casa tiene ventanas*. From what you can see *en este dibujo, la casa tiene dos ventanas* on *la segunda etapa*.

To review then, *esta casa tiene una puerta, un techo con una chimenea*, billowing out of which is black *humo, y naturalmente la casa tiene ventanas— dos ventanas* that you can *ver, dos ventanas* on *la segunda etapa*.

If you could look through *esta ventana*, you could *ver* something inside. You could *ver* that there is *un hombre* sitting at *la ventana*. And he's holding something *en sus manos*. It's a *libro*. He is reading *un libro*. Who is *este hombre*? *Él* is none other than the *dueño de la casa*, who plays a role *en el cuento*.

Other details we need to mention. Growing near *la casa* is *un árbol*. And hanging from a limb *del árbol* is an apple, *una manzana*. On the other side *de la calle* is a forest, *un bosque*. Now you know that danger lurks *en el bosque*, but sometimes *los muchachos* forget about danger.

Well now, what will happen? *¿Qué piensas tú? ¿Piensas que la pelota* breaks *la puerta?* No, *la pelota no rompe la puerta. ¿Piensas que la pelota* lands on *el techo?* No, *la pelota no aterriza en el techo. ¿Piensas que la pelota desciende* through *la chimenea?* No, *la pelota no desciende por la chimenea. ¿Piensas que la pelota* crashes through *la ventana? Exactamente eso es lo que pasa. La pelota* crashes *por la ventana* y hits the *gigante* right in his *nariz…ay ay.*

Now, *¿qué piensas que va a pasar? Piensas que los muchachos* will run away? *Piensas que el hombre, el dueño de la casa,* will punish them? *Piensas que los muchachos* will have to *pagar* the cost of *la ventana?*

Escucha bien to the *continuación del cuento.*

When *la pelota* breaks *la ventana* y smacks the *gigante* on his *nariz, él* jumps up y looks out *la ventana. Él ve a los muchachos. O él is enojado, muy enojado.* Why? *¿Por qué is el hombre enojado?* Well, wouldn't *tú* be *enojado if unos muchachos* threw *una pelota* y broke *la ventana de* your *casa? Y si la pelota* smacked you right on your *nariz?*

So *¿qué pasa* after that? *Piensas que el gigante* jumps out *de la ventana* y pursues— *persigue*—the naughty *muchachos? Piensas que el gigante* climbs up *la chimenea* onto *el techo* y then jumps off? *Bueno,* what does *el hombre* really do?

Él throws *la pelota* back out *de la ventana* y calls out gruffly, *«¡Muchachos!» ¿Y qué piensas que los muchachos* do? *¿Piensas que* they pick up *la pelota* y go knock *a la puerta de la casa* y apologize *al dueño? ¿O piensas que ellos* leave *la pelota* behind y run away? *Exactamente eso es lo que hacen. Ellos* start to run up *la calle. ¿Por qué?* They are afraid. *Ellos tienen miedo* that the *gigante* will catch them. *Ellos tienen miedo que* they will be punished. *Ellos tienen miedo que* they'll have to *pagar el costo de la ventana rota. ¿No piensas tú que el hombre* has a right to punish the *muchachos? ¿No piensas tú que él tiene* the right to make them *pagar por la ventana rota?*

Bueno, to *continuar el cuento.* As *los muchachos corren* up *la calle* (the highway), *ellos* see a lady, *una mujer,* coming toward them. *La mujer ve a los muchachos* go *corriendo* up *la calle.* She calls out to them. *«¡Muchachos!* Wait. *¡Espérense!» Qué piensas que la mujer* wants to do?

Spanish Names

Many names in Spanish are similar to common names in English. In the next section, you'll find short lists of common Spanish names and their English equivalents. (watch for more examples of Spanish names as you work your way through this course.) Many names are spelled the same in both languages, and just pronounced differently.

Now look at the woods. A close look will reveal something sticking out from under *un árbol*. There's an arrow—*una flecha*—pointing to it. *Mira. He aquí la flecha.* What could *la flecha* be pointing to? Could it be a tail? Yes, it could be pointing to *una cola*. Could it be *la cola de un lobo*? A big bad *lobo*? *¿Piensas tú que la flecha indica la cola de un lobo?* Perhaps a ferocious wolf, *un feroz lobo* is hiding under *un árbol* there *en el bosque*.

Are you afraid *que el feroz lobo* is going to eat *los niños? Escucha* closely as *mi cuento* unfolds, *y tú* will find out what *pasa.* After *el gigante* calls out, *« ¡Muchachos! » los muchachos* don't stop. *Ellos* run off into *el bosque. Ellos* are more afraid *del hombre, del gigante,* than they are *del feroz lobo.* Just as *ellos* enter *en el bosque, ellos* see something hiding behind *un árbol.* Could it be *el feroz lobo?* Or is it only *Bobi, un* big dog, *un gran perro* that loves to play *en el bosque con los muchachos?*

It *no es Bobi.* It *es el feroz lobo. Y el lobo es muy* hungry. Just as *el lobo* charges, *los muchachos* catch sight of *el gran perro que* likes to play *en el bosque con los muchachos.* *« ¡Bobi! ¡Bobi! »* cry *los muchachos. Bobi* comes running, chases *el feroz lobo, y* saves *los muchachos. Bobi es un héroe. Los muchachos* run out *del bosque. Ellos* go back to *la casa,* knock *a la puerta, y* offer to *pagar por la ventana rota.*

Now *el hombre no* is angry, *no está enojado. Él dice a los muchachos,* "That's all right. *La ventana rota no importa.* I'm just happy *que el lobo* did not eat you."

You have completed all the activities for

**Section 1.1.1
Day One, 05:15 Hours**

and are now ready to take the section quiz. Before continuing, be sure you have learned the objectives for each activity in this section.

Section Quiz

INSTRUCTIONS Choose the pictograph representation that matches the Spanish phrase. Check your answers on the "Grading Sheet" found on the last page of the book.

1. *Un número, el número uno.*

    A. **3**

    B. **1**

    C. ——

    D. ●

2. *Tres líneas.*

    A. **3 3 3**

    B. —— —— ——

    C. ● ● ●

    D. **4** ●

3. Cinco puntos y dos líneas.

    A. ● ● ● ● ● — —

    B. ● ● ● ● — — —

    C. — — — — ● ●

    D. — ● ● ● ● ●

4. Tres líneas y dos números, los números tres y cuatro.

    A. **3 2 3 4**

    B. — — — ● ●

    C. — — — **3 4**

    D. **3 4** ● ● ●

5. Tres números; los números tres, dos, y uno; y dos líneas.

    A. **3 — 3 2 1**

    B. — — **3 3**

    C. **3 2 1 — —**

    D. ● ● ● **— 1**

INSTRUCTIONS   Read the following problem and do the math to find the answer.

6. **dos + cuatro =**

    A. seis

    B. ocho

    C. cuatro

    D. quince

7. **dos + tres + cinco =**

 A. *ocho*

 B. *quince*

 C. *cuatro*

 D. *diez*

8. **cinco x dos =**

 A. *cuatro*

 B. *ocho*

 C. *diez*

 D. *quince*

9. **cinco x diez x dos =**

 A. *ocho*

 B. *cien*

 C. *mil*

 D. *quince*

INSTRUCTIONS Choose the best answer to the following question.

10. **In *el cuento* about the smashed *ventana*, *¿quién* lives in *la casa?***

 A. *unos muchachos*

 B. *unas muchachas*

 C. *un hombre muy alto, un gigante*

 D. *Bobi, el perro grande*

Isla de Providencia

Day One, 09:00 Hours

Nine Days to Rendezvous

You've finished several activities. Already, your knowledge of the language is growing, as is your confidence in using the language. As you hold the book closer to the dim flashlight, a scrap of paper slips from between two pages and drifts to the floor. You pick it up. It's some sort of note. You read it:

"Hidden on *esta isla* is a treasure of great value, one that may give the finder tremendous wealth. The invaders seek this treasure to steal it. They do not know the treasure's location, nor are they even certain of what it is. Since knowledge of its location is tied closely to an understanding of the Spanish language and culture, chances are excellent that they will never find it. Hidden in this room is *un mapa* that will help you in your search for the treasure, *el tesoro*. To learn the location of *el mapa*, you must complete the next six activities."

You grin broadly and jump to your feet in excitement. Right here, among your Spanish activities, is the first clue you need to proceed with your adventure. You pause, put your ear to the door, and listen carefully. As far as you can tell, there's no one anywhere nearby. You're a bit sorry to start the assigned mission without Stump, but there's no telling when or if he'll catch up with you. You decide you'd better start work on the activities that will lead you to the map. Since you will need to prove your ability to use the language many times before you find the treasure, you may choose to review as often as you feel is necessary.

In this section you will:

→ Pronounce Spanish vowels correctly.

→ Recognize words that are familiar to you as you read.

→ Use words and phrases to find out information.

→ Learn vocabulary through rhythm and cadence.

→ Identify word breaks in Spanish.

Disc **1** Track **6**

ACTIVITY

6

Getting Ready to Read Spanish

INSTRUCTIONS Learn the pronunciation and meaning of the following words. You can guess the approximate pronunciation of most letters, but you might not guess that "h" is always silent ("hotel" is /otel/), that the letters "z" and "s" both make the same sound, and the letters "b" and "v" also make the same sound.

✓ **In this activity you will:**

→ Pronounce Spanish vowels correctly.

◎ Disc **1** Track **7**

The Correspondence of Letter to Sound

INSTRUCTIONS Look at the chart below, then listen to a reading of the Spanish column. Read carefully then listen to the reading of the third column.

Letter	English	Spanish	Meaning
a	ah	*mamá*	mother
ai, ay	eye, sigh, guy	*caites*	sandals
ae	ah-EH	*maestro*	master
alle	AH-yey	*calle*	street
e	eh	*José*	Jose
ei, ey	eight, lay	*ley*	law
i, y	Mimi	*Mimi, y*	Mimi, and
ya, ia	yacht	*ya, fiasco*	already, fiasco
ye, ie	yes	*Yermo, bien*	(place name), well
yo, io	yo-yo	*yo, piojo*	I, louse
o	Lola	*Lola*	Lola
oy, oi	boy, voice	*hoy*	today
u	Lulu	*ruta*	route
uy, ui	phooey	*muy*	very

Spanish Girls' Names

Choose a name from the list to be your Spanish name as you work through the course. If there isn't a name that matches yours, choose one that you like.

English	Spanish
Alicia, Alice	*Alicia*
Anita	*Anita*
Anna	*Ana*
Barbara	*Bárbara*
Carmen	*Carmen*
Caroline	*Carolina*
Catherine, Kathryn	*Catalina*
Claudia	*Claudia*
Christina, Kristen	*Cristina*
Ellen	*Elena*
Lisa	*Elisa*
Lucy	*Lucía*
Margaret	*Margarita*
Mary	*María*
Martha	*Marta*
Sarah	*Sara*
Theresa	*Teresa*

Letter (cont.)	English	Spanish	Meaning
uo	quota	*cuota*	quota
ue	way (clipped)	*bueno*	good
uey	way	*buey*	ox
ua	squash	*guapo*	handsome
uay	"Y," Wye	*Guaymas*	(place name)
z	s as in Sony	*zona*	zone
j	hoe (scraped H)	*ojo*	eye
g (before i, e)	(same as j)	*gente*	people
g (elsewhere)	g	*garganta*	throat

☆

Performance Challenge

Notice the differences between English and Spanish, like the silent "h" and the vowel pronunciation. Listen to the audio several times to become familiar with pronunciation before moving on.

ACTIVITY 6

Spanish Boys' Names

Choose a name from the list to be your Spanish name as you work through the course. If there isn't a name that matches yours, choose one that you like.

English	Spanish
Alexander	*Alejandro*
Anthony	*Antonio*
Carl	*Carlos*
Daniel	*Daniel*
Steven	*Esteban*
Phillip	*Felipe*
James	*Jaime*
George	*Jorge*
Joseph	*José (Pepe)*
Joshua	*Josué*
John	*Juan*
Michael	*Miguel*
Paul	*Pablo*
Peter	*Pedro*
Richard	*Ricardo*
Robert	*Roberto*
Thomas	*Tomás*

In this activity you will:

→ Recognize words that are familiar to you as you read.

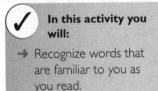

Disc **1** Tracks **8**

Spanish Family Names: *Los Apellidos*

If you have friends or neighbors who are native Spanish speakers, you might have noticed that they usually have two last names, or two *apellidos*.

Example: *Jorge García Sanchez*

Most Hispanics carry on the tradition of keeping the first surname of both the mother and the father. (Note: the family name used to identify the person is the father's last name.)

Example: *Jorge García Sanchez* and *Ana Pérez Arroyo* are married. They name their child *Juan*. He will take the first last name of both his father and mother. His name will be *Juan García Pérez*.

The name by which the family is identified is the father's last name.

If you followed this tradition, what would your last name be? Hint: Your last name goes first, and then your mother's maiden name.

El Alfabeto Romano

The Roman Alphabet

INSTRUCTIONS   Listen to and read the following story. Use this exercise to make sense of spoken and written Spanish. A major step in the learning process of children is to understand the main idea of what they hear or read. Don't worry about understanding every detail; it's more important to understand the main idea.

Existen varios alfabetos: el alfabeto romano, el alfabeto ruso, el alfabeto griego, etcétera.

El alfabeto romano es la lista de letras de español, italiano, inglés, y otras lenguas de Europa, Norte América, y Sudamérica.

El alfabeto romano no es el alfabeto del árabe, ni del hebreo, ni del ruso, ni del griego.

El árabe, el hebreo, el ruso, y el griego tienen su propio sistema de escribir y no usan el alfabeto romano.

Las letras de un alfabeto representan los sonidos de un idioma.

Las letras del alfabeto español representan los sonidos del español.

Las letras del alfabeto italiano representan los sonidos del italiano.

Las letras del alfabeto inglés representan los sonidos del inglés.

El alfabeto de inglés tiene veintiséis (26) letras.

El alfabeto de español tiene veintinueve (29) letras, tres letras más que el alfabeto inglés.

Las tres letras de español que no ocurren en inglés son ñ, rr, y ll.

(La doble-<r> y la doble-<v> son letras, así como la <r> y la <l>.)

El español tiene veinticuatro consonantes y cinco vocales. El inglés tiene veintiún consonantes y cinco vocales.

Entre todas las letras del alfabeto español, cinco son vocales y las otras veinticuatro son consonantes.

El punto (.) y la coma (,) no son letras sino signos de puntuación. El signo de interrogación (?) también es un signo de puntuación: el signo de interrogación.

En el español (como también en el inglés) hay, como ya dije, cinco vocales principales: A E I O U.

La vocal <O> ocurre una vez en NO y dos veces en MONO.

La vocal <A> ocurre una vez en LA, dos veces en CASA, y tres veces en PALABRA.

Estas cinco vocales también son las vocales del inglés: A E I O U, pero en español los nombres de estas letras se pronuncian A E I O U:

- A como en MAMA
- E como en META
- I como en MIMI
- O como en MOLE
- U como en LULU

Repita los nombres de las cinco vocales: A E I O U. Repita otra vez: A E I O U.

ACTIVITY

8

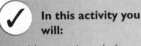

✓ **In this activity you will:**

→ Use words and phrases to find out information.

 Disc **1** Track **9, 10**

Origins of Spanish

Did you know that Spanish is one of the five official languages of the United Nations and that over 340 million people in the world speak it today? Originally, Spanish was a dialect of Latin. It was first recognized as a language in its own right about 700 years ago. Spanish is spoken in Spain (where it originated), in 19 Latin American countries, and in parts of Africa, the Caribbean, and the Philippines. It is also spoken in the United States, where about one out of every ten residents speaks Spanish.

Speed Learning: A Twenty Minute Workshop

Basic Question Words

INSTRUCTIONS Here are some question words. Listen to them; then take the twenty minute workshop.

English	Spanish
Do you understand?	¿Entiende?
I understand.	Entiendo.
How?	¿Cómo?
How much?	¿Cuánto?
Where (at)?	¿Dónde?
When?	¿Cuándo?
Which one?	¿Cuál?
Who?	¿Quién?
What?	¿Qué?
Why? (for what [reason])	¿Por qué?

A Twenty-Minute Workshop

Among the most important words in conversation are question words like "where," "when," "how," etc. The leading question is "Do you understand?" We'll start with that one. You already know *¿comprende?*. The more common way to ask "Do you understand?" sounds like N.T.N.-day (en-tee-ENday). The stress is on the second "en": "en-tee-EN-day." Say it rapidly, speeding up the second syllable so it's "en-tyEN-day." It is written *¿entiende?*. Say it rapidly several times, with its meaning in mind. Pretend you are asking someone if they understand. Equally important is to learn to say "I understand." It sounds like N.T.N.-dough (spelled *entiendo*). Say it rapidly, speeding up the second syllable so it's "en-tyEN-dough." Now put your hands in front of your face, like two puppets facing each other. Have one puppet ask the other: *«¿Entiende?»* And have the other answer: *«Sí, entiendo»*.

Five Question Words

INSTRUCTIONS   Now for more question words. Give these your full concentration, and you will absorb them within minutes. First a set of five.

1. *¿Cómo?* (as in Perry Como)—How?

   • "*Cómo* did you get here?" "*Cómo* can I thank you?"

2. *¿Cuánto?* (as in squanto minus the s-, but as always, the t has a distinct t-sound) —"How much?"

   • Related to our word quantity (just think of asking "What quantity of money?"). "*Cuánto* is this?" "*Cuánto* are the shoes?" "*Cuánto* do I owe you?"

3. *¿Dónde?* (as in Doan-day)—"Where?"

   • Sounds like Doan-day. "Where's Mr. Doan-day?" "It's dark. *Cómo* can I see *dónde* I am?"

4. *¿De dónde?* (put "day" in front of *dónde*)—"From where? Whence?"

   • "*¿De dónde* are you?" "*¿De dónde* are you coming from?"

5. *¿Adónde?* (put "ah" in front of *dónde*)—"To where?"

   • "*¿Adónde* are you going?"

INSTRUCTIONS   Review this first set of words.

English	Spanish
Do you understand?	*¿Entiende?* (or *¿Comprende?*)
I understand.	*Entiendo* (or *Comprendo*).
How?	*¿Cómo?*
How much?	*¿Cuánto?*
Where (at)?	*¿Dónde?*
Where to?	*¿Adónde?*
Where from?	*¿De dónde?*

Stop for a moment to review these and set them firmly in memory. Then take time to do a bit of role-playing with these expressions. For each one, make up sentences like those above, adding English words as needed—or better, adding

Spanish-Speaking Families

Traditionally, Spanish-speaking families have been extended families with grandparents, aunts, uncles, and cousins living under the same roof. You will see very few nursing homes because of the respect and obligation the people feel to take care of the elderly members in their family.

hand motions and facial expressions that will communicate what you need to say to meet an imagined situation. For example, you need a screwdriver. You communicate to your landlady what you need by pantomiming using a screwdriver and asking *¿Dónde?*. Do it as if you really meant it! Then do the same for the following: A telephone. A salt shaker. Scissors. A pen or pencil. A needle. A typewriter.

Ask the cost of the following by naming the item, pausing, then asking *¿Cuánto?* Do it as if you really meant it! Example: (*la blusa* "the blouse") *La blusa…¿cuánto?* (*la fruta*…"the fruit"; *el piano*…"the piano"; *el tren*…"the train"). Do a bit of play acting. Point to a friend's watch and ask, «*¿Cuánto costó?*»—"How much did it cost?" (Possible answers: «*Tres dólares*» "$3," «*Mucho*» "a lot," or «*No mucho*»—"not much.")

One use of *cómo* is in showing that you didn't understand what someone said. To say "How's that?" you would say, «*¿Cómo?*»

To say "How's that? I don't understand," you would say, «*¿Cómo? No entiendo.*»

Four Question Words

INSTRUCTIONS   With these four question words you will multiply the kinds of information you can get.

1. To ask "when," use *cuándo* (not c-when-do but *cuándo*).
   - It begins like *cuánto* but has a d instead of a t. "*Cuándo* will I see you again?" "*Cuándo* will a bus get here?" "*Cuándo* did you leave?"
2. To ask "which," as in "Which is mine?" use *cuál* (like "squall" minus the s).
   - "*Cuál* is mine?" "*Cuál* do you want, this one or that one?"
3. To ask "who," as in "Who came?" use *quién* (sounds like "key-EN"):
   - "*Quién* came?" "*Quién* is that lady?"
   - *Quién* is used alone to mean "Who?" It can refer to the subject that performs something, i.e. (*Quién* hit the ball?). It can also refer to the subject that is something, i.e. (*Quién* is your leader?).
4. To ask "To whom?" put the sound ah before *quién*.
   - "*A quién* shall I give this?" "*A quién* did you deliver the package?"

INSTRUCTIONS   Review this second set of words.

English	Spanish
When?	*¿Cuándo?*
Which one?	*¿Cuál?*
Who?	*¿Quién?*
To whom?	*¿A quién?*

Ask the identity of persons you can point to in an imaginary picture.

Example: *Ese señor…¿quién es?* That gentleman…who is [he]? *Esa señora…¿quién es?* That lady…who is [she]?

A very important application of *cómo* is in asking the question how something is said. The regular spelling of this phrase is *¿Cómo se dice?* It resembles COmo say THEE-say. Say it rapidly two or three times: COmo say THEE-say?

To ask how to say "house" you could say "COmo say THEE-say 'house'?" (The answer can be: "Say THEE-say '*casa*.'" or "It is called '*casa*.'") Now practice using *¿Cómo* say THEE-say? to ask the name of several animals: elephant, tiger, lion.

Two Question Words

Two more words will give you a full set of interrogative expressions.

1. *Qué* sounds like K or Kay and means "what," as in "What do you want?"
   - "*¿Qué* are you doing?" "*¿Qué pasa?*" ("What's happening?")

2. To ask "Why," use *¿por qué?* (literally "for what?").
   - "*¿Por qué* did you do it?" "*¿Por qué* are you laughing?"

INSTRUCTIONS Now review your entire set of expressions. Cover the English except to confirm your response.

English	Spanish
How?	*¿Cómo?*
How do you say __?	*¿Cómo se dice __?*
Where (at)?	*¿Dónde?*
Where to?	*¿Adónde?*
Where from?	*¿De dónde?*
How much?	*¿Cuánto?*
When?	*¿Cuándo?*
Which one?	*¿Cuál?*
Who?	*¿Quién?*
To whom?	*¿A quién?*
Do you understand?	*¿Entiende?*
I understand.	*Entiendo.*
What?	*¿Qué?*
Why? (for what?)	*¿Por qué?*

A Spanish Ditty

Here's a little ditty you can memorize. It takes very little effort.

Phonetic	Spanish	English
Verse 1		
NO SAY k-JUAN-doe	*No sé cuándo,*	I don't know when,
NO SAY KEY-N	*No sé quién,*	I don't know who,
NO SAY NAH-thah	*No sé nada*	I don't know anything
MOO-ey B.N.	*muy bien.*	very well.
Verse 2		
NO SAY th-OWN DAY	*No sé dónde,*	I don't know where,
NO SAY k-WALL	*No sé cuál,*	I don't know which,
SAY MOO-ey POCO	*Sé muy poco,*	I know very little,
E. S.O.C.S. mahl	*Y eso sí es mal.*	And that is indeed bad.

Performance Challenge

As you master the new phrases from this activity, insert them into your English sentences. This is what we call "Spanglish," and it will help you to remember the new words quickly.

Ditties

INSTRUCTIONS Read the "Magic of Ditties and Jingles" and then listen to some.

The Magic of Ditties and Jingles

You likely know these (and countless other) ditties and jingles shared by speakers of American English.

(A)

One potato, two potato, three potato, four,

Five potato, six potato, seven potato more.

(B)

One for the money, two for the show,

Three to get ready, and four to go.

The wonderful thing about such pieces is that they are easily learned and retained without much effort. You don't remember when or how you learned these. You picked them up as a child, on first or second hearing, and even if you haven't heard or spoken them in decades, you still know them by heart. You can use the magic of ditties and jingles to multiply your speed in learning Spanish. A small investment of time in learning a few of them can yield significant dividends.

One caution: being able to sing or say a ditty by heart is not the same as putting the words to real use. It is by using the phrases communicatively that they become functional. After learning each ditty, take its phrases and use them first to role-play in your imagination. Then apply them to real communication.

 In this activity you will:

➔ Learn vocabulary through rhythm and cadence.

 Disc **1** Track **11**

Hispanic Concepts of Time

The Spanish concept of time is that people are more important than schedules, and it is not a problem to start a meeting or an appointment late. They are, however, aware of the United

States' dedication to punctuality and expect their North American friends to be on time.

Conversation is an important part of the Hispanic culture, and they love to talk to other people.

Some Ditties to the Tune of "Good Night Ladies"

I'll demonstrate the first one completely, then only the first and last lines of the rest.

Spanish	English
Hola, joven.	Hi, young man.
Hola, joven.	Hi, young man.
Hola, joven.	Hi, young man.
¿Qué tal está usted?	How are you?
Muy bien, gracias.	Very well, thanks.
Muy bien, gracias.	Very well, thanks.
Muy bien, gracias.	Very well, thanks.
Estoy bastante bien.	I'm quite well.

Spanish	English
Buenos días.	Good morning.
Buenos días.	Good morning.
Buenos días.	Good morning.
Me alegro verles hoy.	I'm glad to see you today.
¿Cómo anda?	How's it going?
¿Cómo anda?	How's it going?
¿Cómo anda?	How's it going?
Pues todo anda bien.	Well, everything's going fine.

Spanish	English
Buenas tardes.	Good afternoon.
Buenas tardes.	Good afternoon.
Buenas tardes.	Good afternoon.
Más tarde volveré.	Later I'll return.
Buenas noches.	Good night.
Buenas noches.	Good night.
Buenas noches.	Good night.
¡Que duerma bien, bien, bien!	May you sleep very well.

Spanish	English
¿Qué tal, viejo?	How is it, old man?
¿Qué tal, viejo?	How is it, old man?
¿Qué tal, viejo?	How is it, old man?
Me siento muy bien.	I feel very well.
Hasta luego.	Till later.
Hasta luego.	Till later.
Hasta luego.	Till later.
Y que le vaya bien.	And may it go well with you.

Spanish	English
Chao, pues, Carlos.	'Bye, then, Carlos.
Chao, pues, Carlos.	'Bye, then, Carlos.
Chao, pues, Carlos.	'Bye, then, Carlos.
Mañana volveré.	Tomorrow I'll return.
Ven conmigo,	Come with me.
Ven conmigo,	Come with me.
Ven conmigo,	Come with me.
O gracias, sí, okey.	Oh thanks, yes, okay.

Performance Challenge

Using ditties is a quick and memorable way to master new vocabulary, but it isn't the same as using the new words and phrases in real situations. Try to find some real life situations in which you can use these words.

ACTIVITY 10

The Puzzle

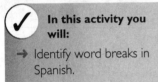

In this activity you will:

→ Identify word breaks in Spanish.

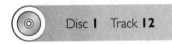

Disc 1   Track 12

The purpose of this activity is to make you prove your ability to tackle the language on your own, figuring out by yourself some fundamental things about the language. Working the puzzle will help you see that learning Spanish is a fascinating and delightful experience. In the process of working through these word strings, you will learn quite a bit about how Spanish works, and you will discover how to form many new sentences.

Puzzle Part 1

Word Breaks 1

INSTRUCTIONS   Below, you will find sentences in normal Spanish, but with no spaces in between the words. Your first task is to figure out where the word breaks are. Do this by comparing the Spanish phrases and their English translation. Don't worry about pronunciation. Mark with pencil or pen the word breaks that you guess. Then do the following:

- Compare the right vs. wrong columns.
- Study the examples and explanations in the help section.
- Fill in the blanks.

Check your answers in Appendix A, on page 452.

INSTRUCTIONS   Listen to a reading of the puzzle sentences.

La Quinceañera

In the United States, turning 16 has traditionally been a special time in a girl's life. We refer to this time as "Sweet 16," when a girl becomes a young lady and is able to get her driver's license. In Hispanic countries this occasion is know as *quinceañera* (note the root word quince) and takes place on a girl's 15th birthday with a special Mass and party that signifies that the girl is becoming a young lady. Traditionally, when a girl turned 15, she would be called *Señorita* (Miss) and was able to marry. The *quinceañera* party includes gifts and a new dress for the young lady. Parents often spend a great deal of money on these special occasions and invite all the family and friends to attend.

	Spanish	English
1.	*PabloyMaría*	Pablo and Maria
2.	*Pabloesunmuchacho.*	Pablo is a boy.
3.	*Maríaesunamuchacha.*	Maria is a girl.
4.	*Pablotienedoshermanas.*	Pablo has two sisters.
5.	*Maríatienetreshermanos.*	Maria has three brothers.
6.	*PabloeselhermanodeMaría.*	Pablo is Maria's brother.
7.	*MaríaeslahermanadePablo.*	Maria is Pablo's sister.
8.	*EllaesunadelashermanasdePablo.*	She is one of Pablo's sisters.

Spanish *(cont.)*	English
9. *La madre y el padre de Pablo y María.*	The mother and the father of Pablo and Maria.
10. *Las hermanas y los hermanos de Pablo.*	The sisters and the brothers of Pablo.

Compare Right with Wrong

INSTRUCTIONS Compare the Spanish translations with their English equivalent. Notice some common mistakes. Circle and correct all the mistakes in the Spanish phrases in the "wrong" column.

English	Right	Wrong
one sister / one brother	*una hermana / un hermano*	*un hermana / una hermano*
the brothers / the sisters	*los hermanos / las hermanas*	*las hermanos / los hermanas*
Pablo is the brother.	*Pablo es el hermano.*	*Pablo es la hermano.*
Maria is the sister.	*María es la hermana.*	*María es el hermana.*
one of the sisters	*una de las hermanas*	*una de los hermanas*

Puzzle 1 Help Section

1. In English, we use the word "the" in all cases. In Spanish, however, there are different ways of saying "the":

English	Spanish
the brother	*el hermano*
the sister	*la hermana*
the brothers	*los hermanos*
the sisters	*las hermanas*

INSTRUCTIONS Similarly, "a brother," "a sister," is *un hermano, una hermana* in Spanish.

2. English has several ways to show possession: the father of the girl = the girl's father. Spanish lacks the 's option, having only the one way: *el padre de la muchacha.*

Personal Space in Hispanic Cultures

The personal space is much smaller in a Hispanic country, and often you will have someone talk to you nose to nose. They may even touch your lapel or sleeve as they talk to you.

Translation 1

INSTRUCTIONS Fill in the translation equivalents. Write one word per line. Check your answers in Appendix A, on page 452.

	English	Spanish Translation
1.	a father	_____ _____
2.	the father	_____ _____
3.	a mother	_____ _____
4.	the mother	_____ _____
5.	a brother	_____ _____
6.	the brother	_____ _____
7.	the brothers	_____ _____
8.	a boy	_____ _____
9.	the boy	_____ _____
10.	a girl	_____ _____
11.	the girl	_____ _____
12.	he has	_____ _____
13.	she has	_____ _____
14.	one of (the sisters)	_____ _____ _____ _____
15.	a sister	_____ _____
16.	the sister	_____ _____
17.	the sisters	_____ _____
18.	Pablo's / of Pablo	_____ _____
19.	Maria's / of Maria	_____ _____

Puzzle Part 2

Word Breaks 2

INSTRUCTIONS Continue as before, marking the word breaks and figuring out the patterns. Check your answers in Appendix A, on page 452.

	Spanish	English
1.	*Estemuchachoesalto…muyalto.*	This boy is tall…very tall.
2.	*Elotronoestanalto.*	The other is not so tall.
3.	*Esteesrico;eltienemuchodinero.*	This one is rich; he has much money.
4.	*Elotronoesrico;elnotienedinero.*	The other one is not rich; he has no money.
5.	*Estahermananoesrica.*	This sister is not rich.
6.	*Peroellaesmuybonita.*	But she is very pretty.
7.	*Esa (laotrahermana) noestanbonita.*	That one (the other sister) is not so pretty.
8.	*Peroellatienemásencanto.*	But she has more charm.

Puzzle 2 Help Section

1. Many adjectives have four forms:

- rich = *rico, rica, ricos, ricas*
- tall = *alto, alta, altos, altas*

Many adjectives (like "tall," "rich") have four forms in Spanish to match a single form in English: the vowel "o," as in *rico* and *alto*, indicates masculine; "a," as in *rica* and *alta*, indicates feminine. Adjectives are pluralized just like the nouns they describe.

The ending of an adjective depends on the gender (masculine or feminine) and number (singular or plural) of the noun that the adjective goes with. Spanish adjectives agree with or reflect the gender and number of the noun they go with. For example, if the noun is masculine and singular, like *hermano*, the adjective will be masculine and singular. This also applies to masculine plural and feminine singular and plural.

English	Spanish
The tall boy.	*El muchacho alto.*
The tall girl.	*La muchacha alta.*
The tall boys.	*Los muchachos altos*
The tall girls.	*Las muchachas altas.*

Which of the forms is selected depends on the gender (masculine or feminine) and number (singular or plural) of the noun that the adjective goes with. Stated in traditional terms, Spanish adjectives agree with or reflect the gender and number of the noun they modify.

2. Negative words always precede the verb; they never follow as in English.

English	Spanish
Pablo is not rich.	*Pablo no es rico.*

Compare Right with Wrong

INSTRUCTIONS   Compare the Spanish translations with their English equivalent. Circle and correct all the mistakes in the Spanish phrases in the "wrong" column.

English	Right	Wrong
this boy	*este muchacho*	*esta muchacho*
this girl	*esta muchacha*	*este muchacha*
this tall girl	*esta muchacha alta*	*esta muchacha alto*
The brother is rich.	*El hermano es rico.*	*El hermano es rica.*
The sister is not so rich.	*La hermana no es tan rica.*	*La hermana no es tan rico.*
The boy is not tall.	*El muchacho no es alto.*	*La hermana es no alto.*

Translation 2

INSTRUCTIONS   Translate the following. Leave space between words you have identified. Check your answers in Appendix A, on page 452.

	English	Spanish Translation
1.	this girl	_____ _____
2.	She is tall and rich	_____ _____
3.	He is tall and rich.	_____ _____
4.	Pablo's money	_____ _____
5.	that boy	_____ _____
6.	He is not very rich.	_____ _____
7.	She is not so tall.	_____ _____
8.	He has much money.	_____ _____

Puzzle Part 3

Word Breaks 3

INSTRUCTIONS   Continue as before, marking the word breaks and figuring out the patterns. Check your answers in Appendix A, on page 452.

	Spanish	English
1.	*Estaserpiente. Esapaloma.*	This snake. That dove.
2.	*Estasserpientesyesaspalomas.*	These snakes and those doves.
3.	*Unaserpiente. Laserpiente. Laotraserpiente.*	A snake. The snake. The other snake.
4.	*Unasserpientes. Lasotrasserpientes.*	Some snakes. The other snakes.
5.	*Laspalomas. Unasotraspalomas.*	The doves. Some other doves.
6.	*Unasserpientesduermenmucho.*	Some snakes sleep a lot.
7.	*Unasserpientesnoduermen.*	Some snakes don't sleep.
8.	*Estapalomaduerme;esaserpientecome.*	This dove sleeps; that snake eats.
9.	*Estaspalomasduermen;esasserpientescomen.*	These doves sleep; those snakes eat.
10.	*Cuandolasotraspalomasduermen…*	When the other doves sleep…
11.	*Unaserpientelasataca.*	A snake attacks them.
12.	*Silaserpienteduerme,laspalomaslaatacan.*	If the snake sleeps, the doves attack it.
13.	*Perosilapalomamuerelaserpientevive.*	But if the dove dies the snake lives.
14.	*Laserpientecomelapaloma.*	The snake eats the dove.
15.	*Perolaspalomasnocomenlaserpiente.*	But the doves don't eat the snake.
16.	*Laspalomaslaatacanperonolacomen.*	The doves attack it but they don't eat it.
17.	*Laspalomaslasatacanperonolascomen.*	The doves attack them but they don't eat them.

Compare Right with Wrong

INSTRUCTIONS   Compare the Spanish translations with their English equivalent. Circle and correct all the mistakes in the Spanish phrases in the "wrong" column.

English	Right	Wrong
these snakes	*estas serpientes*	*esta serpientes*
the snakes	*las serpientes*	*la serpientes*
some snakes	*unas serpientes*	*una serpientes*
The dove eats.	*La paloma come.*	*La paloma comen.*
The doves eat.	*Las palomas comen.*	*Las palomas come.*
The snake hears the dove.	*La serpiente oye la paloma.*	*La serpiente la paloma oye.*
The snake hears it.	*La serpiente la oye.*	*La serpiente oye la.*

Puzzle 3 Help Section

1. Ordering of subject, verb, and object.

The normal order of sentence parts in Spanish is the same as in English:

Subject	Verb	Object
The snake	hears	the doves.
La serpiente	*oye*	*las palomas.*

However, to say "the snake hears them" (where the object is a pronoun), the Spanish sentence order changes to:

Subject	Object	Verb
The snake	them	hears.
La serpiente	*las*	*oye.*

2. Verb forms change with singular and with plural subject.

Singular	Plural
The snake eats.	The snakes eat.
La serpiente come.	*Las serpientes comen.*

3. Negative words go before the verb and before the object.

Singular	Plural
This snake attacks doves.	*Esta serpiente ataca palomas.*
That snake doesn't attack doves.	*Esa serpiente no ataca palomas.*

Singular *(cont.)*	Plural
This snake attacks them.	*Esta serpiente las ataca.*
That snake doesn't attack them.	*Esa serpiente no las ataca.*

Verb Practice

INSTRUCTIONS   Give the Spanish verb form that goes with the subject. Check your answers in Appendix A, on page 453.

English Subject	Spanish Verb
ex. It sleeps	*duerme*
1. It eats	
2. It hears	
3. It attacks	
ex. It doesn't sleep	*no duerme*
4. It doesn't eat	
5. It doesn't hear	
6. It doesn't attack	
ex. They sleep	*duermen*
7. They eat	
8. They hear	
9. They attack	
ex. They don't sleep	*no duermen*
10. They don't eat	
11. They don't hear	
12. They don't attack	
ex. It eats it	*la come*
13. It hears it	
14. It attacks it	
ex. It doesn't eat it	*no la come*
15. It doesn't hear it	
16. It doesn't attack it	

Performance Challenge

Are you getting a feel for Spanish word divisions? Challenge yourself by listening to some Spanish television or radio. Don't try to understand the words. Just see if you can tell where the word breaks are.

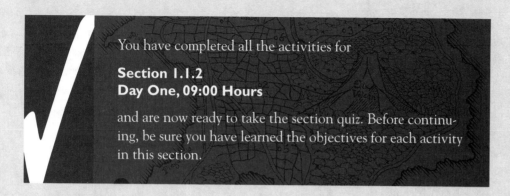

You have completed all the activities for

Section 1.1.2
Day One, 09:00 Hours

and are now ready to take the section quiz. Before continuing, be sure you have learned the objectives for each activity in this section.

Section Quiz

INSTRUCTIONS Select the correct word spacing for the following sentences. Check your answers on the "Grading Sheet" found on the last page of the book.

1. *Maríaesunamuchacha.*
   A. *María es unamuchacha.*
   B. *María es una muchacha.*
   C. *María esuna muchacha.*
   D. *Maríaes una muchacha.*

2. *Maríatienetreshermanos.*
   A. *Maríatiene tres hermanos.*
   B. *María tiene tres hermanos.*
   C. *María tienetres hermanos.*
   D. *María tiene treshermanos.*

3. *PabloeselhermanodeMaría.*
   A. *Pablo es el hermano de María.*
   B. *Pabloes el hermano de María.*
   C. *Pablo esel hermano de María.*
   D. *Pablo es el hermano deMaría.*

4. *ElpadredePabloyMaríaesrico.*
   A. *El padre de Pabloy Maríaes rico.*
   B. *El padre dePablo y María es rico.*
   C. *El padre de Pablo y María esrico.*
   D. *El padre de Pablo y María es rico.*

5. **Lamadredeellosnoesricaperoesmuybonita.**

   A. *La madrede ellos no es ricapero es muy bonita.*

   B. *La madre de ellos no es ricapero esmuy bonita.*

   C. *La madre de ellos no es rica pero es muy bonita.*

   D. *La madrede ellos no es ricapero es muy bonita.*

INSTRUCTIONS For the following questions, choose the correct English translation of the Spanish question word.

6. **¿Cómo?**

   A. Which one?

   B. How?

   C. How much?

   D. When?

7. **¿Cuál?**

   A. How?

   B. Which one?

   C. When?

   D. How much?

8. **¿Cuándo?**

   A. What?

   B. Who?

   C. How much?

   D. When?

9. **¿Cuánto?**

   A. Where (at)?

   B. Do you understand?

   C. How much?

   D. Why? (for what [reason])

10. **¿Dónde?**

    A. When?

    B. How?

    C. Where (at)?

    D. Who?

N

Lago de Reflejos

Avenida Las Palomas

Parque San Cristobal

07

06

03

Río de Plata

Playa Negra

04

02

El Volcán

05

Playa Roja

01

Laguna del Oro

Isla de Providencia

Day One, 12:00 Hours

Nine Days to Rendezvous

After completing the activities, you notice a tiny note at the bottom of the page. It reads, "*La paloma duerme*," which, after your studying, you understand to mean, "The dove sleeps." You wonder what this could mean. You stand up and pace around the small basement room, looking for anything that might help you. You notice that some of the bricks have small letters or pictures carved into them. You start looking for one of a sleeping dove.

After several minutes of searching, you find a brick with a small, sleeping dove carved into it. You carefully dislodge the brick and find the map hidden behind it. It is a road map of the island. Eight locations are marked and numbered in red. You note that one of the marked locations appears to be the *Quintana* residence. You sit down to examine the map more closely and wish that Stump were here to help you figure out what to do next.

Just then, the door cracks open. Quickly, you turn off your flashlight and leap to your feet. The door opens farther, and Stump tiptoes into the room, carrying a tiny flashlight of his own. He closes the door and grins. You heave a sigh of relief. "Long time no see," he says.

"Look at the head start I've gotten in your absence," you reply. You hand him *el mapa* and explain what you have learned so far.

"Nice," Stump replies. "Impressive, even. You missed something, though." He points to the back of the map, on which, in faded brown ink, is written some sort of puzzle. He hands the map back to you, shaking his head. "I don't know all the words to solve that," he tells you.

You look over the puzzle. "Neither do I," you say. "I think we will, though, by the end of this next group of activities."

Stump grins. "What are we waiting for, then?" he asks. "Let's get started!"

In this section you will:

→ Use articles, plurals, and noun/adjective agreement with gender.

→ String together your own narratives.

→ Comprehend, understand, and act on instructions.

→ Develop speed and fluency in spontaneous speech.

→ Comprehend and understand the main idea when listening to a story or conversation.

→ Increase speaking skill.

 Disc **1**   Track **13**

Returning to your seat on the basement floor, you and Stump do exactly that. Remember to pause as often as you need to review.

Puzzle

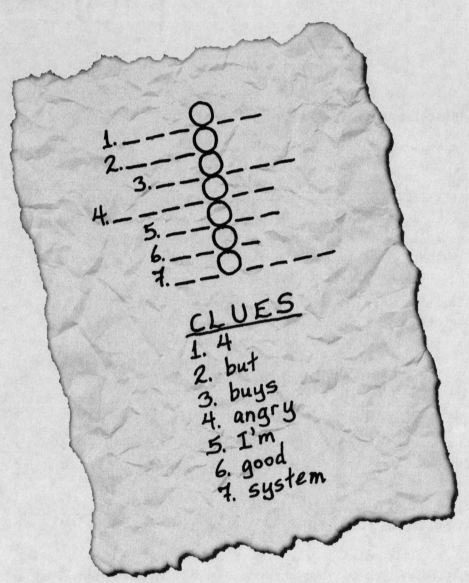

CLUES

1. 4
2. but
3. buys
4. angry
5. I'm
6. good
7. system

After working the puzzle out yourself, check the answers in Appendix A, on page 463.

Reading the Puzzle Sentences

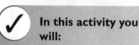

Understanding Basic Sentences

INSTRUCTIONS   Can you say the following sentences? The English translation is found in Appendix A, on page 453.

1. *La paloma come cuando la serpiente duerme.*

2. *Si las serpientes comen, las palomas duermen.*

3. *Esas palomas no oyen a las serpientes.*

4. *Pero estas serpientes ven a las palomas y las oyen también.*

5. *Algunas palomas duermen cuando las serpientes comen.*

6. *Si esta paloma no oye, esa serpiente no ve tampoco.*

7. *Si las palomas duermen, las serpientes las ven.*

8. *Si estas palomas no duermen, las serpientes ven a las otras.*

9. *Algunas serpientes y palomas comen mucho, pero estas serpientes y esas palomas no comen mucho.*

In this activity you will:

→ Use articles, plurals, and noun/adjective agreement with gender.

A Reading of the Puzzle Sentences

INSTRUCTIONS   Practice saying the following puzzle sentences.

Part 1

1. *Pablo y María.*

2. *Pablo es un muchacho.*

3. *María es una muchacha.*

4. *Pablo tiene dos hermanas.*

5. *María tiene tres hermanos.*

6. *Pablo es el hermano de María.*

7. *María es la hermana de Pablo.*

8. *Ella es una de las hermanas de Pablo.*

9. *La madre y el padre de Pablo y María.*

The *Abrazo* as a Greeting

A very common greeting in the Hispanic culture is an *abrazo*, or bear hug. It is common for people who know each other to greet with an *abrazo* or even a kiss on the cheek between women who are friends. A handshake is very important for those who are just being introduced or do not know each other very well.

10. *Las hermanas y los hermanos de Pablo.*

Part 2

1. *Este muchacho es alto…muy alto.*
2. *El otro no es tan alto.*
3. *Este es rico; él tiene mucho dinero.*
4. *El otro no es rico; él no tiene dinero.*
5. *Ésta hermana no es rica.*
6. *Pero ella es muy bonita.*
7. *Esa (la otra hermana) no es tan bonita.*
8. *Pero ella tiene más encanto.*

Part 3

1. *Esta serpiente. Esa paloma.*
2. *Estas serpientes y esas palomas.*
3. *Una serpiente. La serpiente.*
4. *Unas serpientes. Las otras serpientes.*
5. *Las palomas. Algunas otras palomas.*
6. *Algunas serpientes duermen mucho.*
7. *Algunas serpientes no duermen.*
8. *Esta paloma duerme; esa serpiente come.*
9. *Estas palomas duermen; esas serpientes comen.*
10. *Cuando las otras palomas duermen…*
11. *Una serpiente las ataca.*
12. *Si la serpiente duerme, las palomas la atacan.*
13. *Pero si la paloma muere, la serpiente vive.*
14. *La serpiente come la paloma.*
15. *Pero las palomas no se comen a la serpiente.*
16. *Las palomas la atacan pero no se la comen.*
17. *Las palomas las atacan pero no se las comen.*

NOTE

Algunas has the same meaning as *unas*, they both mean "some."

Stringing Together Your Own Narratives

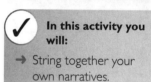

In this activity you will:

→ String together your own narratives.

INSTRUCTIONS   In doing these things, you will be able to compose narratives of your own:

1. Study the words in the scatter chart below.

2. Read the practice sentences.

3. Translate the sentences of the sample story plot.

4. Refer to the chart and use only those words to make up your own stories.

Scatter Chart

farmacia   señora   a

maestra   la

tienda   una

compra   va

en

dice

okey

vende

pero

no   botella de

sí   y   medicina

ella   limonada   naranjada

trae

prueba

es buena

lleva   no es buena

Mediodía

An important time of the day has traditionally been *mediodía*, a time during the middle of the day when a family will get together and have their big meal of the day, socialize, and rest (*siesta*). Many stores and businesses are closed during this time. *Mediodía* was actually started because it was too hot to work during this time of the day.

English Equivalent

pharmacy
(farmasia)

teacher
(ma-eh-stra)

lady

to

the

a

store
(tyenda) *Tienda* also
means tent. Anciently
a store was a tent.

buys

goes

says
(*Dice* is related to
dictate.)

sells
(*Vende* is related to
vend.)

in

okay

no

but

yes

bottle of

she
(eh-ya)

and

medicine

lemonade

orangeade

tries, tastes
(*Prueba* is related to
probe.)

brings
(tra-eh) Relate *trae*
to "tray" as in "bring
on a tray."

is good

takes, carries
(yeva)

is not good

Work

The Hispanic people often work long hours to support their families. It is not uncommon for a man to leave fairly early for work, come home for 2 or 3 hours for *mediodía* to eat and spend time with his family, and then work a second job at night. In many families, the children may also need to start working full time around age 14 or 15 to help support their family.

Sample Sentences

INSTRUCTIONS   Review these sentences which are compiled from the words in the scatter chart.

English	Spanish
A lady comes to the pharmacy.	*Una señora viene a la farmacia.*
She buys medicine.	*Ella compra medicina.*
She tastes the medicine.	*Ella prueba la medicina.*
She says, "The medicine is not good."	*Ella dice, «La medicina no es buena.»*
She sells the medicine.	*Ella vende la medicina.*

Sample Story Plot

INSTRUCTIONS   Translate the following sentences into Spanish. Check your answers in Appendix A, on page 453.

1. A lady goes to the store.

2. She buys a bottle of lemonade.

....

3. She takes the bottle to a teacher.

....

4. The teacher goes to the pharmacy.

....

5. She buys a bottle of medicine.

....

6. She brings the medicine to the lady.

....

7. The medicine is good.

....

8. The lemonade is not good.

....

9. The teacher takes the bottle of lemonade to the store and says, "The lemonade is not good."

....

....

10. The lady in the store says, "The bottle is good."

....

11. The teacher says, "No, the lemonade is not good. The bottle is good, but the lemonade in the bottle is not good."

....

....

12. The lady in the store says, "Okay, the lemonade in the bottle is not good."

....

....

13. The teacher says, "Okay," and takes a bottle of orangeade.

....

14. She says, "The orangeade is good."

....

ACTIVITY 12

Body Parts

English	Spanish	Explanation
foot	*pie*	sounds a bit like P.A.
hand	*mano*	manual—handbook
head	*cabeza*	not caboose-ah but cabase-ah
mouth	*boca*	"Put a coca in your *boca!*"
arms	*brazos*	embrace with arms of brass
legs	*piernas*	Pierre has a pair of *piernas*
face	*cara*	a face on a car is a *cara*
nose	*nariz*	pronounced a lot like gnaw-reese
hair	*pelo*	You pay-low for your *pelo*
bald	*calvo*	Calvin is *calvo*…without *pelo*

Speed Learning

This is a two-minute section. First, recall learning how to say foot, hand, head, mouth. Second, add six more body-part words.

At first, children learn to use language in very limited functions, needing time to get a number of things under control. Then, as need is felt to meet broader and more demanding functions, children gradually extend their repertoires and their skills. Adults are impatient to take on all the functions of language use at once. As a result, they become overburdened with the demands of full-blown language to meet social conditions they are not prepared to meet. The answer may be for adults to take satisfaction in their use of their new language at first for very elementary functions, such as giving monologues and hearing and telling stories. Once the skills involved in such less-demanding communication functions are mastered, they can then proceed to the more demanding functions of two-way conversation.

Challenge

INSTRUCTIONS   Write and say aloud ten sentences using the words in the scatter chart and the body part words you have learned.

1. ....

2. ....

3. ....

4. ....

5.
....

6.
....

7.
....

8.
....

9.
....

10.
....

Performance Challenge

This activity may take more than one study session to complete. Take as much time as you need to review and feel comfortable with the new material.

Chatter at a Royal Ball

ACTIVITY 13

In this activity you will:

→ Comprehend, understand, and act on instructions.

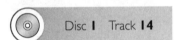

Disc 1   Track 14

INSTRUCTIONS Read and prepare carefully.

Task 1

Getting Ready for Conversation

INSTRUCTIONS This activity aims to help you think in Spanish. This is a different approach to grammar, one that imitates the natural learning process of a child. The goal here is not to make a grammar expert out of you, but to help you communicate in Spanish. As in the learning process of a child, proper grammar use will follow. Be enthusiastic! Push yourself to create new phrases.

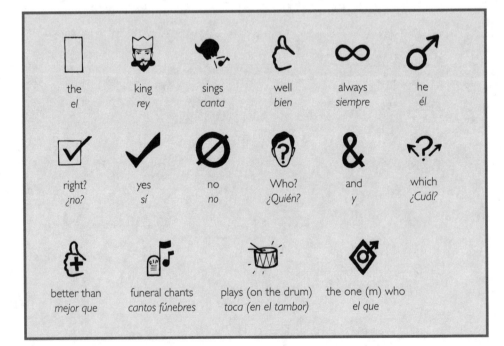

Industries in Hispanic Countries

Each Hispanic country has different basic industries. The jobs in the bigger cities are often similar to those in the United States. In the smaller, rural towns there are a lot of jobs in agriculture. Some examples of the more common products that countries are known for are:

• Spain - grapes and olives
• Central and the north part of South America - fruit, especially bananas
• Columbia - coffee.

Self Quiz on Recognition of the Pictographs

INSTRUCTIONS Select the matching word for each pictograph.

INSTRUCTIONS Read through this list of words and make sure you are familiar with their meanings. Check off words you understand.

Checklist					
○ ¿Quién?	○ sí	○ toca	○ bien	○ canta	○ siempre
○ él	○ el rey	○ ¿cuál?	○ mejor que	○ ¿no?	○ no
○ y	○ el que	○ cantos fúnebres			

Task 2

INSTRUCTIONS With your eyes closed, listen to this dialogue several times until you fully understand the conversation.

The Setting

A royal ball is in process in a royal palace. Two servants are observing and commenting about members of the royal families.

Conversation 1

	English	Spanish
••:	Who is singing?	¿Quién está cantando?
•:	The king, the king is singing.	El rey, el rey está cantando.
••:	Which king?	¿Cuál rey?
•:	The one who always used to play funeral chants on the drum.	El que siempre tocaba cantos fúnebres en el tambor.
••:	Oh, it's the king who used to play funeral chants on the drum.	Oh, es el rey que siempre tocaba cantos fúnebres en el tambor.
•:	Yes, and (he) sings well, doesn't he?	Sí, y canta bien, ¿no?
••:	(He) sings better than (he) plays.	Canta mejor que toca.

Task 3

INSTRUCTIONS Use your hands as puppets and dramatize the dialogue, looking only at the Spanish. Visualize the situation and enjoy the conversation. Aim for fluent Spanish. Then go on to the next task.

Task 4: Pictographic Representation of the Same Dialogue

INSTRUCTIONS Do the same as in Task 3, but now look only at the pictographic representation of the dialogue below. Throw yourself into this performance. Say the dialogue in Spanish without thinking in English. Aim for a high-quality performance.

Performance Challenge

Review the new material in this activity. Try to focus on the Spanish meaning without thinking of the English first.

Toward Fluency 1

Words and Patterns 1

INSTRUCTIONS Review these expressions until you are able to translate from Spanish to English and from English to Spanish.

English	Spanish
Who?	¿Quién? (key-enn)
Who is Pedro? And who is Julio?	¿Quién es Pedro? ¿Y quién es Julio?
So, then...	Entonces…(enTONE-sess)
So then who is José?	Entonces ¿quién es José?
Who is it?	¿Quién es?
Is it Roberto?	¿Es Roberto?
No, it is Carlos.	No, es Carlos.
It is not Carlos.	No es Carlos.
Right? (Isn't it so?)	¿No?
but	pero

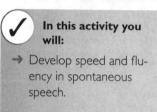

In this activity you will:

→ Develop speed and fluency in spontaneous speech.

Disc 1   Track 15

Rapid Oral Translation Exercise 1

INSTRUCTIONS Rapidly translate each of the following sentences into Spanish. Check your translations in Appendix A, on page 453.

1. Who is Pedro?
2. And who is Julio?
3. So then, who is Alberto?
4. Alberto is Juan.
5. But who is Juan?
6. Who is it?
7. Is it Jorge?
8. No, it is not Jorge.

Meals

Mealtime is very important to a Hispanic family because that is when they spend time together and socialize with each other. A typical meal schedule for a day would be to have a small *desayuno* (breakfast) first thing in the morning consisting of *café* (coffee) or *chocolate* (a thick hot chocolate) and maybe a pastry, donut, or cookies. Around 10:00 or 11:00 they will take a break and have a *merienda* (brunch), which may consist of a *bocadillo* (sandwich) and a drink of some kind. They will have their main meal of the day at around 2:00 during the *mediodía*, which may consist of 3 or 4 courses. *Cena* (dinner) will be served around 9:00 or 10:00 at night when everyone gets home from work or school.

ACTIVITY 14

Family

Family is very important in the Hispanic world and you will find that parents are very devoted to their children. In turn, children are devoted to their parents and will take care of them when they are elderly and unable to take care of themselves. Extended families are traditionally a big part of the Hispanic culture, and it is not uncommon to find *abuelos* (grandparents), *tío* or *tía* (aunt or uncle), or even *primos* (cousins) living in the same household.

The father is the undisputed head of the family, but since he is out of the home so much, the mother is often considered the manager of the household affairs. Most families look forward with a great deal of anticipation to August, when they take their family vacation. These vacations can last the entire month, and it is very difficult to do business during this month.

9. Is it Manuel?

10. It is not Manuel

11. It is Amado, right?

12. No, it's not Amado.

13. Then who is it?

14. It's Jaime.

15. Jaime?

16. Yes, Jaime.

17. Oh, Jaime.

Review

1. Go through the oral translation exercises again, aiming for fluency. Speak with expression and confidence. Imagine you are telling a story to children. Doing this will help your pronunciation by training your mouth muscles to make fluent Spanish sounds.

2. Close your eyes, breathe deeply, and relax, letting your mind create sentences made up of material from this lesson. Don't be afraid of repetition. This review will build your confidence to make sentences on your own, a major step in becoming fluent. See how many meaningful statements you can generate from this material in two minutes. Do it twice.

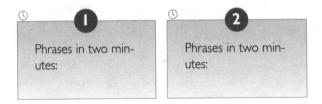

1	2
Phrases in two minutes:	Phrases in two minutes:

Words and Patterns 2

INSTRUCTIONS   Read the following phrases so that you can become aware of words and phrases in Spanish.

English	Spanish
a prince	*un príncipe*
a princess	*una princesa*
a friend (m)	*un amigo*
a friend (f)	*una amiga*

English *(cont.)*	Spanish
a fool	*un bobo*
He is…	*Él es…*
She is…	*Ella es…*
You are…	*Usted es…*
an enemy (m)	*un enemigo*
an enemy (f)	*una enemiga*
formidable	*formidable*
terrible	*terrible*
very	*muy*
also	*también*
either…or…	*o…o…*
the other (m)	*el otro*
the other (f)	*la otra*

ACTIVITY 14

Sample Sentences

INSTRUCTIONS Read and listen to these sample sentences.

English	Spanish
Who is it? It's a friend, Carlos.	*¿Quién es? Es un amigo, Carlos.*
You are not Carlos. You are not a friend.	*Usted no es Carlos. Usted no un amigo.*
Who is Alberto? A friend?	*¿Quién es Alberto? ¿Un amigo?*
Yes, Alberto is a prince.	*Sí, Alberto es un príncipe.*
Renaldo is a friend, right?	*Renaldo es un amigo, ¿no?*
No, he is an enemy.	*No, él es un enemigo.*
A terrible, formidable enemy.	*Un enemigo formidable, terrible.*
And the other prince is an enemy also.	*Y el otro príncipe es un enemigo también.*
Either an enemy or a fool.	*O un enemigo o un bobo.*
But the other princess is a friend.	*Pero la otra princesa es una amiga.*

Rapid Oral Translation Exercise 2

INSTRUCTIONS   Rapidly translate each of the following sentences into Spanish. Check your translations in Appendix A, on page 453.

1. José is a friend.
2. He is a prince.
3. Josefina is a princess, right?
4. Yes, she is a princess and a friend also.
5. And Matilda?
6. She's an enemy.
7. But she's a princess, right?
8. Yes, she's a princess, but also an enemy.
9. A formidable enemy.
10. Alfonzo is a prince, but he is an enemy also.
11. He is a terrible prince but a formidable enemy.
12. So then, who is a fool?
13. You are a fool.
14. He is not a prince, he's a fool.

Review

1. Go through the oral translation exercises again, aiming for fluency. Speak with expression and confidence. Imagine you are telling a story to children.

2. Close your eyes, breathe deeply, and relax, letting your mind create sentences made up of material from this lesson. Once again, don't be afraid of repetition. This review will build your confidence in making sentences on your own, a major step in becoming fluent. See how many meaningful statements you can generate from this material in two minutes. The goal is to reach fourteen statements in two minutes. Can you reach this goal? Do it twice.

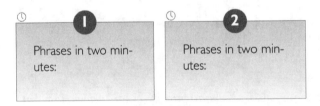

1	2
Phrases in two minutes:	Phrases in two minutes:

★ Performance Challenge

For more practice in rapid translation, look back at an earlier lesson. Just look at one language, and see how quickly you can translate to the other language.

The Key to the Kingdom

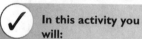

In this activity you will:

→ Comprehend and understand the main idea when listening to a story or conversation.

→ Increase speaking skill.

Disc **1** Track **16**

La Llave del Reino del Rey

INSTRUCTIONS   Listen to and read the following story.

English	Spanish
This is a key, a small key.	*Ésta es una llave, una pequeña llave.*
Here is a king.	*He aquí un rey.*
And here is the king's kingdom.	*Y he aquí el reino del rey.*
In this kingdom, there is a town.	*En este reino hay un pueblo.*
And in this town, there is a park.	*Y en este pueblo hay un parque.*
And in this park, there is a house.	*Y en este parque hay una casa.*

Spain Culture Overview

The Spanish tend to be friendly, helpful, individualistic, and prone to giving advice. Ninety-nine percent of the Spanish population is baptized Roman Catholics. The family is very important in Spain. Divorce rates are low. Businesses have long lunch breaks to accommodate a midday meal with the family and a siesta.

ACTIVITY 15

English (cont.)	Spanish
And in this house, there is a room.	Y en esta casa hay un cuarto.
And in this room, there is a vase.	Y en este cuarto hay un florero.
And in this vase, there's a flower.	Y en este florero hay una flor.
The flower in the vase,	La flor en el florero,
the vase in the room,	el florero en el cuarto,
the room in the house,	el cuarto en la casa,
the house in the park,	la casa en el parque,
the park in the town,	el parque en el pueblo,
the town in the kingdom,	el pueblo en el reino,
and this is the key of the king's kingdom.	y he aquí la llave del reino del rey.
Imagine!	¡Imagínese!

Now listen to the story again in Spanish only.

INSTRUCTIONS After listening, recite the story using the diagram to help you remember the words.

☆ **Performance Challenge**

See if you can recite this story just using the pictures. Take some time to practice, then tell the story to your family and friends.

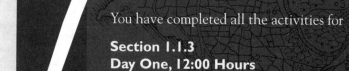

You have completed all the activities for

**Section 1.1.3
Day One, 12:00 Hours**

and are now ready to take the section quiz. Before continuing, be sure you have learned the objectives for each activity in this section.

Section Quiz

INSTRUCTIONS Choose the correct translation of the following sentences. Check your answers on the "Grading Sheet" found on the last page of the book.

1. **A lady goes to the store.**
   A. *Una niña va a la tienda.*
   B. *Una señora va a la tienda.*
   C. *Una niña va a la farmacia.*
   D. *Una señora va a la farmacia.*

2. ***Ella compra una botella de limonada.***
   A. She buys a bottle of lemonade.
   B. She drinks a bottle of lemonade.
   C. She brings a bottle of lemonade.
   D. She sells a bottle of lemonade.

3. **The teacher brings the medicine to the lady.**
   A. *La señora trae la limonada a la maestra.*
   B. *La maestra trae la limonada a la señora.*
   C. *La señora trae la medicina a la maestra.*
   D. *La maestra trae la medicina a la señora.*

4. **Who is Pedro?**
   A. *¿Cuál es Pedro?*
   B. *¿Cómo es Pedro?*
   C. *¿Quién es Pedro?*
   D. *¿Es Pedro?*

5. **No es Manuel.**

   A. No, it's Manuel.

   B. It's not Manuel.

   C. This isn't the manual.

   D. No, this is the manual.

6. **Entonces ¿quién es Carlos?**

   A. Is Carlos angry?

   B. Who is Carlos?

   C. So then, who is Carlos?

   D. Please tell me, who is Carlos?

7. **Where is the vase?**

   A. *en la botella*

   B. *al lado del parque*

   C. *en el cuarto*

   D. *en la llave*

8. **Where is the house?**

   A. *en el parque*

   B. *en el cuarto*

   C. *al lado del florero*

   D. *al lado de la casa*

9. **Where is the town?**

   A. *en el parque*

   B. *en el florero*

   C. *al lado de la casa*

   D. *en el reino*

10. **What is in the room?**

    A. *una llave*

    B. *un florero*

    C. *un cuarto*

    D. *un parque*

 You have completed all the sections for

Module 1.1

and are now ready to take the module test. Before continuing, be sure you have learned the objectives for each activity in this module.

Module Test

INSTRUCTIONS Select the correct word spacing for the following sentences. Check your answers on the "Grading Sheet" found on the last page of the book.

1. **Maríaesunamuchacha.**
   A. María esuna muchacha.
   B. María es una muchacha.
   C. María es unamuchacha.
   D. Maríaes una muchacha.

2. **Maríatienetreshermanos.**
   A. Maríatiene tres hermanos.
   B. María tienetres hermanos.
   C. María tiene tres hermanos.
   D. María tiene treshermanos.

3. **PabloeselhermanodeMaría.**
   A. Pablo es el hermano de María.
   B. Pabloes el hermano de María.
   C. Pablo esel hermano de María.
   D. Pablo es el hermanode María.

4. **ElpadredePabloyMaríaesrico.**
   A. El padrede Pablo y María es rico.
   B. El padre de Pabloy María es rico.
   C. El padre de Pablo y Maríaes rico.
   D. El padre de Pablo y María es rico.

5. *Lamadredeellosnoesricaperoesmuybonita.*

   A. *La madre de ellos noes rica peroes muy bonita.*

   B. *La madrede ellos no es rica pero esmuy bonita.*

   C. *La madre deellos no es rica pero es muy bonita.*

   D. *La madre de ellos no es rica pero es muy bonita.*

INSTRUCTIONS   For the following questions, choose the correct English translation of the Spanish question word.

6. *¿Cuál?*

   A. How?

   B. Which one?

   C. When?

   D. How much?

7. *¿Dónde?*

   A. Where (at)?

   B. When?

   C. How?

   D. Who?

8. *¿Entiende?*

   A. Who?

   B. Why? (for what [reason])

   C. Do you understand?

   D. What?

9. *¿Por qué?*

   A. Why? (for what [reason])

   B. What?

   C. Who?

   D. Where (at)?

10. *¿Cómo?*

   A. How?

   B. How much?

   C. When?

   D. Which one?

··

INSTRUCTIONS   Choose the pictograph representation that matches the Spanish phrase.

11. *Una línea.*

   A. ●

   B. ——

   C. ●● ——

   D. 1

12. *Un punto.*

   A. ——

   B. ╲

   C. ●●

   D. ●

13. *Una línea y seis puntos.*

   A. —— ● ● ● ● ● ●

   B. ● ● ● ● ● —— —— ——

   C. —— 6 ●

   D. —— —— —— —— —— —— ——

14. **Cinco puntos y dos líneas.**

   A. $5 \bullet 2$

   B. — — — — —

   C. ● ● ● ● ● — — —

   D. — ● ● ● ● ● ●

15. **Un número, el número uno.**

   A. ●

   B. —

   C. 3

   D. 1

16. **Cuatro puntos, dos líneas, y un número, el número dos.**

   A. $4\,2$ — —

   B. ● ● ● ● — — 2

   C. — — 2 4

   D. ● ● ● — — 2

INSTRUCTIONS Choose the best answer to the following question.

17. In *el cuento* about the smashed *ventana*, ¿*quién* lives in *la casa*?

   A. *unos muchachos*

   B. *unas muchachas*

   C. *un hombre muy alto, un gigante*

   D. *Bobi, el perro grande*

INSTRUCTIONS   Read the following sentences and do the math to find the answer.

18. **tres + tres =**

   A. ocho

   B. seis

   C. cuatro

   D. quince

19. **dos + cuatro =**

   A. ocho

   B. cuatro

   C. quince

   D. seis

20. **seis - cuatro =**

   A. ocho

   B. cuatro

   C. dos

   D. quince

21. **diez x cien =**

   A. mil

   B. quince

   C. cien

   D. siete

22. **cinco x diez x dos =**

   A. ocho

   B. mil

   C. quince

   D. cien

INSTRUCTIONS For the following questions, choose the correct Spanish translation of the English sentence.

23. **He is a friend.**

    A. *El es un príncipe.*

    B. *Ella es una enemiga.*

    C. *El es un amigo.*

    D. *Una enemiga muy formidable.*

24. **He is a prince.**

    A. *El es un amigo.*

    B. *El es un príncipe.*

    C. *Ella es una enemiga.*

    D. *Una enemiga muy formidable.*

25. **She is a princess, right?**

    A. *Una enemiga muy formidable.*

    B. *Ella es una princesa, ¿no?*

    C. *El es un príncipe, pero es un enemigo también.*

    D. *Pero ella es una princesa, ¿no?*

Nantes
Loire
Bay of Biscay
Bordeaux
Bilbao
Andorra la Vella
PYRENEES
ANDORRA
Zaragoza
Porto
Madrid
Tagus
Lisbon
SPAIN
Valencia
Balearic Sea
Sevilla
Gibraltar (U.K.)
Málaga
Strait of Gibraltar
Ceuta (SPAIN)
Alborán Sea
Melilla (SPAIN)
Oran
Rabat
Casablanca

Module 1.2

Throughout this module we'll be learning about the culture of Spain.

Keep these tips in mind as you progress through this module:

1. Read instructions carefully.

2. Repeat aloud all the Spanish words you hear on the audio CDs.

3. Go at your own pace.

4. Have fun with the activities and practice your new language skills with others.

5. Record yourself speaking Spanish on tape so you can evaluate your own speaking progress.

Nantes

N

Lago de
Reflejos

Avenida Las Palomas

Parque San
Cristóbal

o 7

Río de
Plata

o 3

o 6

Playa Negra

o 4

o 2

El
Volcán

o 5

Playa Roja

o 1

Laguna
del Oro

Isla de
Providencia

Casablanca

Day One, 16:00 Hours

Nine Days to Rendezvous

"*¿Tomates?*" says Stump as you examine the puzzle you just solved. "What kind of clue is that?"

Before you can answer him, though, the door opens again, and *Señora Quintana* slips into the room. She sees the two of you at work and smiles. "*Muy bien,*" she tells you. "You found *el mapa.*" You realize that she speaks a little English. "*Usted habla inglés,*" you say. "I did not want to tell you before. I was afraid there could be spies. But now," she says, "your Spanish learning has already begun, and you will be using the best learning methods available. In order for you to finish this course and complete this mission, you will need to be able to do these things:

1. Use vocabulary on a wide variety of topics.

2. Master question words that will let you request and understand information.

3. Master basic grammar and verb conjugations, without spending hours memorizing dull lists.

4. Be capable of modifying basic conversations to fit different situations.

5. Know how to use the language and be able to converse in a Spanish-speaking country.

"Keep up the good work you have started, and you will be richly rewarded. The invaders have stopped their search, and my sources report they are packing their gear and preparing to leave. Let us hope it is for good. Please join us upstairs."

Upstairs, afternoon sunlight falls softly through the west-facing windows. You're amazed at how quickly your first day on *Isla de Providencia* is flying by. You update the *Quintana* family on what you and Stump have accomplished so far and show them *el mapa* that you found. *Chiquita*, in turn, offers to update you. According to the note you found scrawled in your pocketbook, you can't reach your goal with language mastery alone. You need to learn the Hispanic culture as well. You have already learned a bit about Hispanic culture in general, but *Chiquita* tells you that you'll need to know about Spain if you are to pass your next challenge.

In this section you will:

→ Test your knowledge of basic expressions.

→ Increase usage of adjectives with nouns.

→ Think and communicate in Spanish using targeted vocabulary.

 Disc **1**   Track **17**

Chiquita also has some language learning advice for you. "You may be tempted to take the traditional road and just memorize vocabulary and verb conjugations," she tells you. "Don't give in. Instead, force yourself to use the language. Try to say something new and creative every day. Play with the language, and don't be ashamed of making mistakes. The activities we have included were chosen to encourage you to think creatively in your language learning."

In light of these new hints, you and Stump decide to spend the rest of the day learning more Spanish and acquainting yourselves with basic information on Spain. For dinner, *Señor Quintana* prepares *paella*, one of Spain's traditional dishes. With a bit of persuasion, he agrees to share it with you.

Recipe: *Paella*

- 3/4 cup olive oil
- 8 pieces chicken
- 2 medium onions, chopped
- 2 tomatoes, chopped
- 1 t garlic powder
- 1 green pepper, cut in strips
- 1 red pepper, cut in strips
- 3 cups uncooked rice
- 6 cups water or chicken stock
- 1 large pinch saffron, dissolved in 2 T boiling water
- salt
- pepper
- 1/4 lb. ham, cut in strips
- 1 chorizo sausage, sliced
- 1/2 lb. cleaned shrimp
- 1/2 lb. fillet of any white fish, cut in pieces

Directions   In a large pan, heat oil and brown chicken for 10 minutes. Remove from pan. Saute onions in same pan. Add tomatoes and cook until soft. Stir in garlic powder and peppers. Cook for 2 minutes. Then stir in rice. Cook on high until grains are transparent. Pour on saffron mix and water. Salt and pepper to taste. Place chicken in the rice. Add ham after chicken. Then add—in order—ham, *chorizo*, shrimp, and fish pieces. Bring to a boil and cook over medium heat for 20 minutes. Makes 8 servings.

SECTION 1.2.1

Self Quiz: Basic Expressions

INSTRUCTIONS   Complete this exercise to test your comprehension of the workshop's question words and vocabulary from the beginning of the course. Respond in writing to the conversational statements below. Check your answers in Appendix A, on page 454.

 In this activity you will:

→ Test your knowledge of basic expressions.

ex. You're a security guard at an air base in Florida. Seeing a suspicious character sneaking around, you stop him. In just two words, ask where he's going:

¿Adónde va?
....

1. Surprised, he asks if you speak Spanish:

....

2. You ask him if he speaks English:

....

3. Thinking he can bribe you, he asks to know the amount needed:

....

4. He shows you something you don't recognize. You ask what (it is):

....

5. After handcuffing him, you give him a candy bar. He accepts it, saying:

....

6. He offers you a lollipop. You politely refuse it, saying:

....

7. In explaining something to him, you want to know if he understands. You ask:

....

8. He answers in the affirmative:

....

9. He says, "Watch me!" and does a double backflip. You compliment him:

....

Facts and Figures on Spain

- Spain has four official languages: Castilian Spanish (74%), Catalan (17%), Galician (7%), and Basque (2%).
- The population of Spain is about 39.5 million and is growing by 0.2 percent annually.
- The most popular sports in Spain are soccer and bullfighting.
- Spain's federal government includes a king, a prime minister, other ministries, and a bicameral legislature.

10. You wonder where he is from and ask:

....

11. He tells you he is from Cuba. He says:

....

12. He is curious where you are leading him and asks:

....

13. Coming to the security office door, you bid him to go on in:

....

14. He doesn't see the door and asks its location:

....

15. He sees there are two doors side by side and asks which one:

....

16. You indicate which door you want him to go in:

....

17. He goes in, saying that he understands:

....

18. He asks you how to say, "Gimme a break!" in Spanish:

....

19. You answer truthfully that you don't know:

....

20. Leaving him handcuffed to the chair, you bid him farewell:

....

21. He screams after you, "Why?":

....

22. You answer that you don't know why:

....

23. He screams after you, "Who?":

....

24. You answer that you don't know who:

....

25. Your answer recalls the ditty, so you recite it:

....

....

....

....

26. He laughs and compliments you:

....

More Points, Lines and Figures

✓ **In this activity you will:**

→ Increase usage of adjectives with nouns.

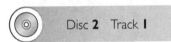

Disc **2**　Track **1**

Points, Lines, and Figures

INSTRUCTIONS　Listen and point to the words that correspond with the words you hear. Use these exercises to increase your listening comprehension through problem-solving tasks that invite you to learn skills in inferring (guessing) meaning.

A. Scatter Chart

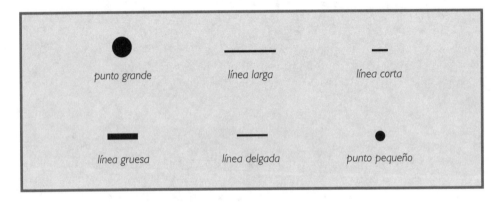

Traditions in Spain

Spain is a country rich in culture and tradition. Spaniards are very hard workers, but enjoy times that are set aside to come together with family and friends to celebrate. Many of the traditions are based on beliefs of the Catholic religion, but are celebrated by people of all faiths. In this activity, we will touch on just a few of the hundreds of traditions popular in Spain.

	Points, Lines, and Figures	Spanish
1.	● ●	*Un punto grande y un punto pequeño.*
2.	▬▬▬ ▬	*Una línea larga y una línea corta.*
3.	▬▬ 5	*Una línea gruesa y un número pequeño, el número cinco.*
4.	● ▬	*Un punto grande y una línea delgada.*

B. Listen, Look, and Read

Points, Lines, and Figures *(cont.)*	Spanish
5. ●● — —	*Dos puntos pequeños y dos líneas cortas.*
6. ●●●●● 6 1	*Cinco puntos grandes y dos números pequeños, los números seis y uno.*
7. ●	*Este punto es pequeño. Es un punto pequeño.*
8. ●	*Este punto es grande. Es un punto grande.*
9. ▬	*Esta línea es gruesa. Es una línea gruesa.*
10. ●●●●●	*Estos puntos son pequeños. Son puntos pequeños.*
11. — —	*Estas dos líneas son delgadas. Son líneas delgadas.*
12. ●●●●●●	*Estos tres puntos son pequeños y estos tres son grandes.*

C. Look and Listen

INSTRUCTIONS   Listen to the audio and follow along with the figures.

Points, Lines, and Figures
1. ● ●
2. — —
3. ▬ 5
4. ● —
5. ●● — —

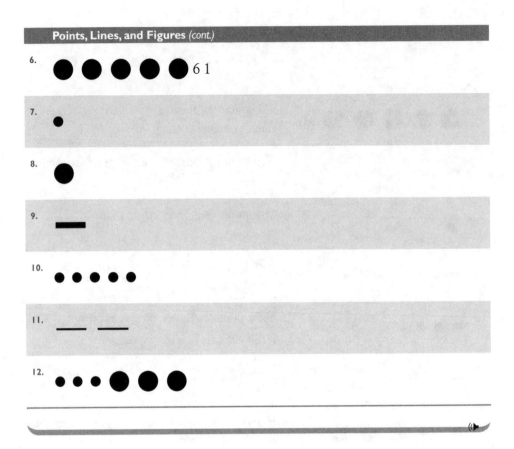

D. Multiple-Choice Frames

INSTRUCTIONS   Point to the section whose contents are described, then listen for the answer. Check your answers in Appendix A, on page 454.

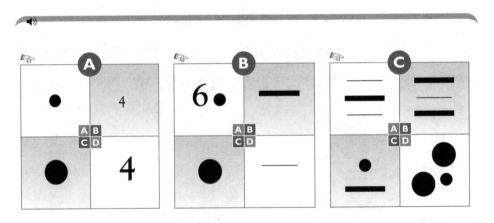

D
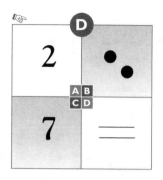

E
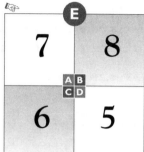

F
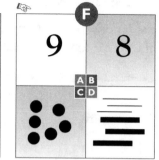

G
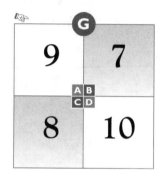

H
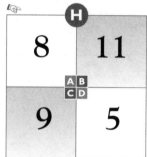

I
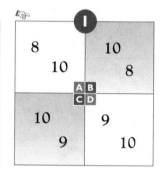

J
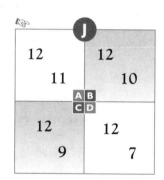

E. Listen and Draw

INSTRUCTIONS Listen to the descriptions and draw what you hear. Stop the audio if the pace is too fast. Check your answers in Appendix A, on page 454.

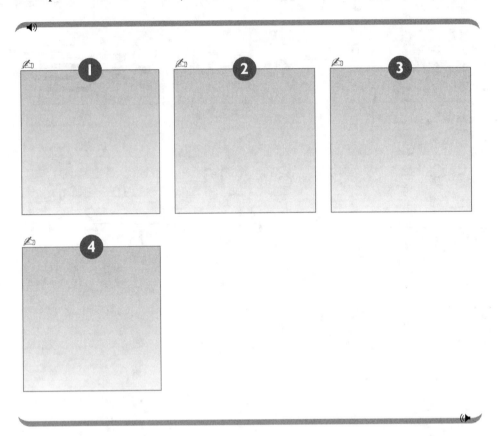

F. Read for Meaning

INSTRUCTIONS Read the Spanish phrases for comprehension. Orally translate them into English. Check your translation in Appendix A, on page 455.

1. *Dos líneas: una gruesa y una delgada.*

2. *Dos más dos son cuatro (2+2=4). Dos puntos más dos puntos son cuatro puntos.*

3. *Tres líneas más dos líneas son cinco líneas.*

4. *Estas líneas son gruesas; estas dos líneas son delgadas.*

5. *Estos son puntos grandes, y estos son puntos pequeños.*

6. *Estos dos puntos son pequeños, y estos dos son grandes. Estos son puntos pequeños y puntos grandes.*

7. *Estas dos líneas son largas, y estas dos son cortas.*

Performance Challenge

Today you learned several new adjectives. In the lesson, you applied them to lines and points. For an extra challenge, use these adjectives to describe other things you see.

Thinking en *Español*

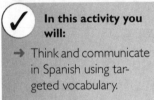

✓ In this activity you will:

→ Think and communicate in Spanish using targeted vocabulary.

INSTRUCTIONS Familiarize yourself with these words and pictographs. You will need these pictographs in order to construct your own sentences and stories. By using pictographs, you will learn to think in Spanish rather than thinking in English and then translating into Spanish.

In becoming bilingual, you will learn to turn your thoughts and feelings directly into Spanish without translation. The following exercises aim to lead you toward that goal. Using pictographs rather than words, you will first create short, simple sentences, then longer, more elaborate sentences that make a story. Give it your best shot!

Part 1: Pictographs and Their Meaning

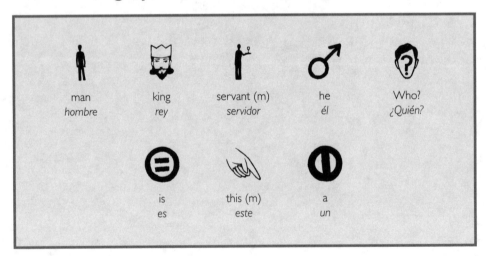

Chart 1: Sentence Building Blocks (Words)

INSTRUCTIONS Use these blocks as a reference for the pictographs below.

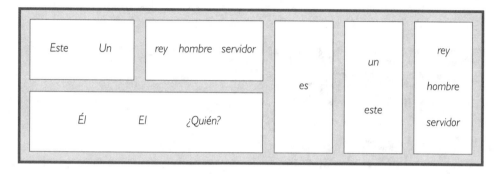

Chart 2: Sentence Building Blocks (Pictographs)

Sample Sentences

INSTRUCTIONS Read and compare the sentences on the left with the pictograph sentences on the right.

Spanish	Pictographic Representation
1. *El rey es un hombre.*	
2. *¿Quién es éste hombre?*	
3. *Él es un rey.*	
4. *El rey es un servidor.*	
5. *¿Quién es este servidor?*	

Reading and Writing 1

INSTRUCTIONS Read the nine pictographic sentences aloud. Then, write the sentence in the space provided below. If you have any difficulty, you may check Appendix A, on page 455, for the Spanish equivalent.

Pictographic Representation	Sentence
1.	
2.	
3.	
4.	
5.	
6.	
7.	
8.	
9.	

Part 2: More Pictographs and Their Meaning

INSTRUCTIONS Familiarize yourself with these words and pictographs. You will need these pictographs in order to construct you own sentences and stories. By using pictographs, you will learn to think in Spanish rather than thinking in English and then translating into Spanish.

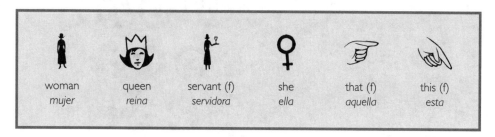

| woman | queen | servant (f) | she | that (f) | this (f) |
| mujer | reina | servidora | ella | aquella | esta |

Chart 3: Sentence Building Blocks (Words)

INSTRUCTIONS Again, use these blocks as a reference for the following pictographs.

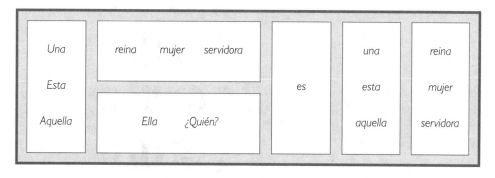

Una Esta Aquella

reina mujer servidora

Ella ¿Quién?

es

una esta aquella

reina mujer servidora

Chart 4: Sentence Building Blocks (Pictographs)

Sample Sentences

INSTRUCTIONS Read and compare the sentences on the left with the pictograph sentences on the right.

	Spanish	Pictographic Representation
1.	*Una mujer es una reina.*	
2.	*La servidora es una reina.*	
3.	*¿Quién es esta mujer?*	
4.	*¿Quién es aquella mujer?*	
5.	*¿Quién es esta servidora?*	
6.	*Ella es una servidora.*	
7.	*Ella es una reina.*	
8.	*Ella es una mujer.*	

Reading and Writing 2

INSTRUCTIONS Read the nine pictographic sentences aloud. Then, write the sentence in the space provided below. If you have any difficulty, you may check Appendix A, on page 455, for the Spanish equivalent.

	Pictographic Representation	Sentence
1.		....
2.		....
3.		....

Pictographic Representation *(cont.)*	Sentence
4. 	....
5.	....
6.	....
7.	....
8.	....
9.	....

ACTIVITY 18

Review Practice

INSTRUCTIONS   Form sentences from these pictographs. Write as many as you can.
From what you've observed, can you guess the male form for *aquella*?

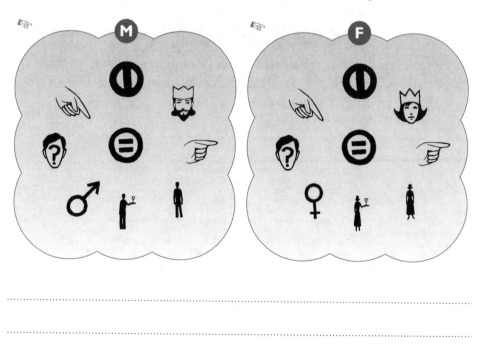

....

....

....

....

....

....

....

....

....

....

....

....

....

....

....

....

....

Performance Challenge

To challenge yourself, go through the activity one more time. This time, try to think all in Spanish. Avoid English as much as you can. This will take some practice, but you can do it.

You have completed all the activities for

Section 1.2.1
Day One, 16:00 Hours

and are now ready to take the section quiz. Before continuing, be sure you have learned the objectives for each activity in this section.

Section Quiz

INSTRUCTIONS Choose the correct response. Check your answers on the "Grading Sheet" found on the last page of the book.

1. **To ask someone if he or she speaks Spanish, you ask:**

   A. *¿Dónde está?*

   B. *¿Cuánto cuesta?*

   C. *¿Habla usted español?*

   D. *¿Habla usted inglés?*

2. **To ask what something is, you ask:**

   A. *¿Qué es esto?*

   B. *¿Quién es?*

   C. *¿Cuál es?*

   D. *¿Cómo se dice esto?*

3. **To politely refuse something, you say:**

   A. *Sí, gracias.*

   B. *Sí, por favor.*

   C. *No tengo una paloma.*

   D. *No, gracias.*

4. **To ask if someone understands, you ask:**

   A. *Entiendo.*

   B. *¿Entiende?*

   C. *¿Hable usted español?*

   D. *¿Dónde está?*

INSTRUCTIONS   Choose the correct English translation for the following Spanish sentences.

5. *Dos líneas: una gruesa y una delgada.*

    A. Two lines: one thick and one thin.

    B. Two lines: one greasy and the other lean.

    C. Two lines: one long and one short.

    D. Two lines: one big and one small.

6. *Tres líneas más dos líneas son cinco líneas.*

    A. Three lines minus two lines is one line.

    B. Three lines plus one line are four lines.

    C. Three lines minus one line are two lines.

    D. Three lines plus two lines are five lines.

7. *Estas dos líneas son largas.*

    A. These two lines are thick.

    B. These two lines are long.

    C. These two lines are short.

    D. These two lines are thin.

INSTRUCTIONS   Choose the correct Spanish translation for the following English sentences.

8. **This man is a king.**

    A. *Este hombre es el rey.*

    B. *Este hombre es un servidor.*

    C. *Este hombre es un rey.*

    D. *Este hombre es el servidor.*

9. **This man is a servant.**

    A. *Este hombre es el rey.*

    B. *Este hombre es un servidor.*

    C. *Este hombre es un rey.*

    D. *Este hombre es el servidor.*

10. **Who is the king?**

    A. *¿Quién es este hombre?*

    B. *¿Quién es el servidor?*

    C. *¿Quién es la reina?*

    D. *¿Quién es el rey?*

Nantes

Lago de
Reflejos

Avenida Las Palomas

Parque San
Cristobal

07

06

03

Playa Negra

04

Río de Plata

El
Volcán

02

05

Playa Roja

01

Laguna
del Oro

Isla de Providencia

Casablanca

Day Two, 08:00 Hours

Eight Days to Rendezvous

Early the next morning, map in hand, you and Stump borrow a couple of bicycles and follow *el mapa* toward the second location, *el segundo lugar*, marked on *el mapa*. The road takes you to the heart of the island's only real town, and finally you pull to a stop in front of the town library.

"I wonder what we're supposed to do in *una biblioteca*," says Stump.

"Let's find out," you suggest. Stump follows you inside. You walk straight to the information desk and catch the librarian's attention.

She asks, "*¿Cómo puedo ayudarles?* How can I help you?"

You realize belatedly that you're really not sure, nor are you sure how much you should tell a complete stranger about your mission here on *Isla de Providencia*. "We're looking for information on Spain," you say after a very awkward pause.

The librarian's face lights up. "On Spain, you say? Well, I've made sure we're well-stocked in that department. Spain is my homeland, you see. I'm afraid the information is all in Spanish, though. Are you certain you can handle that?"

Stump holds up his notebook. "If not, we can always learn more."

The librarian smiles. "Ah, you must be the two Chiquita is looking after. Does this mean you've found the map?"

Feeling a bit confused, you nod your head in silence.

"Splendid!" the librarian exclaims. "I can almost guarantee you'll need to be farther along in those notebooks than you are now. However, the information you need is in this book right here. Let me know if you have any questions. *Mi nombre es Beatriz del Bosque*."

In this section you will:

→ Recognize sentence patterns and build comprehension skills.

→ Increase fluency.

→ Learn numbers 0, 7–19 and how to use them alone, with hundreds, and with thousands.

→ Perform simple math functions in Spanish.

→ Say nouns and adjectives in various types of sentences.

→ String together your own narratives.

Disc **2**   Track **2**

ACTIVITY

19

Toward Fluency 2

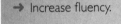

In this activity you will:

→ Recognize sentence patterns and build comprehension skills.

→ Increase fluency.

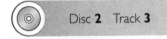

Disc **2**   Track **3**

Words and Patterns 1

INSTRUCTIONS   Read the following phrases so that you can become aware of words and phrases in Spanish.

English	Spanish
Who is this (m)?	¿Quién es éste?
Who is this (f)?	¿Quién es ésta?
This is David; this is Maria.	Éste es David; ésta es María.
my father and my mother	mi padre y mi madre
your father or your mother	su padre o su madre
here	aquí

Sample Sentences

INSTRUCTIONS   Listen to and read the following sentences.

English	Spanish
Who is this? It's a friend (f). It's my friend.	¿Quién es ésta? Es una amiga. Es mi amiga.
She is a princess.	Ella es una princesa.
Where is she from?	¿De dónde es?
She's from here. From Spain. From Madrid.	Es de aquí. De España. De Madrid.
And David? Where is he from?	¿Y David? ¿De dónde es?
David is from Malta.	David es de Malta.
From where? From Malta.	¿De dónde? De Malta.

El Flamenco

While most people think of the flamenco as a dance, its earliest forms are in song and guitar. The development of the flamenco was influenced by many cultures, including the native people of *Andalucía*, the gypsies, the Muslims, and many others. Popular among the young and the old, flamenco is an important part of nearly every festivity in Spain. Women are particularly visible in their beautiful, bright dresses with plenty of frills.

Rapid Oral Translation Exercise 1

INSTRUCTIONS Translate the following sentences into Spanish. Check your translation in Appendix A, on page 455.

1. Where is José from? From Mexico? (or From where is José?)
2. No, he is from Chile.
3. Maria is from Chile too.
4. And is Matilda also from Chile? (or And Matilda is also from Chile?)
5. No, she is from Spain, from Sevilla.
6. And who is this (f)?
7. This is my mother.
8. And this (m)?
9. It's my father.
10. Where is your father from?
11. From here.
12. My mother is from here too.
13. Your father is from here, and your mother is from here too.
14. Your father is your friend, and your mother is your friend too.

Review

1. Go through the three oral translation exercises again found in Toward Fluency 1 and 2, aiming for rapid, smooth delivery. Speak with expression and confidence.
2. Close your eyes, breathe deeply, and relax, letting your mind create sentences made up of material from this lesson. See how many meaningful statements you can generate from this material in two minutes. Your goal is to create 14 phrases in just two minutes. Can you do it? Do it twice.

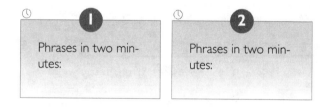

1

Phrases in two minutes:

2

Phrases in two minutes:

Words and Patterns 2

INSTRUCTIONS Read the following phrases so that you can become aware of words and phrases in Spanish.

English	Spanish
Is it certain that...?	*¿Es cierto que...?*
I know that...	*(Yo) sé que...*
Do you know...?	*¿Sabe usted...?*
if, whether	*si*
Who knows if...?	*¿Quién sabe si....?*
I don't know if...	*(Yo) no sé si...*
Of course, indeed.	*Claro.*
Me too.	*Yo también.*
Me neither.	*Yo tampoco.*
I am...	*Soy... (Estoy...)*
We are...	*Somos...*
Roberto's (= of Roberto)	*de Roberto*

Sample Sentences

INSTRUCTIONS Study the following sentences to test your knowledge of the vocabulary you have just learned.

English	Spanish
Who are you? And who am I?	*¿Quién es usted? ¿Y quién soy yo?*
We are friends. We are not enemies.	*Somos amigos. No somos enemigos.*
I am a prince. You are a princess.	*Yo soy un príncipe. Usted es una princesa.*
Am I a princess? And are you a prince?	*¿Soy yo una princesa? ¿Y es usted un príncipe?*
Of course!	*¡Claro!*

English *(cont.)*	Spanish
Sr. Gomez, do you know if Pancho is a friend?	*Señor Gómez ¿sabe usted si Pancho es un amigo?*
Of course. Of course he's a friend.	*Claro. Claro que es un amigo.*
But is it certain that he is a friend?	*¿Pero es cierto que es un amigo?*
Who knows if he is a friend?	*¿Quién sabe si es un amigo?*
I am not a friend of Pancho.	*Yo no soy un amigo* de Pancho.*
I am not a friend of Pancho.	*Yo no soy amigo* de Pancho.*
Me neither.	*Yo tampoco.*

NOTE

Note: *These differ in meaning, but both are right. Compare "He is a friend of Anita" and "He is friends with Anita": *El es un amigo de Anita* and *El es amigo de Anita*.

Rapid Oral Translation Exercise 2

INSTRUCTIONS   Translate the following sentences into Spanish. Check your translation in Appendix A, on page 455.

1. Who is this (m)? I don't know who it is.
2. I don't know if he is a friend or an enemy.
3. Are you my friend (m)?
4. Of course. Aren't you my friend (f)?
5. I am a friend (f) of Alberto. Me too.
6. But I am not a friend (f) of Roberto. Me neither.
7. Do you know if Pancho is a friend of Anita?
8. It's certain that he is a friend of Maria, but I don't know if he is also a friend of Anita.
9. Who is Francisco? I don't know who he is.
10. Of course we are not princes.
11. But it is certain that we are friends.
12. I know that you are my friend, Carlos.
13. Do you know if Pancho is a friend of the prince?
14. No, I don't know.

Review

1. Go through the previous four oral translation exercises again, aiming for fluency.

2. Close your eyes, breathe deeply, and relax, letting your mind create sentences made up of material from this lesson. See how many meaningful statements you can generate from this material in two minutes. Your goal is to create 15 phrases in just two minutes. Can you do it? Do it twice.

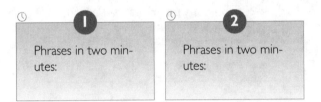

1	**2**
Phrases in two minutes:	Phrases in two minutes:

Performance Challenge

In this activity, remember to do the translations orally. Write them down later to help you remember, but at first, just focus on speaking.

More on Numbers

Más acerca de los Números

INSTRUCTIONS Learn more Spanish numbers by associating them with familiar words or sounds.

You've already learned nine of the seventeen number elements. These are 10, 100, 1000, 1, 2, 3, 4, 5, 6. Look off into space and say them. Now four more numbers.

Zero / *Cero*

The Spanish word for 0 (*cero*) sounds much like "say-doe," not like "zee-row."

Listen and repeat: 0, 1.0, 2.0, 3.0, 0.4, 0.5, 0.6, 1.05.

Seven / *Siete*

The Spanish word for 7 (*siete* or *sete-* or *set-*) comes from Latin sept-. We have it in September (the seventh month of the Roman calendar), septuplets, etc. Listen: *siete*. The main part of it sounds like "see-yet." When you are seven, you can't "see-yet"—*siete*. Repeat *siete* a couple of times with the meaning in mind.

Listen and repeat: 7, 0, 6, 7-0-6, 6.7, 7.0, 2.07, 110, 107

Eight / *Ocho*

Latin octo (8), as in octopus, becomes *ocho* in Spanish. But an octopus is not an ochopuss. Listen: *ocho*. Repeat *ocho* a couple of times with the meaning in mind.

Listen and repeat: 7, 8, 108, 10.5, 7.8, 8.6, 8-0-7, 1008, 108.

Review to yourself. 6, 8, 7, 10, 5, 4, 3, 100, 1000, 1, 2.

If any of these numbers do not come readily to mind, review the memory aids.

In this activity you will:

→ Learn numbers 0, 7-19 and how to use them alone, with hundreds, and with thousands.

→ Perform simple math functions in Spanish.

Disc **2** Track **4**

La Semana Santa

This is the celebration of Easter week, and while there are festivities in all parts of Spain, Seville seems to be the heart of the celebration. Dating back to the 16th century, the *semana santa* is an important Catholic tradition. The most notable parts of the festivities are the processions, which are religious ceremonies where people carry huge wooden figures of saints. Also included in the processions are huge, heavy floats depicting the crucifixion. Groups of men, called *cofradías*, usually carry or walk behind the floats.

Nine / *Nueve*

Nine (9) in both English and Spanish (*nueve* and *nove-*) begins with the letter n. In *nueve*, the n is followed by "wave A": n-wave A—*nueve*. Wave A is a wave with nine peaks and troughs. *Nueve* comes from Latin nove-, as in November (the ninth month in the Roman calendar). Listen: *nueve*. Repeat *nueve* a couple of times with the meaning in mind.

Listen and repeat: 8, 9, 7, 10.9, 8.8, 7.9, 8-0-9, 109, 108.

Now point to the numbers you see in the clusters below as they are spoken in Spanish.

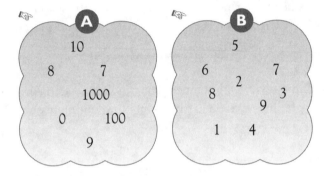

Now say the numbers in cluster B.

Count from 1 to 10. Then count backward from 10 to 0. Test yourself by closing your eyes and imagining one number at a time from 0 to 10. Give the Spanish name for each number.

Forming the "Teens" in Spanish with Dieci- and -ce

You have learned thirteen of the seventeen elements of the Spanish numeric system: 10, 100, 1000, 1, 2, 3, 4, 5, 6, 7, 8, 9, and 0. These are the independent forms. But you have also seen some dependent forms. To review:

Independent	Dependent
cuatro (4)	cator-, cuar-
cinco (5)	quin-

These dependent forms occur in compound numbers such as fifteen, forty-five, and so on, which you will learn now.

Compounds

🔊

From sixteen to nineteen, the numbers are formed like Roman numerals: 10 and 6 (*diez y seis*), 10 y 7 (*diez y seite*), 10 y 8 (*diez y ocho*), 10 y 9 (*diez y nueve*). Note that only the spelling is slightly changed (from *y* to *i*). Listen: *dieciséis* (16), *dieci-siete* (17), *dieciocho* (18), *diecinueve* (19).

Point to the number you hear:

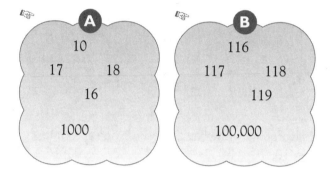

A
10
17   18
16
1000

B
116
117   118
119
100,000

Say each number in cluster A. Count from 16 to 19. Then count backward from 19 to 11.

🔊

Numbers eleven to fifteen are formed with a suffix -ce, which sounds like "say," and means "-teen." A teen has the "say"! With this, the forms you would expect would be uno-ce, dos-ce, tres-ce, cuatro-ce, cinco-ce. However, the "-teen" suffix (-ce) combines with the dependent form of a number. If you recognize the dependent forms *quin-* (five) and *cator-* (four), you can recognize the following numbers: 15, 14, 13, 12, 11.

Note that eleven is *once* (roughly OWN-SAY), not *unce*.

Below is an etymological spelling matched with standard spelling:

Etymological Spelling	Standard Spelling
quin-ce	*quince*
cator-ce	*catorce*
tres-ce	*trece*
dos-ce	*doce*
un-ce	*once*

Listen to the count from eleven to nineteen. 11, 12, 13, 14, 15, 16, 17, 18, 19

Listen and repeat: 18, 15, 11, 19, 14, 12, 16, 13, 13,000, 16,000, 14.05.

Point to the number you hear:

Just to keep active some things learned a while back, say these one at a time before the voice on the CD does: 10,000; 11,000; 12,000; 13,000; 14,000; 16,000; 17,000; 18,000.

Self Quiz

INSTRUCTIONS   Close your eyes and imagine one number at a time from 11 to 19, giving the Spanish name for each number.

Aritmética—Adición / Arithmetic—Addition

10 más 1 son 11
10 más 2 son 12
10 más 3 son ___?
10 más 4 son ___?
10 más 5 son ___?
10 más 6 son ___?
10 más 7 son ___?
10 más 8 son ___?
10 más 9 son ___?

You have now learned nearly all of the elements of the Spanish numeric system. You can say and understand the numbers 100, 1000, and 1–19. All that is lacking is the decades 20–90 and the hundreds 200–900. These are easy. Since they use dependent forms of numbers with a suffix, it will pay to go over the dependent forms once again quickly.

To review:

Number	Independent	Dependent
4	*cuatro*	cator-, cuar-
5	*cinco*	quin-
6	*seis*	ses-
7	*siete*	sete-
9	*nueve*	nove-

Performance Challenge

Practice the numbers until they begin to be second nature to you.

ACTIVITY

Demonstration Lecture 1

In this activity you will:

→ Say nouns and adjectives in various types of sentences.

 Disc **2**   Track **5**

INSTRUCTIONS   Read and listen to the following phrases to learn more vocabulary.

English	Spanish
paper / pencil	*papel / lápiz*
This is a pencil.	*Éste es un lápiz.*
It's a pencil.	*Es un lápiz.*
Paper. This is a (piece of) paper.	*Papel. Éste es un papel.*
Say it: pencil, paper (—,—)	*Dígalo: lápiz, papel (—,—)*
Again: (—,—)	*Otra vez: (—,—)*
Very good.	*Muy bien.*
white / yellow / also	*blanco / amarillo / también*
This pencil is white.	*Este lápiz es blanco.*
It's a white pencil.	*Es un lápiz blanco.*
This paper is white also.	*Este papel es blanco también.*
It's white paper.	*Es papel blanco.*
This paper is yellow.	*Este papel es amarillo.*
It's yellow paper.	*Es papel amarillo.*
This pencil is yellow also.	*Este lápiz es amarillo también.*
It's a yellow pencil.	*Es un lápiz amarillo.*
white pencil and yellow pencil	*lápiz blanco y lápiz amarillo*
white paper and yellow paper	*papel blanco y papel amarillo*

La Navidad

As in many countries, Christmas is a very popular celebration. The nativity scene (called a *nacimiento* or a *belén*) is an important part of the tradition, and can be found in many homes, churches, and public places. People commonly celebrate *Noche Buena* (Christmas Eve) with a big meal and caroling. Bells can be heard, calling people to the *Misa de Gallo* (Midnight Mass). *Papa Noel* (Santa Claus) is becoming more popular in Spain, but most children wait in anticipation for the visit of the three kings.

Stringing Together Your Own Narratives

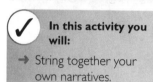

In this activity you will:

→ String together your own narratives.

INSTRUCTIONS Compose narratives of your own by studying the words in the scatter chart and use only those words to invent your stories.

1. Study the words in the scatter chart below.

2. Read the sample story plot.

3. Refer to the chart and use only those words to compose sentences and story plots.

Scatter Chart

(el) mercado		come
	(los) dulces	
		(el) comedor
(un) dulce	vendedor	amigo
		su
vende		prueba
	a	el
	compra	
toma		da
	un	
va		entonces
	y	no
otro		
		dice
él	no son (muy) buenos	
		ella
	más	
		sí
son (muy) buenos		
	viene	
pregunta si...		trae
	(muy) dulce!	
lleva	responde que...	un kilo de...

Día de los Reyes

This holiday falls on January 6th. On the Eve of Epiphany, January 5th, children will fill their shoes with grass or grain for the camels and put them on their doorstep, in anticipation of the arrival of the kings. Tradition holds that during the night, the three kings come and leave gifts in their shoes. (The kings are named Baltasar, Melchor, and Gaspar, with Baltasar being the most popular.) On January 6th, many celebrations include parties and parades.

ACTIVITY 22

English Equivalent

(the) [open] market

(the) sweets, candy

eat

(the) eating place, dining hall

(a) sweet, piece of candy

friend

vendor, salesman

his / her

sells

tries / tastes

to (a place or person)

the

buys

takes / picks up

gives

a

goes

then

and

no

other / another

says

are not (very) good

he

she

more

yes

are (very) good

comes

asks if...

brings

(very) sweet!

takes, carries

answers that...

a kilogram of...

Sample Story Plot

INSTRUCTIONS   Say aloud the Spanish equivalents of the following sentences. Then try writing down the Spanish equivalents. Check your answers in Appendix A, on page 456.

1. A vendor sells sweets in the market.

....

2. His friend Manuel comes to the market.

....

3. Manuel asks if the sweets are good.

....

4. The vendor answers that the sweets are very good.

....

5. He gives a piece of candy to his friend.

....

6. The friend takes the piece of candy.

....

7. He tastes the candy and says, "Mmm, yes, the sweets are very good."

....

8. The vendor sells a kilo of candy to his friend.

....

9. Manuel takes the sweets to a dining hall.

....

10. A friend in the dining hall tastes the sweets.

....

11. He says, "Mmm, very sweet."

....

12. He tries another and says, "Mmm, very, very sweet!"

....

13. Manuel gives the sweets to his friend.

....

14. The friend eats more sweets.

....

15. He eats more and more.

....

16. He eats the kilo of candy.

....

17. Manuel asks, "Very sweet, no?"

....

18. His friend doesn't answer.

....

19. Manuel asks, "Very sweet, no?"

....

20. His friend answers, "No, the sweets are not good."

....

21. The friend goes to the market and buys a kilo of candies.

....

22. He brings the candies to Manuel.

....

23. He gives the candies to Manuel.

....

24. Manuel takes the candies.

....

25. He tastes the candies.

....

26. He eats the candies.

....

27. He says, "The candies are very good."

....

✳

Performance Challenge

On a separate sheet of paper, write twelve or more sentences using the words in this activity's scatter chart (previous ones as well, if you wish). String together the words in ways that make meaningful sentences.

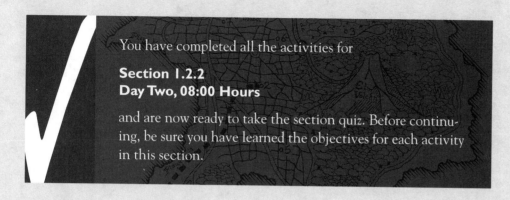

You have completed all the activities for

Section 1.2.2
Day Two, 08:00 Hours

and are now ready to take the section quiz. Before continuing, be sure you have learned the objectives for each activity in this section.

Section Quiz

INSTRUCTIONS   For the following questions, choose the correct Spanish translation of the English sentence. Check your answers on the "Grading Sheet" found on the last page of the book.

1. **Where is he from?**
   A. *¿De dónde es su padre?*
   B. *¿De dónde es él?*
   C. *¿Y quién es ésta?*
   D. *¿Y ella es de Chile también?*

2. **No, he is from Chile.**
   A. *No, ella es de España, de Sevilla.*
   B. *Mi madre es de aquí también.*
   C. *No él es de Chile.*
   D. *Tu padre es de Chile también.*

3. **Is your father from Chile too?**
   A. *¿Tu padre es de Chile también?*
   B. *Su padre es de aquí, y su madre es de aquí, también.*
   C. *No él es de Chile.*
   D. *¿Y ella es de Chile también?*

4. **No, she is from Spain, from *Sevilla*.**
   A. *Su padre es de aquí, y su madre es de aquí, también.*
   B. *Mi madre es de aquí también.*
   C. *Tu padre es de Chile también.*
   D. *No ella es de España, de Sevilla.*

5. **This is my mother.**

   A. *Mi madre es de aquí también.*

   B. *Ésta es mi madre.*

   C. *Es mi padre.*

   D. *De aquí.*

6. **And this (m)?**

   A. *¿Y éste?*

   B. *De aquí.*

   C. *Está aquí.*

   D. *¿Y quién es ésta?*

7. **Where is your father from?**

   A. *¿De dónde es él?*

   B. *¿Y quién es ésta?*

   C. *¿Y éste?*

   D. *¿De dónde es su padre?*

8. **From here.**

   A. *¿Y éste?*

   B. *Es mi padre.*

   C. *De aquí.*

   D. *¿Y quién es ésta.*

9. **My mother is from here too.**

   A. *Es mi padre.*

   B. *Esta es mi madre.*

   C. *Mi madre es de aquí también.*

   D. *No, él es de Chile.*

10. **Your father is from here, and your mother is from here too.**

    A. *Mi madre es de aquí también.*

    B. *Su padre es de aquí, y su madre es de aquí, también.*

    C. *No, ella es de España, de Sevilla.*

    D. *Tu padre es de Chile también.*

Nantes

Lago de
Reflejos

Avenida Las Palomas

Parque San
Cristobal

o7

o6

Playa Negra

o4

o2

o3

Río de
Plata

El
Volcán

o5

Playa Roja

o1

Laguna
del Oro

Isla de Providencia

Casablanca

Day Two, 14:00 Hours

Eight Days to Rendezvous

You finish one section of activities and take a look at the book on Spain that *Beatríz* found for you. You muddle through one page, then Stump shakes his head. "This is too much for me," he says. "A whole book all in Spanish—how are we ever going to read all of it?"

"I don't think we have to read all of it," you say. "We just need to get enough out of it to pass the challenge. Come on, we can learn a lot just from pictures and their captions."

"I'd still feel better if we studied more," Stump says.

"All right," you agree, "but after that, we're going to go ahead and do the best we can. If we sit around trying to remember every single word and detail we encounter, it won't help our language learning or our mission."

You and Stump work your way through a few more Spanish activities, take a fairly thorough look through the library book on Spain, then report to *Beatríz*. She hands you another puzzle. "I wrote a few questions about Spain on it as well," she tells you. "If you can answer them correctly, I shall give you an extra clue. Here's a tidbit to get you started in the right direction, though—be sure to ask your next contact about her special hobbies."

Feeling increasingly confident in your abilities, you and Stump get to work.

✓ In this section you will:

→ Use pictographs to reinforce vocabulary and listening skills.

→ Use identification, description, questions and answers, likes and dislikes, and tensing.

→ Enhance skill of masculine and feminine nouns with various forms of articles.

→ Use singular and plural article agreement.

→ Use infinitive verbs.

→ Express likes.

→ Use passive voice.

→ Understand Spanish translations.

→ Turn statements into questions.

Disc **2**   Track **6**

Puzzle

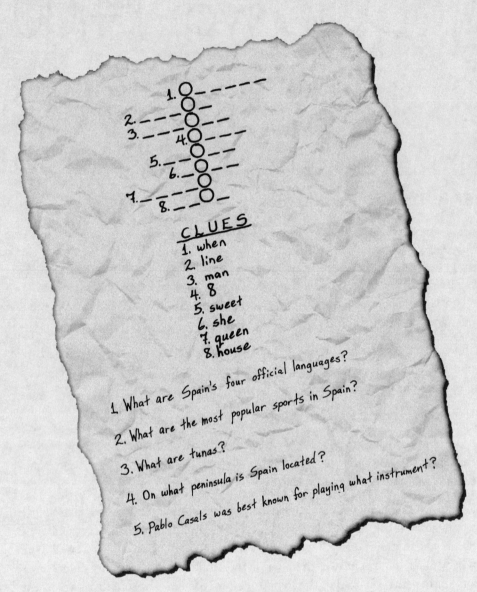

1.
2.
3.
4.
5.
6.
7.
8.

C L U E S
1. when
2. line
3. man
4. 8
5. sweet
6. she
7. queen
8. house

1. What are Spain's four official languages?

2. What are the most popular sports in Spain?

3. What are tunas?

4. On what peninsula is Spain located?

5. Pablo Casals was best known for playing what instrument?

After working the puzzle out yourself, check the answers in Appendix A, on page 463.

Chatter at a Royal Ball

Task 1

Preparation for Conversation

INSTRUCTIONS   Familiarize yourself with these words and pictographs. You will then be able to use these pictographs to construct your own sentences and stories.

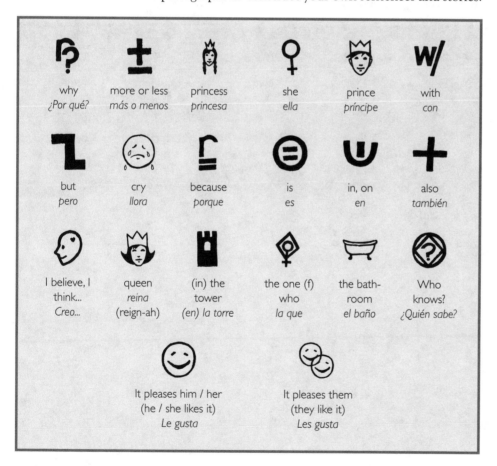

why ¿Por qué?	more or less más o menos	princess princesa
she ella	prince príncipe	with con
but pero	cry llora	because porque
is es	in, on en	also también
I believe, I think... Creo...	queen reina (reign-ah)	(in) the tower (en) la torre
the one (f) who la que	the bath-room el baño	Who knows? ¿Quién sabe?
It pleases him / her (he / she likes it) Le gusta	It pleases them (they like it) Les gusta	

Self Quiz on Recognition of the Pictographs

INSTRUCTIONS   Review some of the previously introduced pictographs.

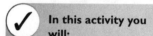

In this activity you will:

→ Use pictographs to reinforce vocabulary and listening skills.

Disc **2**   Track **7**

The Iberian Peninsula

España, a European country with its many diverse landscapes, is located on the Iberian Peninsula. Portugal and parts of France also share this peninsula.

INSTRUCTIONS Read through this list of words and make sure you are familiar with their meanings. Check off words you understand.

Checklist				
○ ¿cuál?	○ porque	○ rey	○ ¿Quién?	○ toc-
○ bien	○ el	○ ella	○ también	○ reina
○ el que	○ cant-	○ y	○ siempre	○ princesa
○ bien	○ llor-	○ sí	○ príncipe	○ pero
○ mejor	○ ¿quién sabe?	○ ¿por qué?	○ no	○ él
○ le gusta	○ más o menos	○ ¿no?	○ cantos fúnebres	

Task 2

INSTRUCTIONS   Listen several times to the reading of this dialogue until you can understand the conversation comfortably with eyes closed.

The Setting

A royal ball is in process in a royal palace. Two servants are observing and commenting about members of the royal families.

Conversation 2

	English	Spanish
●●:	The queen also is singing.	*La reina también está cantando.*
●:	Which queen?	*¿Cuál reina?*
●●:	The one who always cried in the bathroom with the princess, I believe.	*La que siempre lloraba en el baño con la princesa, creo.*
●:	Oh yes, it's the queen who always used to cry in the bathroom with the princess.	*O sí, es la reina que siempre lloraba en el baño con la princesa.*
●●:	She is singing in the tower with the king.	*Ella está cantando en la torre con el rey.*
●:	The king and the queen are singing funeral chants in the tower?	*¿El rey y la reina están cantando cantos fúnebres en la torre?*
●●:	Yes. And don't they sing well?	*Sí. ¿Y no cantan bien?*
●:	Well yes, they sing more or less well. But why do they sing in the tower?	*Pues sí, cantan más o menos bien. ¿Pero por qué cantan en la torre?*
●●:	They like to sing in the tower.	*Les gusta cantar en la torre.*
●:	And why do they sing funeral chants?	*¿Y por qué cantan cantos fúnebres?*
●●:	Who knows?	*¿Quién sabe?*

Task 3

INSTRUCTIONS Use your hands as puppets and dramatize the dialogue, looking only at the Spanish. Drop all shyness and throw yourself into this performance. Aim for flowing Spanish. Then go on to Task 4.

Task 4: Pictographic Representation of the Same Dialogue

INSTRUCTIONS Play the recorded dialogue again, looking only at its pictographic representation below. Then do the same as Task 3 but without the audio. Throw yourself into this performance. Think in Spanish without first thinking in English. Aim for high-quality performance.

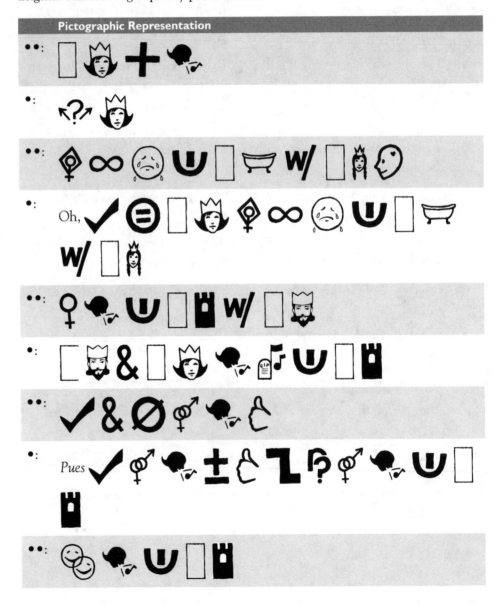

Pictographic Representation *(cont.)*

★

Performance Challenge

You may want to copy the pictographs onto note cards so that you can practice the new vocabulary more easily.

Observing Closely How Spanish Works

ACTIVITY 24

In this activity you will:

→ Use identification, description, questions and answers, likes and dislikes, and tensing.

Northern Spain

Northern *España* is made up of lush, green rolling hills, swift rivers and rugged terrain that are ideal for white water rafting. *Los Pirineos* (the Pyrenees) in northern *España* are a chain of rugged mountains that form a natural border between *España* and *Francia* (France.) The high peaks of *Los Pirineos* offer wonderful vistas (scenic views) to the many hikers who explore the area.

INSTRUCTIONS Take a while now to examine the phrases and sentences below. Go through each group three times. Keep track of how many times you've gone over each group with a checkmark. If you do these things, you will acquire a personal understanding of basic Spanish grammar.

- 1st time through: Compare the Spanish forms and their meaning with the English. (Read the Spanish out loud, then look away and say the phrase while thinking about its meaning and form.)

- 2nd time through: Cover the English and see if you can translate the Spanish into English.

- 3rd time through: Cover the Spanish and see if you can translate the English into Spanish.

Group A

○ 1st time through
○ 2nd time through
○ 3rd time through

English	Spanish
king and queen	*rey y reina*
queen with king	*reina con rey*
the king and the queen	*el rey y la reina*
Which king and which queen?	*¿Cuál rey y cuál reina?*
Which king with which queen?	*¿Cuál rey con cuál reina?*
the queen with the princess	*la reina con la princesa*

English *(cont.)*	Spanish
The queen is with the princess.	*La reina está con la princesa.*
The king and the queen are with the princess.	*El rey y la reina están con la princesa.*

Group B

○ 1st time through

○ 2nd time through

○ 3rd time through

English	Spanish
plays and sings and cries	*toca y canta y llora*
used to play and sing and cry	*tocaba y cantaba y lloraba*
playing and singing and crying	*tocando y cantando y llorando*
Who sings, who plays, and who cries?	*¿Quién canta, quién toca, y quién llora?*
The king sings; the queen plays; the princess cries.	*El rey canta; la reina toca; la princesa llora.*
(He) sings; (they) sing.	*Canta; cantan.*
(He) used to sing; (they) used to sing.	*Cantaba; cantaban.*
(He) is singing; (they) are singing.	*Está cantando; están cantando.*
The king and the queen are singing.	*El rey y la reina están cantando.*
The queen and the princess are crying.	*La reina y la princesa están llorando.*

Group C

○ 1st time through

○ 2nd time through

○ 3rd time through

English	Spanish
The king and queen sing.	*El rey y la reina cantan.*
They are singing in the tower.	*Ellos están cantando en la torre.*
Which king is singing?	*¿Cuál rey está cantando?*
Does he sing well?	*¿Canta bien?*

English (cont.)	Spanish
Which king and which queen are singing?	¿Cuál rey y cuál reina están cantando?
Do they sing well?	¿Cantan bien?
(They) sing more or less well.	Cantan más o menos bien.
The king sings better than (he) plays.	El rey canta mejor de lo que toca.
He plays worse than the queen.	Él toca peor que la reina.
He sings better than the queen.	Él canta mejor que la reina.

Group D

○ 1st time through

○ 2nd time through

○ 3rd time through

English	Spanish
Who cries in the bathroom?	¿Quién llora en el baño?
The princess or the queen.	La princesa o la reina.
Who with? Who does she cry with?	¿Con quién? ¿Con quién llora ella?
Who is she crying with?	¿Con quién está llorando ella?
With which queen?	¿Con cuál reina?
With the one (f) who sings with the king.	Con la que canta con el rey.
Who is singing in the tower?	¿Quién está cantando en la torre?
Which king is with the queen in the tower?	¿Cuál rey está con la reina en la torre?
The one who used to play drums in the bathroom?	¿El que tocaba el tambor en el baño?

Group E

- ○ 1st time through
- ○ 2nd time through
- ○ 3rd time through

English	Spanish	Literal Translation
He likes the queen	*Le gusta la reina.*	The queen pleases him.
They like the queen	*Les gusta la reina.*	The queen pleases them.
She likes the king	*Le gusta el rey.*	The king pleases her.
They like the king	*Les gusta el rey.*	The king pleases them.
He likes to sing	*Le gusta cantar.*	To sing pleases him.
He liked to sing	*Le gustaba cantar.*	To sing used to please him.
She likes to cry	*Le gusta llorar.*	To cry pleases her.
They liked to cry	*Les gustaba llorar.*	To cry used to please them.
He likes to sing; she likes to cry.	*A él le gusta cantar; a ella le gusta llorar.*	To sing pleases [to] him; to cry pleases [to] her.
The queen likes to cry	*A la reina le gusta llorar.*	To cry pleases [to] the queen.
The king likes to sing	*Al rey le gusta cantar.*	To sing pleases [to] the king.
The dukes like to sing	*A los duques les gusta cantar.*	To sing pleases [to] the dukes.
The queens like to sing	*A las reinas les gusta cantar.*	To sing pleases [to] the queens.

INSTRUCTIONS   Review groups A–E above so that you can translate each sentence without hesitation from English to Spanish.

Self Quiz

INSTRUCTIONS   Translate the English into Spanish. Mark for later review those items with which you have difficulty. Check your answers in Appendix A, on page 456.

1. The king sings or plays.

2. The king is singing or playing.

....

3. The king used to sing or play.

....

4. The king and the queen sing.

....

5. They are singing and playing.

....

6. Which princess cries?

....

7. The king used to sing worse…worse than the queen.

....

8. The queen and the princess used to sing better.

....

9. Which princess used to cry?

....

10. She likes to sing in the tower.

....

11. She used to like to sing in the bathroom.

....

12. The queen used to like to sing in the bathroom.

....

13. The king likes to sing in the tower.

....

14. Why does he sing? Because he likes to sing.

....

Focus on the Language 1-7

INSTRUCTIONS Learn to understand more Spanish grammar forms by completing the following exercises.

Focus 1

Masculine and feminine nouns with indefinite articles *un, una.*

English	Spanish
a king and a queen	*un rey y una reina*
one king and one queen	*un rey y una reina*
a cat (m) and a cat (f)	*un gato y una gata*
a drum and a tower	*un tambor y una torre*

1. Every Spanish noun is either of feminine or masculine gender. A noun such as *rey*, referring to a male, is masculine; one such as *reina*, referring to a female, is feminine. Such person nouns as king, queen, prince, princess are said to have "natural gender"—their gender matches their sex. Likewise with other animate nouns: there is a different form for males than for females. (The feminine counterpart of *gato* "cat" is *gata* and of *perro* "dog" is *perra*.) Feminine nouns require feminine-marked modifiers (*una reina, la princesa*) and masculine nouns require masculine-marked modifiers (*un rey, el príncipe*).

2. Nouns such as tower and drum do not have natural gender but do have assigned gender: *una torre* (not *un torre*), *un tambor* (not *una tambor*). Spanish has no neuter nouns; every noun is either masculine or feminine. Why tower is a "she" and drum is a "he" no one knows. There's no logic or reason for the gender of such nouns; it's just a fact of life.

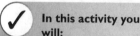

In this activity you will:

→ Enhance skill with masculine and feminine nouns with various forms of articles.
→ Use singular and plural article agreement.
→ Use infinitive verbs.
→ Express likes.
→ Use passive voice.
→ Understand Spanish translations.

Central Spain

Central *España* is different from northern *España* as it is mainly a large, dry plateau called *La Meseta*. The capital of *España* is Madrid, which is a large modern city, and is located in *La Meseta*, which is the geographical center of the country. Madrid is home to more than three million people who are called *madrileños*.

Translate Orally Into Spanish

INSTRUCTIONS   Translate the following phrases to test your knowledge of definite articles.

1. a king and a queen
2. a drum and a tower
3. a duke and a duchess
4. a male cat and a female cat
5. a male dog and a female dog

Focus 2

Four forms of the definite article: *el, la, los, las.*

English	Spanish
the king and the queen	*el rey y la reina*
the kings and the queens	*los reyes y las reinas*

1. Whereas the English definite article "the" doesn't change, its Spanish counterpart has four forms: *el, la, los,* and *las.*
2. *El* always goes with masculine words and *la* goes with feminine words. You'll never hear *la rey* or *el reina*!
3. Before a plural noun, *la* requires an *s: las reinas* (not *la reinas*). Before a plural noun, *el* changes to *los: los reyes* (not *el reyes*) "the kings."

Translate Orally Into English

INSTRUCTIONS   Translate the following phrases to test your knowledge of definite articles.

1. *el rey y la reina*
2. *los reyes y las reinas*
3. *el duque y la duquesa*
4. *los duques y las duquesas*
5. *el tambor y las torres*
6. *el baño y la torre*
7. *la torre y los tambores*

Focus 3

Linking singular with singular, plural with plural.

English	Spanish
The king is in the tower.	*El rey está en la torre.*
The kings are in the tower.	*Los reyes están en la torre.*
NOT: The kings is in the tower.	NOT: *Los reyes está en la torre.*
NOR: The king are in the tower.	NOR: *El rey están en la torre.*
The king sings.	*El rey canta.*
The kings sing.	*Los reyes cantan.*
NOT: The king sing.	NOT: *El rey cantan.*
NOR: The kings sings.	NOR: *Los reyes canta.*

In Spanish (as in standard English) the verb takes different forms when tied to a singular subject as opposed to a plural one. The verb takes the singular form with singular subjects, and the plural form for plural subjects.

Translate Orally Into Spanish

INSTRUCTIONS   Translate the following phrases to test your knowledge of definite articles and subject-verb agreement.

1. The king is in the tower.
2. The dukes are in the tower, too.
3. The king is singing.
4. The dukes are singing, too.
5. The king sings and the dukes sing, too.

Focus 4

The "to" form of the verb—the infinitive:

English	Spanish
The king sings.	*El rey canta.*
The king and queen sing.	*El rey y la reina cantan.*
to sing	*cantar*

You have encountered verbs in different forms, for example *canta, cantan; cantaba, cantaban*. The form *cantar* is called the "to" form, or the "infinitive". For example: to sing, *cantar*; to cry, *llorar*. The "to" form can function as a noun: *Cantar es llo-*

rar—"To sing is to cry" (or "Singing is crying"). *El cantar de la reina*—"The singing of the queen."

Focus 5

How to express "X pleases her"—or the more common English use: "She likes X":

English	Spanish
(Literal) Him pleases the queen.	*Le gusta la reina.*
(Standard English) The queen pleases him.	
OR He likes the queen.	*Le gusta la reina.*
(Literal) Him pleases to sing.	*Le gusta cantar.*
(Standard English) To sing (singing) pleases him.	
OR He likes to sing.	*Le gusta cantar.*
(Literal) Me pleases the king.	*Me gusta el rey.*
(Standard English) The king pleases me.	
OR I like the king.	*Me gusta el rey.*

Carefully compare each paired set. Don't look for an English way to express the idea "to like."

Focus 6

How to express "X pleases the king"—the more common English use: "The king likes X":

English	Spanish
(Literal) To the queen (to her) pleases to sing.	*A la reina *le gusta cantar.*
(Standard English) To sing (singing) pleases the queen.	
OR The queen likes to sing.	*A la reina le gusta cantar.*
(Literal) To the king (to him) pleases to play.	*Al rey *le gusta tocar.*
(Standard English) To play (playing) pleases the king.	

English (cont.)	Spanish
OR The king likes to play.	*Al rey le gusta tocar.*
(Literal) To me (me) pleases the queen.	*A mí *me gusta la reina.*
(Standard English) The queen pleases me.	
OR I like the queen.	*A mí me gusta la reina.*

In the Spanish above, *le and *me refer to the preceding indirect object (to the queen / to me) and not to something or something else. They cannot be translated into English and make sense.

Translate Orally Into English

INSTRUCTIONS   Translate the following phrases to test your knowledge of the verb *gustar*.

1. *A la princesa le gusta el duque.*
2. *Al duque le gusta la princesa.*
3. *A las princesas les gusta el duque.*
4. *A los duques les gusta la princesa.*
5. *A las duquesas les gusta el rey.*
6. *A los duques no les gusta el rey.*
7. *A mí no me gusta el rey.*

Focus 7

INSTRUCTIONS   Learn one way of forming simple questions. (Other ways are presented in other activities.) Look at the following sentences. Note how a statement can be made into a question by simply placing the verb at the beginning of the sentence.

English	Spanish
The king sings.	*El rey canta.*
Does the king sing?	*¿Canta el rey?*
The princess used to sing.	*La princesa cantaba.*
Did the princess use to sing?	*¿Cantaba la princesa?*
The queen is playing the drum.	*La reina está tocando el tambor.*
Is the queen playing the drum?	*¿Está tocando el tambor la reina?*

NOTE

Note that in the last sentence the phrase "*está tocando el tambor*" is kept and is followed by "*la reina*"—literally "Is playing the drum the queen?" That sounds strange to English speakers, but putting the elements of the Spanish sentence in the English order (*¿Está la reina tocando el tambor?*) would sound strange to Spanish ears.

Performance Challenge

Remember that some sentences don't translate the same way in English, so get a feel for Spanish grammar and don't worry that it might not make perfect sense in English. Make sure you understand each focus well before moving on to the next activity.

Questions in Spanish

INSTRUCTIONS   Learn to understand more Spanish grammar forms by completing the following exercises.

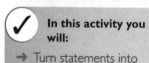

In this activity you will:

→ Turn statements into questions.

Spanish Question Form

INSTRUCTIONS   Study the examples of question forms below. Note that the Spanish question pattern parallels the Old English question pattern.

Normal English Form	Old English Form	Spanish Equivalent
Does the king cry?	Cries the king?	*¿Llora el rey?*
Did the queen cry?	Cried the queen?	*¿Lloraba la reina?*
Do they sing?	Sing they?	*¿Cantan ellos?*
Do the king and queen sing songs?	Sing songs the king and queen?	*¿Cantan cantos el rey y la reina?*
Did the king and queen sing songs?	Sang songs the king and queen?	*¿Cantaban cantos el rey y la reina?*

Caution: Don't try to translate the English *do*, *does*, *did* in question sentences like those above—it just won't work. Instead, rephrase normal English questions into the Old English form that parallels the Spanish question pattern.

Normal English Form	Old English Form	Spanish Equivalent
Is the king singing?	Is singing the king?	*¿Está cantando el rey?*
Are the king and queen crying?	Are crying the king and queen?	*¿Están llorando el rey y la reina?*
Is the queen playing the drum?	Is playing the drum the queen?	*¿Está tocando el tambor la reina?*

Having looked at the above examples of question formation, note also that rising voice inflection (or intonation—how you emphasize a word to give it meaning) can also be used to indicate that a question is being asked.

Southern Spain

Southern *España* is known for having some of the most beautiful beaches in Europe. With its beautiful white sands and Mediterranean blue waters, the beaches in Southern *España* attract many tourists each year.

Practice in Translation

INSTRUCTIONS Cover the Spanish sentences as you translate each of the following English sentences into Spanish.

English	Spanish
Who likes to sing?	¿A quién le gusta cantar?
Does Robert like to sing?	¿A Roberto le gusta cantar?
Do Maria and Anita like to sing?	¿A María y Anita les gusta cantar?
Which king likes to sing?	¿A cuál rey le gusta cantar?
Doesn't the princess like to sing?	¿A la princesa no le gusta cantar?
Didn't the king used to like to sing?	¿Al rey no le gustaba cantar?

Self Quiz

INSTRUCTIONS Translate out loud. Remember that the Spanish question form parallels the Old English form. Mark those items with which you have difficulty.

1. Does the king sing?
2. Does he like to sing?
3. Did the queen used to cry?
4. Did she like to cry?
5. Do the king and the queen sing?
6. Do they like to sing?
7. Did the prince and the king use to sing better?
8. Is the princess singing or crying?
9. Are the king and the princess singing?
10. Does the dog sing well too?
11. Do the dog and the cat sing worse?
12. Were the princesses singing?
13. Or were they crying in the bathroom?
14. The princess likes to cry in the bathroom.
15. The king likes to sing in the tower.
16. Does the princess like to sing?
17. Doesn't the duchess like to sing?
18. Who doesn't like to sing?
19. Which duke likes to sing?

Performance Challenge

The questions you learned in this activity often put the verb before the subject. This is not how we usually ask questions in English, so you'll need some practice to remember how it works. Using the words from this activity, try to make five questions of your own.

√ You have completed all the activities for

Section 1.2.3
Day Two, 14:00 Hours

and are now ready to take the section quiz. Before continuing, be sure you have learned the objectives for each activity in this section.

Section Quiz

INSTRUCTIONS   Read the following English story excerpt. Fill in the blanks using the choices given. Check your answers on the "Grading Sheet" found on the last page of the book.

1. **A vendor sells sweets in the market. = *Un vendedor vende ... en el ....***

    A. *buenos / mercado*

    B. *dulces / mercado*

    C. *los dulces / prueba*

    D. *dulces / toma*

2. **Manuel asks if the sweets are good. = *Manuel ... los dulces son buenos.***

    A. *compra da*

    B. *compra si*

    C. *pregunta si*

    D. *vende y*

3. **The vendor answers that the sweets are very good. = *El ... responde que los dulces son muy ....***

    A. *vendedor / prueba*

    B. *comedor / buenos*

    C. *amigo / dulces*

    D. *vendedor / buenos*

4. **He gives a piece of candy to his friend. = *El da un dulce a su ....***

    A. *comedor*

    B. *vendedor*

    C. *amigo*

    D. *pregunta*

5. The friend takes the piece of candy. = *El amigo ... el dulce.*

   A. *toma*

   B. *viene*

   C. *vende*

   D. *compra*

6. He tastes the candy and says, ... = *El ... el dulce y dice, ...*

   A. *toma*

   B. *beba*

   C. *lleva*

   D. *prueba*

7. "Mmm, yes, the sweets are very good." = «*Mmm, sí, los ... son buenos.*»

   A. *dulceses*

   B. *otro*

   C. *dulces*

   D. *entonces*

8. The vendor sells a kilo of candy to his friend. = *El vendedor ... un kilo de dulces a su amigo.*

   A. *viene*

   B. *toma*

   C. *vende*

   D. *responde*

9. Manuel takes the sweets to a dining hall. = *Manuel ... los dulces a un ....*

   A. *lleva / comedor*

   B. *responde / pregunta*

   C. *toma / vendedor*

   D. *viene / comedor*

10. A friend in the dining hall tastes the sweets. = *Un amigo en el comedor prueba los ....*

    A. *buenos*

    B. *dulces*

    C. *dice*

    D. *entonces*

11. He says, "Mmm, very sweet." He tries another and says, "Mmm, very, very sweet!" = El dice, «Mmm, muy dulce.» El prueba ... y dice: «¡Mmm, ..., ... dulce!»

   A. responde / no / no

   B. viene / más / más

   C. otro / muy / muy

   D. come / toma / y

12. Manuel gives the sweets to his friend. The friend eats more sweets. = Manuel da los dulces a su amigo. El amigo ... más dulces.

   A. vende

   B. a

   C. come

   D. trae

13. He eats more and more. = El come ... y ....

   A. muy / muy

   B. otro / más

   C. lleva / toma

   D. más / más

14. He eats the kilo of candy. Manuel asks, "Very sweet, no?" His friend doesn't answer. Manuel asks, "Very sweet, no?" = El come el kilo de dulces. Manuel pregunta, «Muy dulce, ¿no?» Su amigo no responde. Manuel ..., «Muy dulce, ¿no?»

   A. kilo

   B. responde

   C. pregunta

   D. compra

15. His friend answers, "No, the sweets are not good." = Su amigo ..., «No, los dulces no son buenos.»

   A. responde

   B. viene

   C. pregunta

   D. come

16. The friend goes to the market and buys a kilo of candies. = *El amigo va al mercado y ... un kilo de dulces.*

   A. *vende*

   B. *compra*

   C. *entonces*

   D. *prueba*

17. Manuel takes the candies. = *Manuel ... los dulces.*

   A. *son*

   B. *compra*

   C. *tomas*

   D. *toma*

18. He tastes the candies. = *El ... los dulces.*

   A. *prueba*

   B. *toma*

   C. *come*

   D. *compra*

19. He eats the candies. = *El ... los dulces.*

   A. *toma*

   B. *come*

   C. *compra*

   D. *y*

20. He says, "The candies are very good." = *El ..., «Los dulces son muy buenos.»*

   A. *lleva*

   B. *dice*

   C. *pregunta*

   D. *trae*

You have completed all the sections for

Module 1.2

and are now ready to take the module test. Before continuing, be sure you have learned the objectives for each activity in this module.

Module Test

INSTRUCTIONS Choose the pictographic representation that matches the Spanish phrase. Check your answers on the "Grading Sheet" found on the last page of the book.

1. *un punto grande y un punto pequeño*

   A.

   B. ●● •

   C. — 5

   D. — ●

2. *una línea gruesa y un número pequeño, el número cinco*

   A.

   B. ●● —

   C. — 5

   D.  ●

3. **Estas dos líneas son delgadas. Son líneas delgadas.**

   A. ● ●

   B. —— ——

   C. ——

   D. **2**

....

INSTRUCTIONS   For the following questions, choose the correct Spanish translation of the English phrase or sentence.

4. **Where is he from?**

   A. *¿De dónde es él?*

   B. *¿Y ella es de Chile también?*

   C. *¿Y quién es ésta?*

   D. *¿De dónde es su padre?*

5. **Where is your father from?**

   A. *¿Y quién es ésta?*

   B. *¿De dónde es su padre?*

   C. *¿De dónde es él?*

   D. *¿Y éste?*

6. **From here.**

   A. *¿Y éste?*

   B. *Es mi padre.*

   C. *¿Y quién es ésta?*

   D. *De aquí.*

....

INSTRUCTIONS   Read the following sentences and do the math to find the answer.

7. **dos + siete =**

   A. *ocho*

   B. *nueve*

   C. *cuatro*

   D. *quince*

8. **seis - cuatro - uno =**

   A. dos

   B. ocho

   C. uno

   D. seis

9. **cinco x tres =**

   A. quince

   B. dieciocho

   C. tres

   D. seis

....

INSTRUCTIONS Read the following English story excerpt. Fill in the blanks using the choices given.

10. **A vendor sells sweets in the market. = Un vendedor vende ... en el ....**

    A. buenos / mercado

    B. los dulces / prueba

    C. dulces / mercado

    D. dulces / toma

11. **His friend Manuel comes to the market. Manuel asks if the sweets are good. = Su amigo Manuel viene al mercado. Manuel ... los dulces son buenos.**

    A. pregunta si

    B. compra da

    C. compra si

    D. vende y

12. **The vendor answers that the sweets are very good. = El ... responde que los dulces son muy ....**

    A. vendedor / prueba

    B. comedor / buenos

    C. amigo / dulces

    D. vendedor / buenos

INSTRUCTIONS For the following questions, choose the correct English translation of the Spanish sentence.

13. **El rey canta o toca.**

   A. The king is singing or playing.

   B. The king used to sing worse than the queen.

   C. The king sings or plays.

   D. The king used to sing or play.

14. **El rey cantaba o tocaba.**

   A. The king used to sing or play.

   B. The king sings or plays.

   C. They are singing and playing.

   D. The king is singing or playing.

15. **¿Por qué canta? Porque le gusta cantar.**

   A. To sing used to please him. [He liked to sing.]

   B. Why does he sing? Because he likes to sing.

   C. Which princess cries?

   D. Which princess used to cry?

INSTRUCTIONS Determine whether or not the following statements are true or false.

16. **The indefinite articles in *una rey y un reina* are used correctly.**

   A. True

   B. False

17. **The definite articles in *el rey y la reina* are used correctly.**

   A. True

   B. False

18. **The definite articles in *la torre y los tambores* are used correctly.**

   A. True

   B. False

19. **The subject and verb agreement in *el rey están en la torre* is used correctly.**

   A. True

   B. False

20. The subject and verb agreement in *el rey está cantando* is used correctly.

    A. True

    B. False

21. The subject and verb agreement in *el rey canta y los duques cantan también* is used correctly.

    A. True

    B. False

22. The verb *cantar* is infinitive.

    A. True

    B. False

23. The verb *come* is infinitive.

    A. True

    B. False

24. The verb *comer* is infinitive.

    A. True

    B. False

25. There is a simple, English-like way to express the idea "to like" in Spanish.

    A. True

    B. False

Module 1.3

Throughout this module we'll be learning about the cultures of Mexico and Guatemala.

Keep these tips in mind as you progress through this module:

1. Read instructions carefully.
2. Repeat aloud all the Spanish words you hear on the audio CDs.
3. Go at your own pace.
4. Have fun with the activities and practice your new language skills with others.
5. Record yourself speaking Spanish on tape so you can evaluate your own speaking progress.

Isla de Providencia

Day Two, 18:00 Hours

Eight Days to Rendezvous

"*Tomates, cebollas, y chiles verdes,*" you mutter after thanking *Beatríz* and leaving the library.

"I'm not even sure what *cebollas* are," Stump adds.

"Onions, I think," you say.

"So, our clues so far are tomatoes, onions, and green chili peppers," says Stump. "What are we after, do you think? The lost grocery list?"

"I don't know," you reply. "Give us a few days, though, and I'm sure we'll find out."

"Good," says Stump. "A few days is all we have, if we're going to meet our ride home."

You pedal back to the Quintana residence in silence. Chiquita has a warm, tasty meal of *enchiladas de queso* waiting for you. Over this tasty meal, you brief Chiquita on your day's adventures. "*¡Excelente!*" she congratulates you. "I suppose this meal is a good introduction to the next country you'll need to study. This *enchiladas* recipe comes from *México*, which, if I recall correctly, is where your next contact spent much of her childhood."

After the meal, Chiquita shows you to the other room in her small basement. She's set up a fairly sophisticated computer system, complete with high-speed internet connections. "This is great!" exclaims Stump. "We can email the submarine captain from here."

You and Stump stay up rather late doing exactly that, then finally get some rest. Early the next morning, before departing for the third location on your list, you study some more Spanish.

In this section you will:

→ Use geometrical shapes.

→ Increase listening comprehension.

→ Learn mini dialogues quickly.

→ Read and comprehend the meaning of a text.

→ Add body parts to your vocabulary base.

→ String together narratives.

→ Listen to and read a story.

 Disc **2**   Track **8**

Recipe: *Enchiladas de Queso*

- 12 corn tortillas
- 1 cup mild salsa
- 1 6 oz. can tomato paste
- 1 1/2 cups shredded cheese
- 1 1/2 cups chopped green onion

Directions   Heat tortillas in oven or microwave just until soft. Do NOT cook until crisp. Meanwhile, mix salsa and tomato paste thoroughly in big bowl or round cake pan. Dip one tortilla in salsa mixture. Place on shallow ungreased baking pan. Top with 2 tablespoons of shredded cheese and 2 tablespoons of green onion. Dip next tortilla in salsa mixture and place on top of first. Top with cheese and green onion. Repeat process with remaining tortillas. Pour remaining salsa mix over top of tortilla stack. Sprinkle remaining cheese on top of sauce. Bake, uncovered, in 350º oven for 15 to 20 minutes. Cut in wedges to serve. Makes 4 servings.

Points, Lines, and Figures

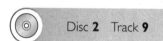

INSTRUCTIONS   Use these exercises to increase your vocabulary and reading skills.

✓ **In this activity you will:**
→ Use geometrical shapes.

◎ Disc **2**   Track **9**

A. Scatter Chart

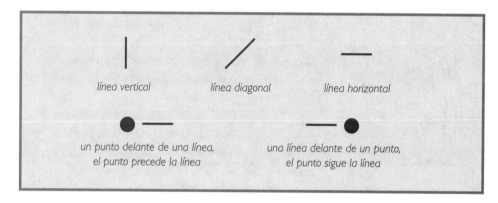

B. Listen, Look, and Read

INSTRUCTIONS   Cover the Spanish and just listen to the audio if you like.

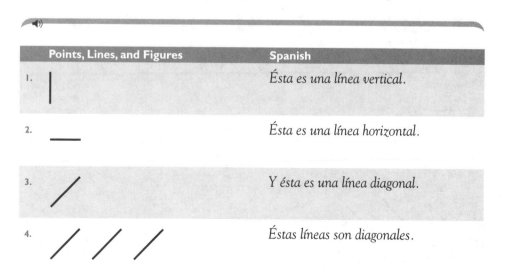

Points, Lines, and Figures	Spanish
1.	*Ésta es una línea vertical.*
2.	*Ésta es una línea horizontal.*
3.	*Y ésta es una línea diagonal.*
4.	*Éstas líneas son diagonales.*

Mexico Culture Overview

Spanish is the official language of Mexico, but as many as 100 Indian languages are still spoken in parts of Mexico. The majority of Mexicans (91%) are Roman Catholic. Family unity is very important in Mexico. Common foods include *tortillas, frijoles refritos* (refried beans), *quesadillas* (tortilla baked with cheese), and *enchiladas*. It is polite to eat with both hands—but not the elbows—above the table, and it is common to stay at the table after the meal for conversation. Mexicans are very hospitable. Visitors are welcomed and served refreshments. It is impolite to refuse these refreshments. The standard greeting is a handshake or a nod of the head.

Points, Lines, and Figures *(cont.)*	Spanish
5. 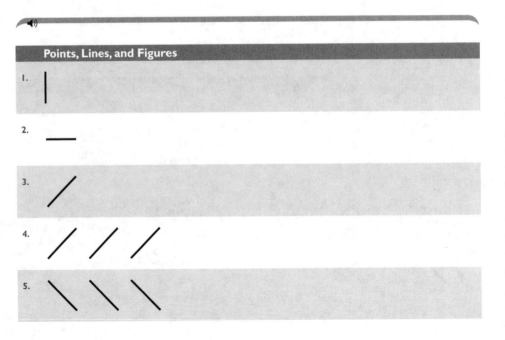	*Éstas líneas son diagonales también.*
6. ──	*¿Es vertical esta línea? No, es horizontal.*
7. ──	*¿Es horizontal esta línea también? Sí.*
8. //	*¿Son horizontales estas líneas? No, son diagonales.*
9. |||	*¿Son verticales estas líneas? Sí. (Son verticales.)*
10. |	*Ésta no es una línea diagonal.*
11. ●|	*Éste es un punto delante de una línea vertical. (El punto precede la línea.)*
12. ||●	*Éstas son dos líneas verticales delante de un punto. (El punto sigue las líneas.)*

C. Listen and Look

Points, Lines, and Figures
1. |
2. ──
3. /
4. ///
5. \\\\\\

Points, Lines, and Figures *(cont.)*

6. —

7. —

8. / /

9. |||

10. |

11. ● |

12. || ●

D. Multiple-Choice Frames

INSTRUCTIONS Listen to the audio and choose the correct frame. Check your answers in Appendix A, on page 456.

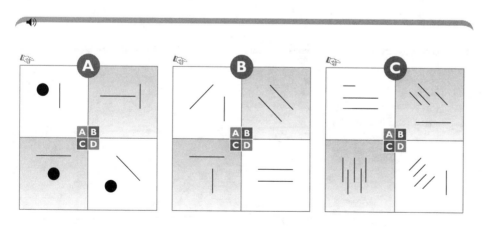

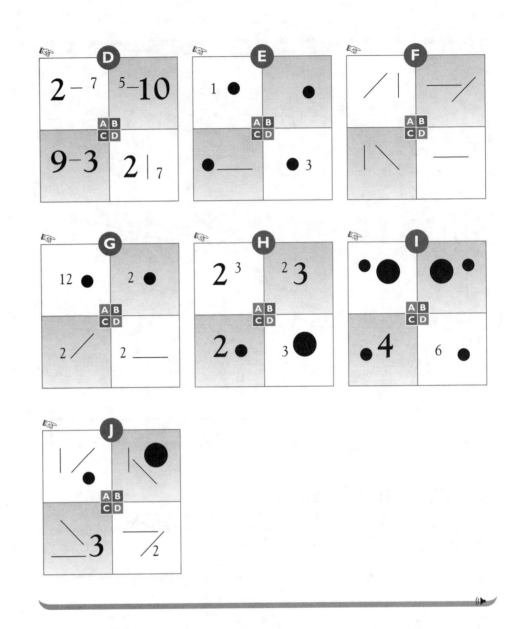

E. Listen and Draw

INSTRUCTIONS   Pause the audio if the pace is too fast. Check your answers in Appendix A, on page 457.

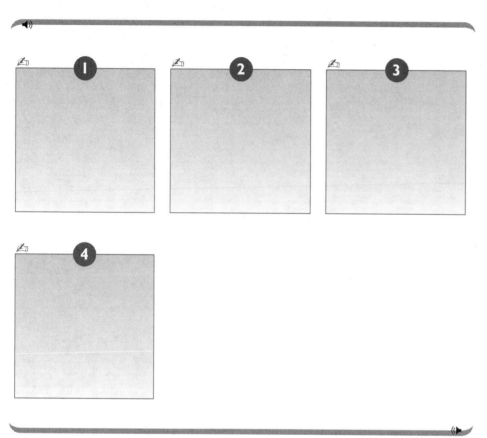

F. Read for Meaning

INSTRUCTIONS   Read the following sentences and see if you can understand them. Check the translations in Appendix A, on page 457.

1. *Ésta no es una línea horizontal, es una línea diagonal.*

2. *Éstas son dos líneas verticales y otras dos líneas horizontales.*

3. *Éste es el número seis delante de una línea larga y gruesa.*

4. *Y éste es el número siete delante de un punto grande.*

5. *Ésta es una línea delgada delante de una línea gruesa y de un punto pequeño.*

6. *Ésta es una línea vertical y una línea diagonal delante de una letra grande, la letra M.*

7. *Éste es un punto pequeño y un punto grande delante de una línea larga y delgada.*

Performance Challenge

In this activity, you learned some prepositions, words used to describe where something is in relation to other things. Set some pencils or erasers on your study table and use the words you learned today to describe where they are.

Speed Learning: Five Mini-Dialogues

INSTRUCTIONS Learn these five dialogues and perform them, cueing only from the Spanish. Try to do it after only 15 minutes. This exercise will show you that with some help, you can learn many useful Spanish sentences in a very short period of time.

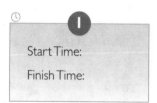

Start Time:

Finish Time:

In this activity you will:

→ Increase listening comprehension.

→ Learn mini dialogues quickly.

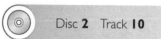 Disc **2**   Track **10**

Dialogue 1

	English	Phonetic Spelling	Spanish
●●:	How have you all been?	KAY TALL HONEST STAr THOUGH?	*¿Qué tal han estado?*
●:	More or less well.	MOSS oh MAY nose B.N.	*Más o menos bien.*

Dialogue 2

English	Phonetic Spelling	Spanish
●●: Where are you going?	AH th-OWN DAY VOSS?	¿Adónde vas?
●: I'm going to my house.	BOY A MI CASA	Voy a mi casa.
●●: Till later.	AH-stall WAY-go	Hasta luego.
●: G'bye.	CHOW	Chao.

Dialogue 3

English	Phonetic Spelling	Spanish
●●: That's it. That's surely it!	S.O.S! S.O.C.K.S!	Eso es. ¡Eso sí que es!
●: Maybe.	Key SAUCE or Key SAW	Quizás / Quizá.
●●: I'm not lying.	No me -N.-toe (myento)	No miento.
●: I know [it], but nevertheless...	Low-SAY, PAY-row scene-embargo...	Lo sé, pero sin embargo...

Dialogue 4

English	Phonetic Spelling	Spanish
●●: It's that way.	S. ah-C.	Es así.
●: Perhaps.	Tall VASE	Tal vez.
●●: That's how it is.	Ah-SEE S.	Así es.
●: No, it's not that way.	No, no S. ah-C.	No, no es así.

Facts and Figures on Mexico

- Its population is over 100,000,000 people and it is continually growing.
- Education is mandatory and free from ages six to fourteen. Students are required to wear uniforms, whether in public or private schools.
- The federal government is a *república federal* (federal republic), led by a president and a bicameral legislature. The president serves one term, and legislators can serve only two consecutive terms.
- The Mexican currency is *el nuevo peso* (the new peso).
- Agriculture employs 26 percent of the labor force, with crops consisting of: *algodón* (cotton), *café* (coffee), *trigo* (wheat), *arroz* (rice), *caña de azúcar* (sugar cane), *fruta* (fruit), *maíz* (corn) and *verduras* (vegetables).
- Mexico's main exports are agricultural products, like shrimp, cotton, oil, and coffee. Along with its main exports, Mexico's industry also includes mining *plata* (silver), producing *acero* (steel), textiles, and *caucho* (rubber).
- Like many Hispanics throughout the world, the majority of Mexicans (91%) are Roman Catholic.

Dialogue 5

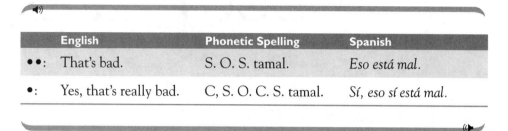

	English	Phonetic Spelling	Spanish
••:	That's bad.	S. O. S. tamal.	*Eso está mal.*
•:	Yes, that's really bad.	C, S. O. C. S. tamal.	*Sí, eso sí está mal.*

How long did it take you to complete the task? Stop your memorization and perform the five dialogues the best you can.

Performance Challenge

Time yourself. See how many of this activity's new phrases you can say in one minute.

Body Parts

 In this activity you will:

→ Read and comprehend the meaning of a text.

→ Add body parts to your vocabulary base.

 Disc **2** Track **11**

Our Southern Neighbor

Mexico is the southern neighbor of the United States. Physically, Mexico is about three times the size of the state of Texas.

Una Madre Habla a Su Niñito

INSTRUCTIONS This activity imitates the natural learning process of children. Children learn very simple words and then, as they are exposed to more and more of the language, they gradually learn to put these words into more advanced sentences. In this activity, you will first review very simple phrases, then you will gradually build to more advanced sentences. Learn many body parts in Spanish.

English	Spanish
Hand. Foot.	*Mano. Pie.*
Hands. Feet.	*Manos. Pies.*
One hand. Two hands.	*Una mano. Dos manos.*
One foot. Two feet.	*Un pie. Dos pies.*
Two hands and two feet.	*Dos manos y dos pies.*
This is my hand.	*Ésta es mi mano.*
This is my foot.	*Éste es mi pie.*
These are my hands.	*Éstas son mis manos.*
These are my feet.	*Éstos son mis pies.*
These are my hands and my feet.	*Éstas son mis manos y mis pies.*
Two hands and two feet.	*Dos manos y dos pies.*
Arm. Leg.	*Brazo. Pierna.*
This is my arm.	*Éste es mi brazo.*
This is my leg.	*Ésta es mi pierna.*
These are my arms.	*Éstos son mis brazos.*
These are my legs.	*Éstas son mis piernas.*
Two arms, two legs, two hands, and two feet.	*Dos brazos, dos piernas, dos manos, y dos pies.*
This is Maria.	*Ésta es María.*

English *(cont.)*	Spanish
This is Juan.	*Éste es Juan.*
These are Maria's arms.	*Éstos son los brazos de María.*
These are her feet.	*Éstos son sus pies.*
These are John's hands.	*Éstas son las manos de Juan.*
These are his legs.	*Éstas son sus piernas.*
This is Maria's head.	*Ésta es la cabeza de María.*
And this is her face.	*Y ésta es su cara.*
Her face is pretty.	*Su cara es bonita.*
These are her eyes.	*Éstos son sus ojos.*
She has pretty eyes, doesn't she?	*Ella tiene ojos bonitos, ¿no?*
Two pretty eyes. Very pretty.	*Dos ojos bonitos. Muy bonitos.*
Maria is beautiful.	*María es bonita.*
This is John's face.	*Ésta es la cara de Juan.*
This is John's nose.	*Ésta es la nariz de Juan.*
This is his mouth.	*Ésta es su boca.*
And these are his ears.	*Y estas son sus orejas.*
His nose, his mouth, and his ears.	*Su nariz, su boca, y sus orejas.*
One nose, one mouth, and two ears.	*Una nariz, una boca, y dos orejas.*
John's face.	*La cara de Juan.*
Look at Maria's mouth.	*Mira la boca de María.*
She has a delicate mouth with pretty lips and teeth.	*Ella tiene una boca delicada con labios y dientes bonitos.*
Red lips and white teeth.	*Labios rojos y dientes blancos.*
Yes, she has a very pretty face with red lips and white teeth.	*Sí, ella tiene una cara muy bonita con labios rojos y dientes blancos.*

Performance Challenge

Listen to the audio as many times as necessary. Then try this activity with a young child and see how much Spanish you can teach him or her.

From Words to Discourse

De la palabra al discurso

INSTRUCTIONS Use this vocabulary and the words you already know to compose narratives of your own. Here is a scatter chart of words that you must learn to string together to make sentences. Sample strings are given below.

✓ **In this activity you will:**

→ String together narratives.

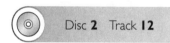 Disc **2** Track **12**

Scatter Chart

aquí hay			esa(s)
	es / son	otra(s)	
esta(s)		cosa(s)	y
	la(s)		
una(s)			negra(s)
		grande(s)	
chica(s)			no
		sí	
blanca(s)			

Sample Strings of Words

INSTRUCTIONS Carefully study these sentences. Notice the grammatically incorrect ones with the asterisk. Work out in your mind the rules for the correct formation of these kinds of word strings.

◀))

	English	Spanish
1.	A thing. The thing.	Una cosa. La cosa.
2.	The things. Some things.	Las cosas. Unas cosas.
		*La cosas. *Una cosas.
3.	Here is a thing.	He aquí una cosa.

Mexico's Other Neighbors

The river *Río Bravo Del Norte* forms a natural border between Mexico and the United States. We know this river as the Rio Grande. Mexico is the northernmost country of the Latin American countries. To the south of Mexico, the countries Belize and Guatemala are its neighbors. In this southern area of Mexico you will also find the Yucatan Peninsula. This peninsula is a low, limestone plateau. Many centuries ago great pits were formed into the limestone by the rain. The Mayan Indians used these pits as sacred wells.

	English (cont.)	Spanish
4.	Here is a white thing.	He aquí una cosa blanca.
		*He aquí una blanca cosa.
5.	And here is a black thing.	Y he aquí una cosa negra.
		*Y he aquí una negra cosa.
6.	Here are the things.	He aquí las cosas.
		*He aquí la cosas.
7.	Here are the other things, large things and small things.	He aquí las otras cosas, cosas grandes y cosas chicas.
		*He aquí las cosas otras.
8.	Here are some other things.	He aquí unas otras cosas.
9.	Some white things and some black things.	Unas cosas blancas y unas cosas negras.
10.	This thing is black.	Esta cosa es negra.
11.	The one is white; the other is black.	La una es blanca; la otra es negra.
12.	The black thing is large.	La cosa negra es grande.
		*La negra cosa es grande.
13.	The white thing is small.	La cosa blanca es chica.
		*La blanca cosa es chica.
14.	This thing is small, and that thing is large.	Esta cosa es chica, y esa cosa es grande.
15.	These things are small.	Estas cosas son chicas.
		*Estas cosas son chica.
16.	These small things are white.	Estas cosas chicas son blancas.
		*Estas chica cosas son blancas.
17.	Those large things are black.	Esas cosas grandes son negras.
		*Esas cosas grandes es negras.
18.	Is the black thing large? Yes, it's large.	¿Es grande la cosa negra? Sí, es grande.
		*¿Es la cosa negra grande?
19.	Is the white thing large? No, it's not large.	¿Es grande la cosa blanca? No, no es grande.

English (cont.)	Spanish
	*¿Es la cosa blanca grande? *No, es no grande.
20. Are these things large and white?	¿Son grandes y blancas estas cosas?
	*¿Son estas cosas grandes y blancas?
21. No, they aren't large and white.	No, no son grandes y blancas.
	*No, son no grandes y blancas.

INSTRUCTIONS Look at the twenty-one sentences above again, but cover the Spanish with your hand or a piece of paper. Translate them into Spanish and check your version with the version next to it.

Preparing to Deal with Real Objects

INSTRUCTIONS For each sentence below, orally give the Spanish equivalent. Do the same for a new, different sentence of parallel structure.

Example

English Sentence	Spanish Equivalent
A white thing. Here is a white thing.	Una cosa blanca. Aquí hay una cosa blanca.

Parallel Structure	Spanish Equivalent
A large thing. Here is a large thing.	Una cosa grande. Aquí hay una cosa grande.

1. And here is a black thing.
2. One white thing and one black thing.
3. Here are the white things.
4. Some white things and some black things.
5. This thing is small.
6. These things are large.
7. These large things are black.
8. The other things are white and small.

ACTIVITY 30

Dealing with Real Objects

INSTRUCTIONS   Set out on a table before you a number of small white things and large black things. They can be pieces of paper or whatever, as long as the smaller things are white and the larger ones are black. (You can even write "black" on larger pieces of white paper to represent black things.) Referring to these objects in front of you, see how many meaningful statements you can generate about them in two minutes. Keep a tally. Start with very short statements, then advance to more ambitious ones. The goal is for you to create twelve statements in two minutes. Can you reach this goal?

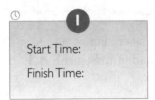

Start Time:

Finish Time:

○ Check here after concentrating at least 40 minutes on this assignment.

Performance Challenge

Concentrate on learning new vocabulary and using the new words in sentences. You may notice that *he aquí* is used in this activity for "here is." *Aquí está* is another way of saying "here is." Both are grammatically correct.

A Lesson in Spanish

Una Lección de Español

INSTRUCTIONS Listen to and read the following lesson. Learn vocabulary from this lesson.

In this activity you will:

→ Listen to and read a story.

Disc 2   Track 13

English	Spanish
What is this?	*¿Qué es esto?*
A leaf. Another leaf. The other leaf.	*Una hoja. Otra hoja. La otra hoja.*
What's the difference?	*¿En qué está la diferencia?*
One is yellow. The other is white.	*Una es amarilla. La otra es blanca.*
What is this?	*¿Qué es esto?*
A sheet of paper.	*Una hoja de papel.*
And this?	*¿Y ésto?*
Another sheet of paper.	*Otra hoja de papel.*
What's the difference?	*¿En qué está la diferencia?*
Correct. Exactly. Precisely.	*Correcto. Exactamente. Precisamente.*
Thing. The thing. This thing.	*Cosa. La cosa. Esta cosa.*
One thing yellow and one thing white.	*Una cosa amarilla y una cosa blanca.*
This yellow thing, what is it?	*Esta cosa amarilla ¿qué es?*
It's a pencil.	*Es un lápiz.*
This white thing, what is it?	*Esta cosa blanca ¿qué es?*
It's a sheet of paper.	*Es una hoja de papel.*
Yes, a white sheet of paper and a yellow pencil.	*Sí, una hoja de papel blanco y un lápiz amarillo.*
More. Two more things. So…	*Más. Dos cosas más. Entonces…*

Mexico's Mountains, Forests, and Bodies of Water

The Pacific Ocean lies to the west of Mexico and the Gulf region of Mexico lies to the east. The northern part of the Gulf of Mexico is dry and covered with low, thorny bushes and trees. The southern part of the Gulf region is a tropical rain forest. Many of Mexico's ancient ruins are hidden throughout this region. Mexico has many mountains. Two of its great mountain ranges run along its coastal borders. The *Sierra Madre Occidental* lies along Mexico's west coast and the *Sierra Madre Oriental* lies along its east coast. (What do you think the words *occidental* and *oriental* mean?) Another one of Mexico's mountain ranges, *Sierra Madre del Sur*, is found in the southern part of Mexico. The Aztecs found much of their gold in this area of Mexico. (What do you think the word *sur* means?)

English *(cont.)*	Spanish
Two more things: a yellow sheet of paper and a white pencil.	*Dos cosas más: una hoja de papel amarillo y un lápiz blanco.*
Two yellow things and two white things.	*Dos cosas amarillas y dos cosas blancas.*
So, a total of four things: two sheets of paper and two pencils.	*Entonces, un total de cuatro cosas: dos hojas de papel y dos lápices.*
These two things are white.	*Estas dos cosas son blancas.*
These two things are yellow.	*Estas dos cosas son amarillas.*

Performance Challenge

Try to make some of your own sentences using the new vocabulary. If you apply the new vocabulary, you will remember it more easily.

You have completed all the activities for

**Section 1.3.1
Day Two, 18:00 Hours**

and are now ready to take the section quiz. Before continuing, be sure you have learned the objectives for each activity in this section.

Section Quiz

INSTRUCTIONS Choose the Spanish sentence that best describes the pictographic representation. Check your answers on the "Grading Sheet" found on the last page of the book.

1.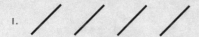

   A. *Estas son líneas diagonales.*

   B. *Estas no son líneas verticales.*

   C. *Estas son líneas horizontales.*

   D. *Estos son puntos.*

2.

   A. *Estas son dos líneas verticales.*

   B. *Estas son dos líneas horizontales.*

   C. *Estos son dos líneas horizontales y dos puntos.*

   D. *Estos son dos líneas verticales y dos puntos.*

INSTRUCTIONS Choose the correct response.

3. **¿Qué tal han estado?**

   A. *Hasta luego.*

   B. *Eso es.*

   C. *Eso está mal.*

   D. *Más o menos bien.*

INSTRUCTIONS Choose the correct Spanish translation of the underlined English word or phrase.

4. **Estos son <u>the hands</u> de Enrique.**
   A. *los pies*
   B. *la cabeza*
   C. *las manos*
   D. *los brazos*

5. **Mira <u>the eyes</u> de la reina.**
   A. *los dientes*
   B. *los labios*
   C. *las orejas*
   D. *los ojos*

6. **La cosa es <u>big</u>.**
   A. *grandes*
   B. *chicos*
   C. *negro*
   D. *grande*

INSTRUCTIONS Choose the correct Spanish translation of the English phrase.

7. **a white thing**
   A. *una cosa chica*
   B. *una cosa blanca*
   C. *la cosa blanca*
   D. *la cosa chica*

INSTRUCTIONS Choose the correct Spanish translation of the underlined English word or phrase.

8. **Y en este pueblo <u>there is</u> una flor.**
   A. *está*
   B. *en*
   C. *aquí*
   D. *hay*

9. **Esta cosa amarilla. <u>What is it?</u>**

   A. ¿Qué es?

   B. ¿Aquí está?

   C. ¿Qué es la diferencia?

   D. ¿Y ésto?

10. **Dos cosas <u>yellow</u> y dos cosas <u>white</u>.**

   A. blancos / amarillas

   B. amarillas / blancas

   C. blancas / amarillas

   D. amarillos / blancos

Isla de Providencia

Day Three, 10:00 Hours

Seven Days to Rendezvous

Mounted once again on borrowed bicycles, you and Stump set out for the third location marked on *el mapa*. It's more than halfway across the island from the *Quintana* residence. Even pedaling hard, it's past noon by the time you pull to a stop in front of a large, old-fashioned *hacienda*.

"Well, this should be it," you say. You ring the bell at the imposing wrought-iron gate.

"*¿Sí? ¿Quién es?*" emerges a very proper voice from the box above the doorbell.

"*Somos amigos de Beatríz del Bosque,*" you reply.

"*¿Amigos de Beatríz?*" the voice queries. "Ah, *sí*, she told me you might be coming. *Pase, por favor.*" With that, the gate smoothly opens, and you're able to proceed down the broad brick-paved driveway to the elegant red-roofed mansion at the center of the *hacienda*.

A pleasant-looking and very well-dressed middle-aged woman opens the door. "Let me see, you must be Rumpelstiltskin, and you must be Stumpelriltskin," she says. "*Beatríz* visited me last night and told me all about you. My name is *Bárbara*, by the way—*Bárbara Buenaventura*. *Beatríz* and I are in the same botany club, you see."

"Oh, is that your hobby?" Stump asks.

"No, actually, my hobby is writing," *Bárbara* replies. "Right now, I'm working on a narrative article on growing up in *México*, and another on the Mayan ruins of Guatemala. What do you two know of these countries?"

While showing you the first set of activities you'll need to complete your next challenge, *Bárbara* proceeds to bring you up to date on *México* and *Guatemala*.

In this section you will:

→ Use pictographs to reinforce vocabulary and listening skills.

→ Recognize sentence patterns and structures.

→ Re-tell stories using visuals.

→ Use pictographs to master words and dialogues.

→ Master new vocabulary and sentence patterns and increase translation skills.

→ Use geography vocabulary.

Disc **2**   Track **14**

Chatter at a Royal Ball

ACTIVITY 32

In this activity you will:

→ Use pictographs to reinforce vocabulary and listening skills.

Disc **2** Track **15**

INSTRUCTIONS Use pictographs to master the following words and dialogue.

Preparation for Conversation

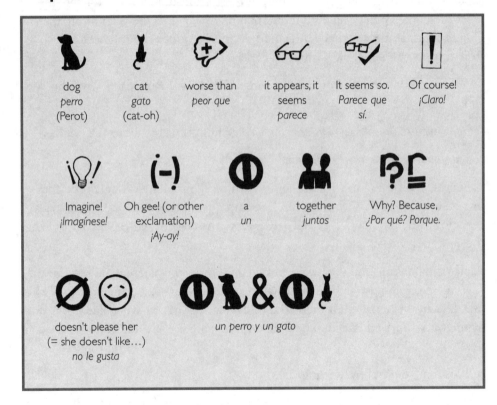

The Volcanoes of Mexico

In the south of Mexico there are also many mountains that include chains of volcanoes. Three of Mexico's highest mountain peaks are actually volcanoes. These peaks are called *Orizaba*, *Popocatepetl*, and *Ixtacihuatl*. *Paricutin* is another one of Mexico's main volcanoes. These volcanoes form a series of volcanoes known as the Volcanic Axis. The Volcanic Axis extends across Mexico. Many of these volcanoes are active!

Self Quiz on Recognition of the Pictographs

INSTRUCTIONS Review previously introduced pictographs.

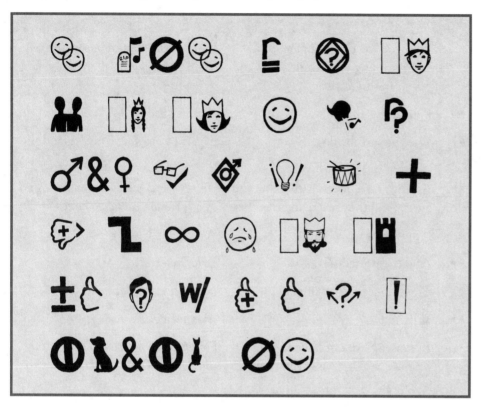

INSTRUCTIONS Read through this list of words and make sure you are familiar with their meanings. Check off words you understand.

Checklist			
○ ¿cuál?	○ bien	○ mejor que	○ con
○ siempre	○ el que	○ el rey	○ la reina
○ quien	○ ¿quién sabe?	○ juntos	○ pero
○ peor que	○ no le gusta	○ claro!	○ la torre
○ llora	○ porque	○ también	○ le gusta
○ él y ella	○ el príncipe	○ toca	○ no les gusta
○ ¿por qué?	○ la princesa	○ ¡imagínese!	○ les gusta
○ parece que sí	○ canta	○ un perro y un gato	○ más o menos bien
○ cantos fúnebres			

Conversation 3

	English	Spanish
•:	Polo and Misti are singing, too. They are singing with the king and queen in the tower.	*Polo y Misti están cantando también. Están cantando con el rey y la reina en la torre.*
••:	Polo and Misti?	*¿Polo y Misti?*
•:	The cat and the dog.	*El perro y el gato.* (The dog and the cat.)
••:	A king and a queen with a dog and a cat. And they're singing together?	*Un rey y una reina con un perro y un gato. ¿Y están cantando juntos?*
•:	It appears so.	*Parece que sí.*
••:	And the princess?	*¿Y la princesa?*
•:	The princess is not singing.	*La princesa no está cantando.*
••:	Why not?	*¿Por qué no?*
•:	Because she doesn't like to sing. She doesn't sing well. She sings worse than the dog.	*Porque a ella no le gusta cantar. No canta bien. ¡Canta peor que el perro!*
••:	But better than the cat!	*¡Pero mejor que el gato!*
•:	Of course. Imagine!	*Claro. ¡Imagínese!*
••:	Oh gee!	*¡Ay ay!*

Go back and listen several times to this conversation until you can understand it with eyes closed.

Task 1

INSTRUCTIONS   Use your hands as puppets and dramatize the dialogue, looking only at the Spanish. Don't be shy! Throw yourself into this performance.

Task 2

INSTRUCTIONS   Do the same as in the previous task, but look only at the pictographic representation of the dialogue and express your thoughts in Spanish without thinking in English.

Pictographic Representation of the Same Dialogue

Pictographic Representation
•: Polo & Misti ... + ... w/ ... & ...
••: Polo & Misti?
•: ... & ...
••: ... & ... w/ ... & ... & ...
•: ...
••: & ...
•: ...
••: ?
•: ...
••: ...
•: !
••: (-)

☆

Performance Challenge

Copy the pictographs from this activity onto note cards as well. Use them with the cards you made earlier, and make as many new sentences as you can. Say each sentence aloud for practice.

Focus on the Language 8-10

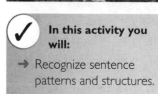

INSTRUCTIONS Complete the following grammar exercise.

Focus 8

Gustar (to please)

To express "She likes X" in Spanish, it is helpful to think of the statement in this form: "X pleases her." If you insist on making a word for word translation, you will likely get confused. Remember, English and Spanish have different ways of saying the same thing.

English	Spanish
The queens please him / her.	*Le gustan las reinas.*
OR He / she likes the queens.	
To sing pleases them.	*Les gusta cantar.*
OR They like to sing.	
To write doesn't please me.	*No me gusta escribir.*
OR I don't like to write.	

NOTE

Note: To say, "I like (something or someone)," you could say, "Me pleases (something or someone)." Don't try to form a more direct translation equivalent! It may seem awkward or backward to express the idea of liking in this way, but that's how it is expressed in Spanish.

✓ In this activity you will:

→ Recognize sentence patterns and structures.

Mexico's Plateau Region

Do you remember learning about a large, dry plateau called *La Meseta*, in *España*? Well, Mexico has a region similar to *La Meseta*. The Plateau of Mexico is where most of the people in Mexico live and it is also the country's main agricultural region. The capital of Mexico, Mexico City, is found in this region in an area known as *el Distrito Federal* (the Federal District).

Focus 9

Gustar (with personal noun).

English	Spanish
The queen likes to sing.	*A la reina le gusta cantar.*
The king likes to sing, too.	*Al rey le gusta cantar también.*
Who likes to sing with the cat?	*¿A quién le gusta cantar con el gato?*

The noun must have an *a* before it when using *gustar*: *a la reina*, for example. *Le* in the three examples above must also be used before *gustar*. This is nearly untranslatable in English, but it is required in Spanish.

Focus 10

Gustar (with object pronoun after an infinitive)

English	Spanish
(Literal) To him / her it pleases to sing it.	*Le gusta cantarlo.*
OR He / she likes to sing it.	NOT **le gusta lo cantar.*
(Literal) To him / her it pleases to drink it.	*Le gusta tomarlo.*
OR He / she likes to drink it.	NOT: **le gusta lo tomar.*

Translate Orally From and Into Spanish

INSTRUCTIONS Now incorporate Focus 8, 9, and 10.

English	Spanish
The queen pleases me.	*Me gusta la reina.*
I like the queen.	*Me gusta la reina.*
I like the dogs.	*Me gustan los perros.*
I don't like the queen.	*No me gusta la reina.*
To smoke doesn't please me.	*No me gusta fumar.*
I don't like to drink.	*No me gusta tomar.*
He (or she) likes to sing.	*Le gusta cantar.*
But he doesn't like to sing with the cat.	*Pero no le gusta cantar con el gato.*

English (cont.)	Spanish
Who likes the dog?	¿A quién le gusta el perro?
Who likes the cat and the dog?	¿A quién le gustan el gato y el perro?
Pablo likes Maria and Ana.	A Pablo le gustan María y Ana.
The dukes eat this.	Los duques comen esto.
They like to eat this.	Les gusta comer esto.
But they don't like to eat it in the tower.	Pero no les gusta comerlo en la torre.
Who likes to sing and who likes to dance?	¿A quién le gusta cantar y a quién le gusta bailar?
I don't like to drink it.	No me gusta tomarlo.
The king pleases the queen.	A la reina le gusta el rey.

NOTE

Note that the word *quiere* ("want") is used differently from *gustar*: *El rey quiere cantar*. The king wants to sing. *Quiere* follows regular usage for verbs, unlike *gustar*.

Performance Challenge

Work on mastering each grammar focus. Try to match the grammar you just learned with vocabulary you've learned in other activities to make sentences that use the new grammar focuses.

In this activity you will:

➜ Re-tell stories using visuals.

➜ Use pictographs to master words and dialogues.

The People and Culture of Mexico

At the beginning of this unit you learned about the physical aspects of Mexico. Now let's learn more about this beautiful country, its people and culture. Mexico is a rich and diverse country with many resources and history. Did you know that even though Spanish is the official language of Mexico, there are as many as 100 Indian languages still spoken in parts of Mexico? It is known as the "cradle" of advanced civilizations. Many Mexicans are of mixed indigenous and European descent.

Wrap-Up Activities

Reading and Responding to Questions

INSTRUCTIONS   This activity simulates a very important step in the natural language learning process: putting together many different parts of what you have learned to create new and meaningful statements. In preparation, have the following materials ready:

1. The set of 3" x 5" pictograph cards taken from all the previous pictograph exercises.

2. A new set of 3" x 5" cards (that you make) with the question word pictographs (see below).

Question Words and Their Pictographs

INSTRUCTIONS   Read through the following chart to cement your knowledge of the following Spanish question words.

English	Spanish	Pictograph	Memory Aid
Who?	¿Quién? (key-N.)		(person)
(To) whom?	¿A quién?		(arrow to…)
From whom?	¿De quién?		(arrow from…)
Which?	¿Cuál?		
Why?	¿Por qué? (for what?)		(R for "reason")
How?	¿Cómo?		(H for "how")

English (cont.)	Spanish	Pictograph	Memory Aid
Where?	*¿Dónde?*		(@ for "at")
(To) where?	*¿Adónde?*		(arrow to…)
From where?	*¿De dónde?*		(arrow from…)
What?	*¿Qué?* ("K")		(thing)
When?	*¿Cuándo?*		
How much?	*¿Cuánto?*		
activity, doing	*haciendo*		

English	Spanish	Pictograph
What is she doing?	*¿Qué está haciendo ella?*	
With whom is she singing?	*¿Con quién está cantando?*	

Mini-Story: The Musical Royal Family

INSTRUCTIONS Read the story just below, preparing to respond to the questions that follow it.

En esta historia hay (= there is) *un rey y una reina. Éste es el rey* y *ésta es la reina*

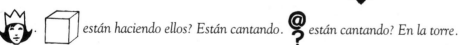

[pictograph] canta mejor que [box] [queen], [box] [queen] canta mejor que el perro, y el perro canta mejor que el gato. Hay una princesa también. Esta es la princesa [princess]. ¿Está cantando [box] [princess]? No, ella no está cantando. [face]no? Pues ella no canta bien. Canta peor que el perro. ¿Peor que el perro? Sí, peor que el perro…pero mejor que el gato. [cube] [arrow] [box] [princess]? ¿No está llorando en el baño? ¿[face] sabe? [face] llora [box] [princess] en el baño? [face] sabe? ¿Llora [box] [queen] con [box] [princess] en el baño? Sí, las dos lloran en el baño.

Questions

INSTRUCTIONS Put the following questions into pictographs. Answer them according to the pictograph answers given. A review of the previous pictographs may be helpful.

	Question	Answer
ex.	¿Qué está haciendo el gato? [sad face]	[cube] [arrow] [box] [cat]? El gato llora.
1.	¿Qué está haciendo el rey? [note]	
2.	¿Cómo canta el rey? [thumb]	
3.	¿Qué está haciendo la reina? [note] **+**	
4.	¿Quién canta mejor, el perro o el gato? [dog]	
5.	¿Qué clase de cantos tocaba el rey en el tambor? [note]	

Question (cont.)	Answer
6. ¿Dónde está cantando el rey?	....
7. ¿Con quién está cantando el rey?	....
8. ¿Él canta mejor que el perro?	....
9. ¿La princesa está cantando con el rey?	....
10. ¿Quién canta peor, el gato o la princesa?	....

Generating Your Own Sentences

INSTRUCTIONS   Suppose you knew only four nouns: butcher, baker, dog, cat, and five possible interactions between them: hates, loves, catches, ignores, hugs. Suppose also that you had this simple rule for combining these elements into meaningful statements: place a noun before an interaction word (a verb), and place a noun after the verb. Here is a combination chart of those elements. Pick any item in column 1, then any in column 2, then any in column 3, and say them in that order: 1-2-3.

Sentence Generation Chart

INSTRUCTIONS   Read through the following chart to learn how to generate sentences correctly.

1: Agent (noun)	2: Impact (verb)	3: Patient (noun)
The butcher	hates	the dog.
The baker	loves	the cat.
The dog	catches	the butcher.
The cat	ignores	the baker.
	hugs	

Here are some sample sentences from this sentence "machine": The butcher ignores the baker. The cat loves the butcher. The dog catches the butcher.

Sring several sentence combinations from this chart into a story line. To do this, you just need to pay attention to the logic of the story possibilities of the sequence. Here, for example, is a story line: The baker loves the cat. The baker loves the dog. The dog hates the cat. The cat hates the dog. The dog catches the cat. The dog ignores the cat. The baker hates the dog.

A language learner gains a lot by practicing telling such stories (and longer ones) fluently and expressively.

Here is some help in organizing your own sentence machine, one that will be much more powerful than the chart shown above. From the statements you can form various combinations. From the various combinations of words, you can create stories.

Sentence and Phrase Parts You Know How to Express

Sentence and Phrase Part	Example
Actor / patient noun	*rey, reina, princesa, gato (reyes, reinas, princesas, gatos)*
Modifiers	*el, la, un, una, este, esta (los, las, estos, estas)*
Pronouns	*ella, él (ellos, ellas)*
Location nouns	*baño, torre*
Location or accompaniment	*en, con*
Action verb stems	*cant-, llor-, toc-*
Action verb endings	*-a(n), -aba(n), -ando*
Auxiliary verb	*está(n)*
Manner	*mejor / peor (que); (muy) bien, mal*
Information question words	*¿Qué? ¿Quién? ¿Dónde? ¿Cómo? ¿Cuál? ¿Por qué?*
Answers or rejoinders	*Sí. No. ¡Imagínese!*
Other words	*y, pero, también*

Arrange your cards into separate piles according to the categories listed above.

INSTRUCTIONS Using the words listed above (represented by your pictographs on cards), do the following:

1. Take three actor nouns and three action-verb stems, like {rey} and {llor-}. By adding the proper grammatical details, make up three quick sentences on the model of *El rey llora*.

2. Make your three sentences plural, on the model *Los reyes lloran.* (Be sure to put the plural marker *-n* on the action word.)

3. Turn these sentences into yes / no questions by reversing the noun and the verb on the model of *¿Llora el rey?* (the reverse of *El rey llora*).

4. Turn the sentences into who questions or where questions as in *¿Quién llora? ¿Dónde llora la reina?*

5. Change the sentences to what action questions as in *¿Qué hace el rey?* or *¿Qué hacen las princesas?*

6. Make three new sentences by joining two actors as sentence subjects, on the model *El rey y la reina lloran.* (Be sure to put the plural marker *-n* on the action word.)

7. Expand your last three sentences by adding a location phrase (*en…*) and a "with" phrase (*con…*) on the model *El rey y la reina lloran en la torre con el gato.*

8. Choosing from this material, make up equally complex or even more complex sentences of your own.

Creating Your Own Mini-Story Plots

INSTRUCTIONS Create your own mini-story plots. Plan them out–perhaps even write them–then give them orally, aiming for a smooth flow of speech without hesitation. Limit yourself to words you know, supplemented by a selection of a few additional words given below.

How to prepare using new vocabulary:

1. Write each of the new words below on a separate card and put the cards in their appropriate piles.

2. Select certain cards that together can form meaningful statements and arrange them in the order you want.

3. Aim at performing your story plots orally without reading. Aim at smooth-flowing diction.

Subjects or Agents of Action

Use these words as the subjects of your sentences.

English	Spanish
preacher	*predicador, predicadora*
student	*(el / la) estudiante*
director	*director, directora*
trombone player	*(el / la) trombón*
violinist	*(el / la) violinista*
drummer	*(el / la) tambor*

English (cont.)	Spanish
secretary	(el / la) secretaria
helper	(el / la) ayudante
actress	(la) actriz
actor	(el) actor
doctor	(el) médico
chief, boss	(el / la) jefe
commander	(el / la) comandante
teacher	profesor, profesora
person	persona

Action Without Impact on Anyone Else *(Intransitive Verbs)

Verbs are action words. They tell us what the subject does. From the verbs you have learned so far, we can divide them into two types: some verbs describe actions that impact others, while others do not. For example, we say "I like (cake, the drummer, the school...)". However, it does not make sense to say "I sleep (cake, the drummer, the student...)". To sleep does not have an impact on others, whereas to detest does.

English	Spanish
enters	entra
exits	sale
dies	muere
relaxes	relaja
dances	baila
sleeps	duerme

Action With Impact on Persons or Things *(Transitive Verbs)

Verbs that impact others are called transitive verbs. Verbs that do not impact others are called intransitive verbs. You can remember this by thinking that when there is an impact on others (a transitive verb), there is a transition of the action from one to another. When there is not an impact on another, there is not a transition of the action from one to another.

English	Spanish
attacks	ataca
defends	defiende

English (cont.)	Spanish
detests	detesta
loves	ama
accepts	acepta
receives	recibe
fabricates	fabrica
preaches	predica
observes	observa
prepares	prepara
studies	estudia
cures	cura
helps	ayuda
insults	insulta
practices	practica
commands / sends	manda

Settings

Use these words as the setting or location for your subjects and verbs.

	English	Spanish
Place:	school	escuela
	theater	teatro
	church	iglesia
Time:	one day	un día
	one night	una noche

Concrete Objects and Associated Verbs

Use these words as the objects upon which your subject performs an action.

English	Spanish
a document	un documento
The secretary prepares a document.	La secretaria prepara un documento.
a sermon	un sermón
The preacher preaches a sermon at church.	El predicador predica un sermón en la iglesia.

English *(cont.)*	Spanish
a package	*un paquete*
The trombonist receives a package from the violinist.	*El trombón recibe un paquete de la violinista.*
a letter	*una carta*
The chief sends a letter to the actress.	*El jefe manda una carta a la actriz.*
the lesson	*la lección*
The student studies the lesson in school.	*La estudiante estudia la lección en la escuela.*
the cause	*la causa* ("cow-sa")
The helper helps the cause.	*El ayudante ayuda la causa.*

Sample Beginning of a Mini-Story Plot

INSTRUCTIONS Below is the beginning of a story based on some of the vocabulary that was presented above. Read it once attempting to understand the meaning, then check the translation in Appendix A, on page 457.

1. *Hay tres personas: un trombón, una violinista, y un tambor.*
2. *El trombón ama a la violinista.*
3. *Pero la violinista no ama al trombón.*
4. *Ella odia…detesta al trombón.*
5. *La violinista ama al tambor.*
6. *Pero el tambor no ama a la violinista.*
7. *Él ama a una actriz.*
8. *El tambor canta y baila con la actriz.*
9. *Él le manda cartas a la actriz, y la actriz le manda cartas al tambor.*
10. *Un día el trombón le manda una carta a la violinista.*
11. *La violinista recibe la carta del trombón.*
12. *La violinista ataca al trombón.*

You now have everything you need to create a mini-story of your own. It may help to begin by selecting some of your pictographs and laying them out in front of you, subjects in one group, action verbs in another, etc. You don't need to create great pieces of fiction, just string statements together in some meaningful order.

The more statements you can weave into each story, the better. Write two or more stories on paper, but then tell them without reading. Or better yet, sit back and relax, letting your mind spin off meaningful strings of statements that form a story line. In telling your stories out loud, aim for fluency of delivery, imitating a Spanish accent as well as you can.

Performance Challenge

Read the sample mini-story plot, then create your own. Work on using correct grammar, but don't worry if it's not perfect. At this point, just focus on being creative with the Spanish language.

ACTIVITY
35

Toward Fluency 3

INSTRUCTIONS Use these exercises to master new vocabulary and sentence patterns.

In this activity you will:

→ Master new vocabulary and sentence patterns and increase translation skills.

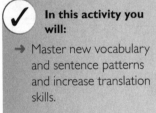

Disc **2** Track **16**

Mexican Families

Family unity is very important in Mexico. The traditional Mexican family is large and close knit. As you continue to read about families in Mexico, think about your family. Are there any similarities? In a traditional Mexican family you will find that not only are there parents and children living in the home, but often there are grandparents and sometimes even aunts and uncles. Child-care, parties, music, and meals are some of the activities shared by all members of the family. The concept of privacy is different in Spanish-speaking countries including Mexico. People spend less time alone and more time with their family and friends.

Words and Patterns 1

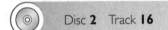

English	Spanish
a gentleman	*un señor*
the gentleman	*el señor*
a young lady	*una señorita*
the young lady	*la señorita*
lady	*señora*
a friend who…	*un amigo que…*
he / she was	*él / ella era*
you were	*usted era*
I was	*Yo era (estaba)*
It was me.	*Era yo.*
of the princess	*de la princesa*
of the prince	*del príncipe*
I believe so.	*Creo que sí.*
I believe not.	*Creo que no.*

English	Spanish
You know who Albert was, don't you?	*Usted sabe quién era Alberto, ¿no?*
I know that he was a prince.	*Sé que él era un príncipe.*
He was the prince who was the friend of Anita.	*El era el príncipe que era amigo de Anita.*
And do you know who Richard was?	*¿Y sabe quién era Ricardo?*

English *(cont.)*	Spanish
I believe he was a friend of the princess.	*Creo que él era amigo de la princesa.*
Was he a friend of the prince too?	*¿Era amigo del príncipe también?*
No, he wasn't. For certain he wasn't.	*No, no era. Es cierto que no era.*
Who is it that was the prince's friend?	*¿Quién es que era amigo del príncipe?*
Wasn't it the gentleman from Verona?	*¿No era el señor de Verona?*
Who was it? Was it you? Yes, it was me.	*¿Quién era? ¿Era usted? Sí, era yo.*
Wasn't it him? No, sir, it was her.	*¿No era él? No, señor, era ella.*
Who is it? It's me / I am I, Don Quixote.	*¿Quién es? Soy yo, Don Quijote.*

Rapid Oral Translation Exercise 1

INSTRUCTIONS   Translate the following sentences into Spanish. Check your translations in Appendix A, on page 457.

1. Rolando was a prince and is a prince.

2. Richard was not a prince and is not a prince.

3. José is a friend of Juanita, who is a princess.

4. Josefina's friend isn't a princess.

5. Pedro's friend was a prince, yes.

6. He was from Spain, and he was a friend of your mother. Maria too, right?

7. Who is Juanita? She's the princess who was Jose's friend.

8. You were a friend of José, right? Yes, I was a friend of the prince and the princess, but I was not Josephine's friend.

9. Was she an enemy? Yes, she was.

10. Yes, we're enemies. She was my enemy and she still is my enemy.

Review

1. Go through the previous oral translation exercises in the "Toward Fluency" activities, aiming for rapid, smooth delivery. Speak with expression and confidence. Imagine you are telling a story to children.

2. Close your eyes, breathe deeply, and relax, letting your mind create sentences made up of material from this lesson. See how many meaningful statements you can generate from this material in two minutes. Keep a tally. Try to make fifteen statements in two minutes. Do it four times.

ACTIVITY 35

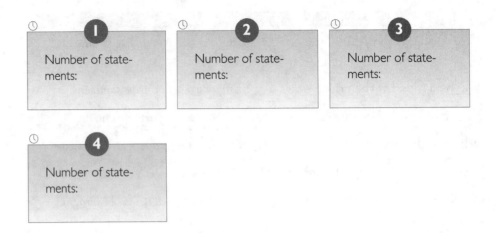

1 Number of statements:	2 Number of statements:	3 Number of statements:

4 Number of statements:

Words and Patterns 2

English	Spanish
Where is…?	¿Dónde está…?
Where is the house?	¿Dónde está la casa?
He, she, or it is here.	Está aquí.
Where was…?	¿Dónde estaba…?
Where was the house?	¿Dónde estaba la casa?
He, she, or it was here.	Estaba aquí.
in the hospital	en el hospital
in the garden	en el jardín
in the house	en la casa
at home	en casa
now	ahora
not now	ahora no

English	Spanish
Where is she? She's in the house.	¿Dónde está ella? Está en la casa.
But the prince is not at home.	Pero el príncipe no está en casa.
Is it certain he is not [there]?	¿Es cierto que él no está?
Where is he?	¿Dónde está él?
Is he here now?	¿Está aquí ahora?

English *(cont.)*	Spanish
Not now. He's not here; he's there.	*Ahora no. El no está aquí; está allá.*
Was she there?	*¿Estaba ella allá?*
No, she was not there; she was here.	*No, no estaba allá; estaba aquí.*

Contrast the use of the verb:

1. *El es de España. El es un amigo.*
   - BUT NOT: *El está de España. El está un amigo.*
2. *El está aquí.*
   - BUT NOT: *El es aquí.*

"To be (located somewhere)" takes the "to be" verb *estar.* "To be (originated from somewhere)" and "to be (a friend)" take the verb *ser.*

Rapid Oral Translation Exercise 2

INSTRUCTIONS   Translate the following sentences into Spanish. Check your translations in Appendix A, on page 457.

1. Where is the prince? Where is he from?
2. Do you know if he is from Spain?
3. Do you know if he is at home now?
4. Is the gentleman in the house?
5. Was the gentleman in the house?
6. Is the gentleman at home?
7. Was the gentleman home?
8. Where is the lady? Is she in the garden?
9. Where was the lady? Was she in the hospital?
10. The young lady who was here is not my friend.
11. Roberto is my friend, but he was not here.
12. Who was here and who was there?
13. Who was your friend (m) and who was your enemy (m)?

Review

1. Go through the oral translation exercises again, aiming for fluency. Speak with expression and confidence. Imagine you are telling a story to children.
2. Close your eyes, breathe deeply, and relax, letting your mind create sentences made up of material from this lesson. See how many meaningful statements you can generate from this material in two minutes. Your goal is to make sixteen statements in two minutes. Can you do it? Do it four times.

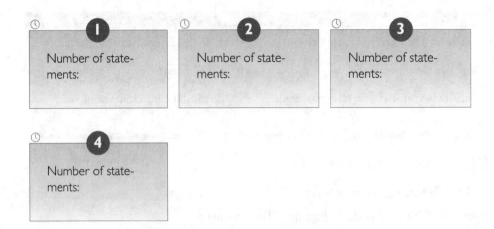

Number of statements:

Number of statements:

Number of statements:

Number of statements:

Performance Challenge

In this activity, you worked with the past tenses of *ser* and *estar*. Both these verbs mean "to be," but they're used differently. Go over the activity one more time, this time trying to pick out the nuances that distinguish the two verbs.

More on the Alphabet

INSTRUCTIONS Read and listen to this next activity.

Más acerca del Alfabeto

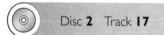

Los Nombres de las Consonantes en Español

La pronunciación de los nombres de las consonantes es así:

Letter		Letter		Letter	
B	be-grande	C	ce	D	de
F	efe	G	ge	H	hache
J	jota	K	ka	L	ele
LL	elle	M	eme	N	ene
Ñ	eñe	P	pe	Q	qu
R	ere	RR	erre	S	ese
T	te	V	be-corta	W	doble-ve
X	equis	Y	i-griega	Z	zeta

La primera letra del alfabeto no es una consonante sino una vocal—la vocal <A>. <A> no es una consonante, ni en inglés ni en español. <A> siempre es una vocal.

La última letra del alfabeto no es una vocal sino una consonante—la consonante <Z>. <Z> no es una vocal, ni en inglés ni en español. <Z> siempre es una consonante.

En otras palabras, <A> es la primera letra del alfabeto romano y es una vocal, y <Z> es la última letra del alfabeto romano y es una consonante.

Después de la letra <A> viene la letra <B>, y después de la <B> viene la <C>. Antes de la letra <N> viene la letra <M>, y antes de la <M> viene la <L>. ¿Cuál letra viene antes de la <L>? La <K>. ¿Cuál letra viene entre la <A> y la <C>? La letra <B> viene entre la <A> y la <C>. Y la <C> viene entre la <B> y la <D>, ¿no?

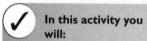

In this activity you will:

→ Master new vocabulary and sentence patterns and increase translation skills.

Disc **2** Track **17**

Meals in Mexico

Mealtime is an important family time in Mexico. At mealtimes Mexican families come together to share. Common foods eaten in Mexico include *tortillas, frijoles refritos* (refried beans), *quesadillas* (tortilla baked with cheese), and *enchiladas*. Here are some Mexican meal time guidelines for proper etiquette:

- It is polite to eat with both hands—but not the elbows—above the table.
- It is common to stay at the table—even if you finish your meal before everyone else—after the meal for conversations.

En el alfabeto español, la letra <M> viene antes de la <N> y la <N> antes de la <Ñ>. Estos sonidos nasales son los únicos en el alfabeto. ¿Cuántas consonantes nasales hay en el alfabeto? Tres. ¿Y cuáles son? La <M>, la <N>, y la <Ñ>. ¿Cuál viene primero en el alfabeto? La letra <M> viene primero. La <O> viene después de la <Ñ> y no después de la <N>, como en el alfabeto del inglés. De estas cuatro letras, la <M>, la < N>, la < Ñ> y la <O>, ¿cuál es una vocal?

¿Es la <Y> siempre una consonante? No, no siempre. Ordinariamente la <Y> sirve como una consonante.

En las palabras ya, yeso, yo, yuca, por ejemplo, la <Y> sirve como una consonante. Pero en la palabra Y que significa "and," la <Y> es una vocal. Y en las palabras soy y doy, la <Y> es una semi vocal—como en inglés.

Las letras <K> y <W> no son letras ordinarias del español. Estas letras—la <K> y la <W>—no ocurren en palabras de origen español. El alfabeto del inglés tiene dos letras nasales: la <M> y la <N>. El alfabeto del español tiene tres letras nasales: Las dos que hay en inglés más la letra <Ñ>.

La <D> más la <O> más la <S> construyen la palabra dos. La primera letra de dos es la <D>; la <O> es la segunda, y la <S> es la tercera y última letra.

En el alfabeto, ninguna letra viene antes de la letra <A> y ninguna letra viene después de la <Z>. Es decir, la <A> es la primera letra y la <Z> es la última letra del alfabeto. Aquí se ve el alfabeto.

Aa, Bb, Cc, Dd, Ee, Ff, Gg, Hh, Ii, Jj, Kk, Ll, LLll, Mm, Nn, Ññ, Oo, Pp, Qq, Rr, RRrr, Ss, Tt, Uu, Vv, Xx, Yy, Zz

Nótese que cada letra tiene dos formas, la forma mayúscula y la forma minúscula. Las letras mayúsculas son más grandes que las letras minúsculas. Las letras mayúsculas se usan con nombres de personas en la posición inicial. Por ejemplo, mi nombre es Carlos. Así se escribe mi nombre: Carlos. Nótese que la <C> inicial se escribe con mayúscula, pero las otras letras se escriben con minúscula.

Todas las letras, sean mayúsculas o minúsculas, se pueden escribir en letra de bloque o en letra cursiva. Por ejemplo, aquí está mi nombre escrito en letra de bloque: Carlos. Aquí en letra cursiva:

Carlos

A Geography Lesson

In this activity you will:

→ Use geography vocabulary.

Disc **2**   Track **18**

Mexican Hospitality

Mexicans are very hospitable people. Visitors are welcomed and served refreshments whenever they stop by, announced or unannounced. It is impolite to refuse these refreshments. The standard greeting is a handshake or a nod of the head, although between family and friends it is common to greet one another with a kiss on the cheek and a hug.

Una Lección de Geografía

INSTRUCTIONS   Learn vocabulary related to geography as you listen to and read this story.

English	Spanish
Here is a map of the world.	*He aquí un mapa del mundo.*
The earth is our spaceship.	*La tierra es nuestra nave espacial.*
It is one of nine planets that revolve around the sun.	*Es uno de los nueve planetas que giran alrededor del sol.*
Most of the surface of the earth is covered with water.	*La mayoría de la superficie de la tierra está cubierta de agua.*

English (cont.)	Spanish
There are three great oceans: the Pacific Ocean, the Atlantic Ocean, and the Indian Ocean.	*Hay tres océanos grandes: el Océano Pacífico, el Océano Atlántico, y el Océano Indico.*
Here is the Pacific Ocean.	*Aquí está el Océano Pacífico.*
It is the largest ocean.	*Es el océano más grande.*
Also the deepest.	*También el más profundo.*
Here is the Atlantic Ocean.	*Aquí está el Océano Atlántico.*
It is situated between Europe and North America, also between Africa and South America.	*Está situado entre Europa y Norteamérica, también entre África y Sudamérica.*
Here is the Indian Ocean, which extends from	*Aquí está el Océano Índico, que se extiende de*
Africa to Australia and touches Arabia and India.	*África hasta Australia y toca Arabia e India.*
The largest continent in the world extends from Europe to China.	*El continente más grande del mundo se extiende de Europa hasta la China.*
It is called Eurasia.	*Se llama Eurasia.*
This continent here is Africa.	*Este continente (aquí) es África.*
Africa is large, but it's not so large as Eurasia.	*Africa es grande, pero no es tan grande como Eurasia.*
Here on the other side of the Atlantic is situated another great continent, the one called South America.	*Aquí al otro lado del Atlántico está situado otro continente, el que se llama Sudamérica.*
And here is found the largest river in the world.	*Y aquí se halla el río más grande del mundo.*
It is called the Amazon River.	*Se llama el río Amazonas.*

Performance Challenge

Take a moment to notice the differences in English and Spanish spellings of geography words. Watch, read, or listen to the news tonight and see if you can express in Spanish any of the things that the reporters discuss.

You have completed all the activities for

Section 1.3.2
Day Three, 10:00 Hours

and are now ready to take the section quiz. Before continuing, be sure you have learned the objectives for each activity in this section.

Section Quiz

INSTRUCTIONS   Choose the answer that best completes the following sentences. Check your answers on the "Grading Sheet" found on the last page of the book.

1. **A las muchachas ... cantar canciones románticas.**

   A. *le gustan*

   B. *les gusta*

   C. *les gustan*

   D. *le gustamos*

2. **... me gusta estudiar la lección.**

   A. *Yo*

   B. *A mí*

   C. *Ella*

   D. *A él*

3. **¿... están los reyes?**

   A. *Quiénes*

   B. *Qué*

   C. *Dónde*

   D. *Cuándo*

4. **¿...? El actor trabaja con la actriz.**

   A. *¿Dónde trabaja el actor?*

   B. *¿Por qué trabaja el actor?*

   C. *¿Cómo trabaja el actor?*

   D. *¿Con quién trabaja el actor?*

INSTRUCTIONS   Choose the correct response.

5. **¿Cuál de estos NO es un continente?**

   A. Sudamérica

   B. Norteamérica

   C. África

   D. Eurasia

6. **¿Cuál de las letras es una vocal?**

   A. E

   B. T

   C. L

   D. M

7. **¿Cuál de los nombres tiene la letra inicial mayúscula?**

   A. elena

   B. ELENA

   C. Elena

   D. eLena

8. **¿De dónde son los profesores?**

   A. España

   B. la casa

   C. la escuela

   D. el jardín

9. **Which of the following sentences is written in the correct order?**

   A. Está en el hospital el médico.

   B. El médico está en el hospital.

   C. El médico en el hospital está.

   D. En el hospital el médico está.

INSTRUCTIONS   Choose the best verb to complete the sentence.

10. *El gato ... en el suelo.*

   A. *estudia*

   B. *practica*

   C. *sale*

   D. *duerme*

N

Lago de
Reflejos

Avenida Las Palomas

Parque San
Cristóbal

Río de Plata

Playa Negra

El Volcán

Playa Roja

Laguna
del Oro

Isla de Providencia

Day Three, 16:00 Hours

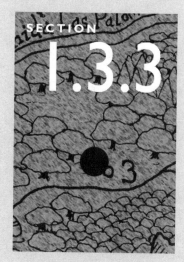

Seven Days to Rendezvous

Just as you're finishing the first set of activities *Bárbara* gave you, her cook brings out a tasty late afternoon snack. You munch through it contentedly while working on the next set of activities.

"*¡Muy bien!*" *Bárbara* exclaims when she sees your work. "Here is the puzzle you must solve, if you wish to receive your next clue. Look for your next contact near the shores, for he is the oldest of those who live at the sea's whim."

Wondering at this strange clue, you finish the last of the activities, then tackle *Bárbara's* puzzle. Despite all the odd turns your adventure has taken, you're delighted at how rapidly your language mastery is progressing.

✓ In this section you will:

→ Create your own sentences.

→ Correct errors in writing.

→ Express needs and opinions.

→ Ask questions and understand answers.

→ Increase speaking fluency.

→ Use correct verb tenses.

◎ Disc **2** Track **19**

Puzzle

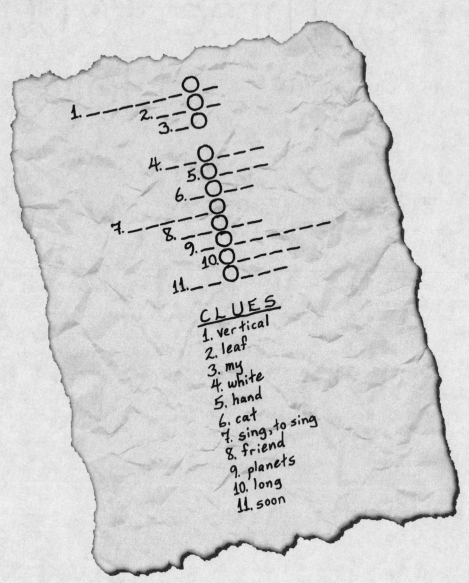

After working the puzzle out yourself, check the answers in Appendix A, on page 463.

From Words to Discourse

INSTRUCTIONS Review previous scatter charts and sample sentences. Then carefully examine the following scatter chart and sample sentences. Use the following words to make new and original sentences.

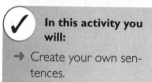

In this activity you will:

➜ Create your own sentences.

➜ Correct errors in writing.

Scatter Chart

ésta(s)

ésa(s)

¿verdad?

es / son

hay [pronounced "eye"]

(no) está(n) aquí

toda(s)

otra(s)

cosa(s)

varilla(s)

y

(no) está(n) allí [pronounced *ayi* or "all ye"]

chica(s)

pero

también

sí

corta(s)

no

colorada(s)

la(s)

larga(s)

grande(s)

una(s)

sobre

(no) está(n) parada(s)

blanca(s)

(no) está(n) acostada(s)

negra(s)

NOTE

Note: In Spanish, you'll encounter *esta, ésta,* and *está.* The first, *esta,* means "this" and is used before a noun: *esta cosa* ("this thing"). The second, *ésta,* means "this one" and is used by itself: *Sí, ésta es blanca* ("Yes, this one is white"). The third, *está,* is a form of the "be" verb: *La cosa blanca está sobre la cosa negra* ("The white thing is on the black thing"). Remember, accents are typically dropped when the letter is capitalized: *ésta, Esta.* Al: Like *esta* and *ésta, esa* and *ésa* follow the same usage: *esa cosa* ("that thing") and *Sí, ésa es blanca* ("Yes, that one is white").

Mexican Holidays

¡A celebrar! (Let's party!) We all like parties and holidays. The Mexican people are no different and have actually taken this activity to greater heights. Many visitors or newcomers to Mexico are amazed at how many different holidays are celebrated. Some of the reasons for so many holidays are:

a. National holidays, such as *el cinco de mayo* (May 5th), which celebrates their independence from France.

b. Religious holidays, such as *El día de los Reyes.* King's Day or Epiphany, to celebrate the coming of the three kings to visit the Christ child. This is traditionally when gifts are given, instead of at Christmas.

c. Local holidays where *pueblos* (villages) have local patron saints that they remember and honor. The people are very proud of their patron saints and look forward to these celebrations held annually.

English Equivalent

this one

is that so?

that one

is / are

there is / are

is / isn't here   all   others

things

rod(s) or stick(s)   and

is / isn't there

small, little   but

also

short   yes

no   colored

the

big   large

a

on, on top of

is / isn't standing

is / isn't lying down

white

black

Sample Sentences

INSTRUCTIONS Study the following sentences. The sentences with asterisks are incorrect.

English	Spanish
1. There is a rod, a white rod.	*Hay una varilla, una varilla blanca.*
2. There is another rod, a black rod.	*Hay otra varilla, una varilla negra.*
3. This rod is black; that one is white.	*Esta varilla es negra; ésa es blanca.*
4. And this one is long, but that one is short.	*Y ésta es larga, pero ésa es corta.*
	*Y ésta una es larga, pero esa una es corta.
5. These ones are long, but those ones are short.	*Éstas son largas, pero ésas son cortas.*
6. Is this black rod short?	*¿Es corta ésta varilla negra?*
	*¿Es ésta negra varilla corta?
7. No, this one is long.	*No, ésta es larga.*
8. Is that one also long? Yes, that one is long too. It's long.	*¿Es larga ésa también? Sí, ésa es larga también. Es larga.*

	English (cont.)	Spanish
9.	A black rod on a white rod.	Una varilla negra sobre una varilla blanca.
10.	The black rod is on the white rod.	La varilla negra está sobre la varilla blanca.
11.	It is a short rod.	Es una varilla corta.
12.	This black rod and this white one are short.	Esta varilla negra y ésta blanca son cortas.
		*Ésta varilla negra y ésta blanca son cortas.
13.	That black rod and that white one are long.	Esa varilla negra y ésa blanca son largas.
		*Esa varilla negra y ésa blanca una son largas.
14.	This short rod is standing on the black rod.	Esta varilla corta está parada sobre la varilla negra.
15.	This other rod is also here, standing on the black rod.	Esta otra varilla también está aquí, parada sobre la varilla negra.
16.	Some white rods are standing on the black rod.	Unas varillas blancas están paradas sobre la varilla negra.
		*Varillas blancas están parad…
17.	The black rod is long, but…	La varilla negra es larga, pero…
18.	The white rods are short.	Las varillas blancas son cortas.
		*Las varillas blanca son corta.
19.	All the white rods are standing.	Todas las varillas blancas están paradas.
		*Toda la varillas blancas están parada.
20.	The black rod is lying there.	La varilla negra está acostada allí.
21.	These two white rods are standing, but these two are lying.	Estas dos varillas están paradas, pero estas dos están acostadas.
		*… pero estas dos están acostada.
22.	These black rods are long, but these white rods are short, right?	Estas varillas negras son largas, pero estas varillas blancas son cortas, ¿verdad?

English *(cont.)*	Spanish
23. One is short, and the others are long.	*Una es corta y las otras son largas.*
24. Are all the black rods long? No, there are long ones and short ones.	*¿Son largas todas las varillas negras? No, hay unas largas y unas cortas.*
25. Are the white rods black? No, the white rods are white, and the black rods are black.	*¿Son negras las varillas blancas? No, las varillas blancas son blancas, y las varillas negras son negras.*
26. The white ones are here; the black ones are there.	*Las blancas están aquí, las negras están allí.*
27. Two white ones lying on one black one.	*Dos blancas acostadas sobre una negra.*

Practice Translation

INSTRUCTIONS Look at the twenty-seven sentences above again, but cover the Spanish with your hand or a piece of paper. Translate them into Spanish and check your version with the version next to it.

Performance Challenge

Create fifteen sentences using the words in this activity's scatter chart. Look at the chart and string words together in ways that make meaningful and well-formed sentences, and remember to work toward fluency.

Communication With Limited Means

In this activity you will:

→ Express needs and opinions.

INSTRUCTIONS Children learning their first language are able to communicate a great deal before they have mastered many words. This activity will help you imitate how children learn by guiding you in making many sentences from a few words. Read over these words until you understand them.

English	Spanish
for, for the purpose of	*para*
there	*allá*
to work, working	*trabajar*
to eat, eating	*comer*
to be happy	*estar contento*
to be unhappy	*estar descontento*
well	*bien*
but	*pero*
without	*sin*
to live, living (compare "vivid," "vivify")	*vivir*
to be able, being able (compare "power")	*poder*
to sleep, sleeping (compare "dorm")	*dormir*
to rest, resting (compare "repose")	*reposar*
much, a lot	*mucho*
One must (you have to, it's necessary to)	*Hay que*

Details on Five Popular Holidays

- *Carnaval:* The week before Lent when many parties and parades are held.
- *Semana Santa:* Literally, this means Holy Week. It is celebrated the week before Easter.
- *El día de los muertos:* This holiday is celebrated on October 31 and November 1. According to traditional beliefs, the spirits who have died in the past year all come together on this night and begin their trek to heaven. Cakes and cookies are taken to the cemeteries to give the spirits strength for their voyage, and many families keep candles lit all night at the graves of their loved ones, while the living quietly reminisce about those who have passed on.
- *El día de independencia :* On September 16, Mexico celebrates its independence from Spain.
- *El día de la raza*—Race day: We celebrate this holiday in the United States as well, but we call it Columbus Day. In Mexico, it's celebrated on October 12.

English (cont.)	Spanish
(It) is stupid.	*Es estúpido(a).*
It is (im)possible.	*Es (im)posible.*

NOTE

Note: The word "*estúpido*" in Spanish has a strong connotation, "*tonto*" is a milder word to use.

Useful Spanish Sentences

INSTRUCTIONS   Get the meaning of the following sentences.

1. *Hay que trabajar allá.*
2. *Hay que trabajar mucho allá.*
3. *Hay que trabajar sin reposar y sin comer.*
4. *Hay que trabajar para comer.*
5. *Hay que trabajar bien para vivir bien.*
6. *Hay que trabajar bien para estar contento.*
7. *Hay que comer mucho para poder trabajar mucho.*
8. *Hay que dormir bien para trabajar bien.*
9. *Hay que trabajar para poder estar contento.*
10. *Trabajar es vivir.*
11. *Vivir es comer.*
12. *Trabajar sin poder dormir es vivir sin poder estar contento.*
13. *Es imposible trabajar sin reposar y sin comer.*
14. *Reposar sin dormir es posible.*

Equivalents of Spanish Sentences

INSTRUCTIONS   In case you have doubts, here are the same sentences in English. Orally translate these back into Spanish.

1. One has to work there.
2. You have to work a lot there.
3. It's necessary to work without resting and without eating.
4. You have to work in order to eat.
5. One has to work well in order to live well.
6. It's necessary to work well in order to be happy.
7. You have to eat a lot in order to be able to work a lot.

8. You have to sleep well in order to work well.

9. One has to work in order to be able to be happy.

10. To work is to live (or, working is living).

11. To live is to eat (or, living is eating).

12. To work without being able to sleep is to live without being able to be happy.

13. It is impossible to work without resting and without eating.

14. It's possible to rest without sleeping (or, resting without sleeping is possible).

Translation Exercise

INSTRUCTIONS   Orally translate the following sentences into Spanish. Check your translations in Appendix A, on page 458.

1. Eating is living.

2. Sleeping is impossible there (or, it is impossible to sleep there).

3. Working without being happy is impossible there (or, it is impossible to work there without being happy).

4. It is stupid to eat a lot in order to sleep well (or, eating a lot in order to sleep well is stupid).

5. It is impossible to sleep without resting, but it is possible to rest without sleeping.

6. It is possible to work without resting, but it is stupid.

Bonus: Spelling Rules of Cognate Words

In many cognate words—words that are very similar in different languages—double letters in English correspond to single letters in Spanish:

Letters	Spanish
bb > b	*abreviación, sábado* (compare "Sabbath")
cc > c	*ocupación, acomodación, aceptar, acumulación*
dd > d	*adición*
ff > f	*efecto, aflicción*
gg > g	*agresor, agravación*
ll > l	*ilusión, colección*
mm > m	*comentario, acomodación*
nn > n	*conexión, anual*
pp > p	*opresión*

Letters (cont.)	Spanish
ss > s	*misión imposible, asociación, necesario*
tt > t	*atención, atractiva*

In many cognate words, consonant clusters are reduced to a single consonant:

Letters	Spanish
ct > t	*respetable*
ph > f	*foto, elefante, geografía, profeta*
ks > j	*complejo* (complex)

Speed Learning and Self Quiz

A Fifteen-Minute Workshop

INSTRUCTIONS   Give this lesson fifteen minutes of quiet concentration. It will help you expand your ability to ask questions. First review the question words you previously learned. Also review the pictographs used to represent these meanings. Learn new question words and phrases.

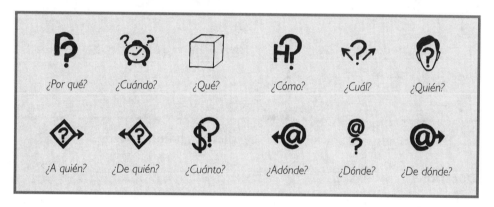

| ¿Por qué? | ¿Cuándo? | ¿Qué? | ¿Cómo? | ¿Cuál? | ¿Quién? |
| ¿A quién? | ¿De quién? | ¿Cuánto? | ¿Adónde? | ¿Dónde? | ¿De dónde? |

Here are some additional question words and phrases you can tie to the ones you already know.

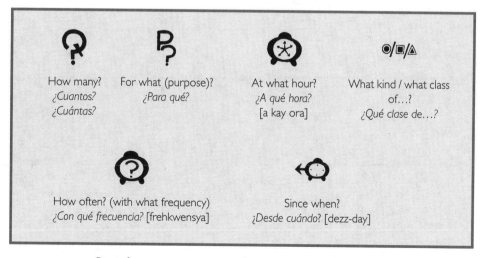

How many?
¿Cuantos?
¿Cuántas?

For what (purpose)?
¿Para qué?

At what hour?
¿A qué hora?
[a kay ora]

What kind / what class of...?
¿Qué clase de...?

How often? (with what frequency)
¿Con qué frecuencia? [frehkwensya]

Since when?
¿Desde cuándo? [dezz-day]

INSTRUCTIONS   Stop for a moment to set these in memory. Then take time to role-play. Use hand motions and facial expressions that will communicate the ideas

Mexico's Two Independence Days

In Mexico there are two independence days because they gained their independence from two different countries, Spain and France. On *el Cinco de Mayo*, Mexico celebrates its independence from France. On *el Día de Independencia*, Mexico celebrates its independence from Spain.

✓ **In this activity you will:**
→ Ask questions and understand answers.

for which you lack vocabulary. For example, some people ask you to get some gentlemen and ladies to help them. Using your fingers as counters, you ask, *¿Cuantos señores? ¿Cuantas señoras?* Do this now. Then imagine situations where the other new questions would be appropriate.

Self Quiz

1. In the scatter chart below, write the correct Spanish word below each pictograph.

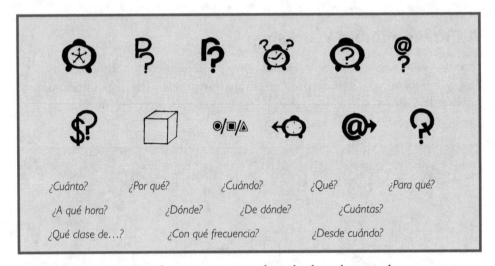

¿Cuánto?	*¿Por qué?*	*¿Cuándo?*	*¿Qué?*	*¿Para qué?*
¿A qué hora?	*¿Dónde?*	*¿De dónde?*	*¿Cuántas?*	
¿Qué clase de…?	*¿Con qué frecuencia?*	*¿Desde cuándo?*		

2. Create 10 questions of your own, using these high-utility words.

Questions

1. ....

2. ....

3. ....

4. ....

5. ....

6. ....

7. ....

8. ....

9. ....

10. ....

Chatter at a Royal Ball

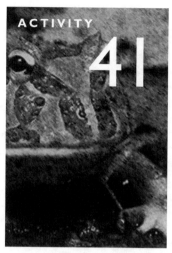

INSTRUCTIONS   Use pictographs to master the following words and dialogue.

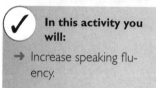

In this activity you will:
→ Increase speaking fluency.

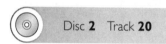

Disc **2**   Track **20**

Preparation for Conversation

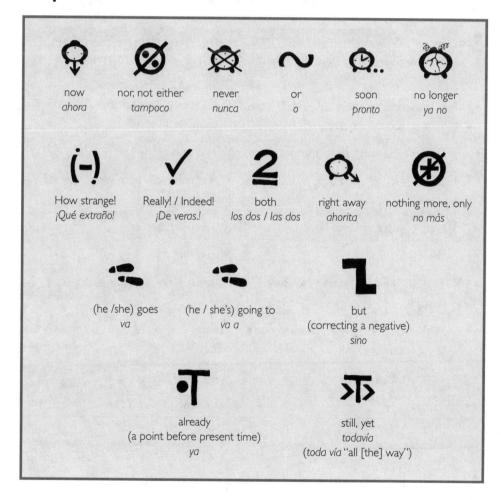

now *ahora*	nor, not either *tampoco*	never *nunca*	or *o*	soon *pronto*	no longer *ya no*
How strange! *¡Qué extraño!*	Really! / Indeed! *¡De veras.!*	both *los dos / las dos*	right away *ahorita*	nothing more, only *no más*	
(he /she) goes *va*	(he / she's) going to *va a*	but (correcting a negative) *sino*			
already (a point before present time) *ya*	still, yet *todavía* (*toda vía* "all [the] way")				

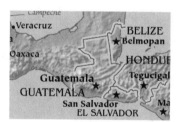

Guatemala Culture Overview

Guatemalans are proud of their country and seek opportunities to improve their lives. Personal honor is important, and Guatemalans will defend it vigorously, even physically. Hence, it is a good idea to avoid personal criticism.

Most Guatemalans are Roman Catholic, though many Indian groups practice Catholicism in conjunction with their own religious traditions. Due to the year-round mild climate in its capital city, Guatemala has been nicknamed "the Land of the Eternal Spring."

Sample Sentences

English	Spanish
He's going to sing soon.	*Él pronto va a cantar.*
Carlos no longer sings.	*Carlos ya no canta.*
Jose doesn't sing. Juan doesn't either. Me neither.	*José no canta. Juan tampoco. Yo tampoco.*
Not a king but a duke.	*No un rey sino un duque.*
The duke sings. The duchess too.	*El duque canta. La duquesa también.*

Conversation 4

	English	Spanish
•:	Now the king isn't playing but singing.	*Ahora el rey no está tocando sino cantando.*
••:	Yes, the king is only singing. It's the queen that is playing.	*Sí. El rey está cantando no más. Es la reina que está tocando.*
•:	Doesn't the king play anymore?	*¿Ya no toca el rey?*
••:	Yes, he still plays, but now he's not playing.	*Sí, todavía toca, pero ahora no está tocando.*
•:	Is he going to play soon?	*¿Va a tocar pronto?*
••:	Yes, right away.	*Sí, ahorita.*
•:	The dog and cat, what are they doing?	*El perro y el gato, ¿qué están haciendo?*
••:	Both are singing with the king and the queen.	*Los dos están cantando con el rey y la reina.*
•:	How strange!	*¡Qué extraño!*
••:	Truly.	*De veras.*

Pictographic Representation of the Same Dialogue

Task 1

INSTRUCTIONS Use your hands as puppets and dramatize the dialogue, looking only at the Spanish. Visualize the situation and get into the spirit of the dialogue. Aim for a flowing Spanish quality. Then go on to the next task.

Task 2

INSTRUCTIONS Do the same as in Task 1, but now look only at the pictographic representation below. Review pictographs from previous activities as necessary. Throw yourself into this performance. Think in Spanish without first thinking in English.

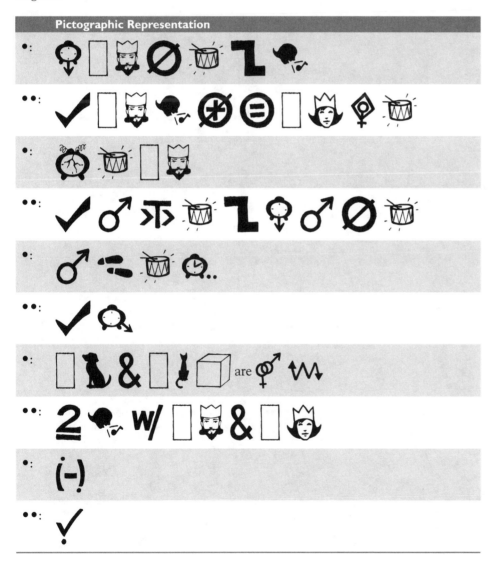

Performance Challenge

Copy the pictographs for this activity onto note cards as well, and spend a few minutes creating new sentences with them. Then go over this activity one more time, this time trying to work all in Spanish. Don't look at the English at all, unless you need to.

Observing Closely How Spanish Works

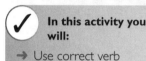

In this activity you will:

→ Use correct verb tenses.

INSTRUCTIONS Use these exercises to master more Spanish grammar patterns. Make three passes through the sentences in A, B, and C.

- 1st pass: Compare the Spanish forms and their meaning with the English. (Read the Spanish out loud, then look away and say it, thinking of its meaning and form. Also without looking at the Spanish, see if you can repeat the line just above.)

- 2nd pass: Cover the English and see if you can translate the Spanish into English.

- 3rd pass: Cover the Spanish and see if you can translate the English into Spanish.

Group A

○ Repeat Spanish
○ Spanish to English
○ English to Spanish

English	Spanish
He is playing the piano and singing.	*Él está tocando el piano y cantando.*
He and she are playing the piano.	*Él y ella están tocando el piano.*
Who (all) play the piano and who (all) sing?	*¿Quiénes tocan piano y quiénes cantan?*
Who plays the piano and who sings?	*¿Quién toca piano y quién canta?*
She plays the piano and he sings.	*Ella toca el piano y él canta.*
That princess doesn't play the piano.	*Aquella princesa no toca piano.*

Facts and Figures on Guatemala

- The population of Guatemala is about 10.8 million and is growing by 2.4% annually.
- Spanish is the official language of Guatemala, but about 20 Indian languages are also spoken.
- Guatemala has several active volcanoes.
- *Tortillas* are eaten with every meal in Guatemala.
- Guatemala's federal government consists of a president, a 100-member legislature, and an independent judicial branch.

English (cont.)	Spanish
That prince is not singing.	*Aquel príncipe no está cantando.*
He is talking.	*Está hablando.*

Group B

○ Repeat Spanish
○ Spanish to English
○ English to Spanish

English	Spanish
Do the prince and princess sing?	*¿El príncipe y la princesa cantan?*
Yes, both sing.	*Sí, los dos cantan.*
Now they are both singing.	*Ahora los dos están cantando.*
The princess already sings.	*La princesa ya canta.*
The king no longer sings.	*El rey ya no canta.*
The prince sings a lot.	*El príncipe canta mucho.*
He used to speak Spanish a lot.	*El hablaba mucho español.*
He still speaks Spanish a little.	*Todavía habla un poco de español.*
The princess doesn't speak Spanish yet.	*La princesa todavía no habla español.*

Group C

○ Repeat Spanish
○ Spanish to English
○ English to Spanish

English	Spanish
They don't drink milk.	*Ellos no toman leche.*
(They) don't eat either.	*Tampoco comen.*
They're not playing but singing.	*No están tocando sino cantando.*
Now the queen is singing a little. Not much.	*Ahora la reina está cantando un poco. No mucho.*
The king used to play the drum.	*El rey tocaba el tambor.*

English *(cont.)*	Spanish
They both play a little.	*Los dos tocan un poco.*
Neither the king nor the queen plays very well.	*Ni el rey ni la reina tocan muy bien.*

Self Quiz

Part I

INSTRUCTIONS   Match the numbered English with the lettered Spanish. Check your answers in Appendix A, on page 458.

	English		Spanish
1. _____	how many	A.	*más que*
2. _____	who?	B.	*¿quién?*
3. _____	how?	C.	*aquella*
4. _____	which one?	D.	*mejor que*
5. _____	fewer than	E.	*¿cuántos?*
6. _____	that one (f)	F.	*¿cuál?*
7. _____	better than	G.	*¿dónde?*
8. _____	worse than	H.	*aquel*
9. _____	more than	I.	*menos que*
10. _____	right?	J.	*peor que*
11. _____	what?	K.	*¿verdad?*
12. _____	why?	L.	*¿por qué?*
		M.	*¿qué?*
		N.	*¿cómo?*
13. _____	not anymore	A.	*un poco*
14. _____	not either	B.	*también*
15. _____	a lot	C.	*ni…ni*
16. _____	neither…nor	D.	*todavía no*
17. _____	but rather	E.	*sino*
18. _____	a little	F.	*tampoco*
19. _____	and…and	G.	*pero*

	English *(cont.)*		Spanish
20. _____	also	H.	*antes*
21. _____	either...or	I.	*nunca*
22. _____	not yet	J.	*y...y*
23. _____	there is	K.	*ahora*
		L.	*o...o*
		M.	*hay*
		N.	*mucho*
		O.	*ya no*

Part 2

INSTRUCTIONS   Translate the following phrases and sentences. Do your best.

Group A

1. This king doesn't play the piano.

   ....

2. He also doesn't sing.

   ....

3. This queen isn't crying.

   ....

4. The princess isn't either.

   ....

5. The prince and princess drink water.

   ....

6. The prince also drinks milk.

   ....

7. This king doesn't drink milk.

   ....

8. This queen doesn't either.

   ....

Group B

9. *Ese rey todavía no toca el piano.*

   ....

10. *Éste príncipe todavía canta mucho.*

....

11. *El rey todavía canta y toca.*

....

12. *El rey y la reina todavía no tocan el piano.*

....

Group C

13. The prince already sings.

....

14. He no longer plays.

....

15. They already sing.

....

16. Does the king no longer play?

....

17. They no longer cry.

....

Group D

18. *¿Quién ya toca el piano?*

....

19. *Aquella princesa ya toca el piano.*

....

20. *Aquel príncipe y esta princesa ya tocan el piano.*

....

21. *Esta reina no toca el piano;*

....

22. *este rey tampoco.*

....

Group E

23. The king that used to play now sings.

....

24. The king that used to sing is now playing the drum.

....

Group F

25. *Ni él ni ella cantan.*

....

26. *Y el perro y el gato cantan.*

....

27. *Los dos lloran también.*

....

Take some time now for review. Go back to any words or sentences you had difficulty with and see if you can iron things out now. Then go on.

✩

Performance Challenge

This activity doesn't use audio, so say each Spanish sentence aloud so that you can hear yourself speak.

You have completed all the activities for

**Section 1.3.3
Day Three, 16:00 Hours**

and are now ready to take the section quiz. Before continuing, be sure you have learned the objectives for each activity in this section.

Section Quiz

INSTRUCTIONS   Choose the answer that best completes the following sentences. Check your answers on the "Grading Sheet" found on the last page of the book.

1. *¿De quién es … varilla?*

    A. *ésa*

    B. *está*

    C. *esta*

    D. *ésta*

2. *Las varillas son muy ….*

    A. *largo*

    B. *grande*

    C. *largos*

    D. *grandes*

INSTRUCTIONS   Choose the correct Spanish translation of the English sentence.

3. **It is important to study.**

    A. *Hay que estudia.*

    B. *Es importante estudia.*

    C. *Hay que estudian.*

    D. *Es importante estudiar.*

INSTRUCTIONS Choose the correct Spanish spelling of the phrase.

4. **mission impossible**

   A. *mission impossible*

   B. *mission imposible*

   C. *misión imposible*

   D. *misión impossible*

INSTRUCTIONS Choose the correct Spanish translation of the English sentence.

5. **It's necessary to eat in order to live.**

   A. *Hay que come vivir.*

   B. *Hay que comer para vivir.*

   C. *Es tonto comer para vivir.*

   D. *Es importante come a vivir.*

INSTRUCTIONS Choose the answer that best completes the following sentence.

6. **¿... es la clase de matemáticas?**

   A. *A qué hora*

   B. *Cuánto*

   C. *Por qué*

   D. *De dónde*

INSTRUCTIONS Choose the correct Spanish translation of the English sentence.

7. **I don't like to sing either.**

   A. *No me gusta cantar también.*

   B. *No me gusta cantar ya no.*

   C. *No me gusta cantar tampoco.*

   D. *No me gusta cantar todavía.*

INSTRUCTIONS Choose the correct response.

8. **What is the predominant religion in Guatemala?**

   A. Presbyterian

   B. Roman Catholic

   C. Native Indian religions

   D. Islam

INSTRUCTIONS Choose the correct Spanish translation of the underlined English word or phrase.

9. *El rey y la reina* <u>are playing</u> *el piano.*

   A. *tocan*

   B. *estar tocando*

   C. *están tocando*

   D. *tocaban*

10. *El príncipe* <u>used to sing</u>.

    A. *cantaba*

    B. *cantar*

    C. *está cantando*

    D. *canta*

You have completed all the sections for

Module 1.3

and are now ready to take the module test. Before continuing, be sure you have learned the objectives for each activity in this module.

Module Test

INSTRUCTIONS Determine whether or not the following phrases or sentences are grammatically correct. Check your answers on the "Grading Sheet" found on the last page of the book.

1. *una cosa*

   A. True

   B. False

2. *la cosas*

   A. True

   B. False

3. *una cosas*

   A. True

   B. False

4. *He aquí una blanca cosa.*

   A. True

   B. False

5. *Y aquí una negra cosa.*

   A. True

   B. False

6. *He aquí la cosas.*

   A. True

   B. False

7. *Aquí están las otras cosas.*

   A. True

   B. False

8. *La negra cosa es grande.*

   A. True

   B. False

9. *La cosa blanca es chica.*

   A. True

   B. False

10. *Estas cosas son chica.*

    A. True

    B. False

11. *Estas chica cosas son blancas.*

    A. True

    B. False

12. *Esas cosas grandes es negras.*

    A. True

    B. False

....

INSTRUCTIONS   Choose the correct Spanish translation of the English sentence.

13. **The queen pleases me.**

    A. *Los duques comen ésto.*

    B. *Pero no le gusta cantar con el gato.*

    C. *Me gusta la reina.*

    D. *Me gustan los perros.*

14. **I like the house.**

    A. *No me gusta la reina.*

    B. *Le gusta cantar.*

    C. *Les gusta comer ésto.*

    D. *Me gusta la casa.*

15. **I like the dogs.**

   A. *Me gustan los perros.*

   B. *No me gusta tomarlo.*

   C. *Me gusta la casa.*

   D. *Les gusta comer ésto.*

16. **I don't like the queen.**

   A. *No me gusta la reina.*

   B. *A mi me gusta la reina.*

   C. *Me gusta la reina.*

   D. *No me gusta el rey.*

17. **To sing doesn't please me.**

   A. *No me gusta tomar.*

   B. *No me gusta cantar.*

   C. *Le gusta cantar.*

   D. *Me gustan los perros.*

18. **I don't like to drink.**

   A. *No me gusta cantar.*

   B. *Le gusta cantar.*

   C. *No me gusta tomar.*

   D. *Les gusta comer ésto.*

19. **He (or she) likes to sing.**

   A. *Les gusta comer ésto.*

   B. *Me gustan los perros.*

   C. *Me gusta la reina.*

   D. *Le gusta cantar.*

20. **But he doesn't like to sing with the cat.**

   A. *¿A quién le gusta el perro?*

   B. *Él canta con el gato.*

   C. *No me gusta la reina.*

   D. *Pero no le gusta cantar con el gato.*

21. **Who likes the dog?**

    A. ¿A quién le gustan el gato y el perro?

    B. ¿A quién le gusta cantar y a quién le gusta bailar?

    C. ¿A quién le gusta el perro?

    D. Pero no le gusta cantar con el gato.

22. **Who likes the cat and the dog?**

    A. ¿A quién le gustan el gato y el perro?

    B. ¿A quién le gusta el perro?

    C. A Pablo le gustan María y Ana.

    D. ¿A quién le gusta cantar y a quién le gusta bailar?

23. **Pablo likes Maria and Ana.**

    A. Los duques comen ésto.

    B. No me gusta tomarlo.

    C. No me gusta la reina.

    D. A Pablo le gustan María y Ana.

24. **The dukes eat this.**

    A. Los duques comen ésto.

    B. Pero no le gusta cantar con el gato.

    C. Me gustan los perros.

    D. Me gusta la reina.

25. **They like to eat this.**

    A. Los duques comen ésto.

    B. Les gusta comer ésto.

    C. No me gusta cantar.

    D. No les gusta comerlo en la torre.

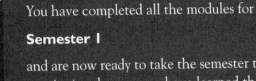

You have completed all the modules for

Semester 1

and are now ready to take the semester test for credit. Before continuing, be sure you have learned the objectives for each activity in this semester. If you do not desire to receive credit, continue to Semester 2.

Semester Test for Credit

In order to provide as complete a foreign language experience as possible for our learners, Power-Glide enables learners to receive high school credit for their course work. For more information on how to receive credit, please visit our website at: <http://www.power-glide.com/credit>.

Semester 2

Iquique

Campo
Grande

PARAGUAY

Antofagasta

Salta

Asunción

San Miguel
de Tucumán

a San Ambrosio
(CHILE)

Resistencia

CHILE

Cerro Aconcagua
(highest point in
South America, 6962 m)

Córdoba

Santa Fe

Pôrto Alegre

Salto

Valparaíso

Mendoza

Rosario

URUGUAY

Santiago

P
A
M
P
A
S

Buenos Aires

La Plata

Montevideo

Concepción

ARGENTINA

A
N
D
E
S

Bahía Blanca

Mar del Plata

San Carlos de
Bariloche

P
A
T
A
G
O
N
I
A

Puerto Montt

Península Valdés
(lowest point in
South America, -40 m)

Comodoro Rivadavia

00

Strait of
Magellan

rojection

Río
Gallegos

Stanley

Falkland Islands
(Islas Malvinas)
(administered by U.K.

0 Miles

Punta Arenas

Module 2.1

Throughout this module we'll be learning about the culture of Argentina.

Keep these tips in mind as you progress through this module:

1. Read instructions carefully.
2. Repeat aloud all the Spanish words you hear on the audio CDs.
3. Go at your own pace.
4. Have fun with the activities and practice your new language skills with others.
5. Record yourself speaking Spanish on tape so you can evaluate your own speaking progress.

N

Campo Grande

PARAGUAY

Lago de Reflejos

Avenida Las Palomas

Parque San Cristobal

o7

o6

o3

Río de la Plata

o2

El Volcán

Playa Negra

o4

o5

Playa Roja

o1

Laguna del Oro

Isla de Providencia

Day Three, 23:30 Hours

Seven Days to Rendezvous?

It's very late by the time you and your fellow secret agent, Stump, make it back to the home of Chiquita *Quintana*, your main contact. She and her husband are waiting up for you, afraid you'd gotten lost. Chiquita also has news for you. Evidently the submarine captain who is supposed to rendezvous with you in another seven days has replied to your email message—but her news is not good.

You trudge sleepily downstairs and read the message. Chiquita is right—it's not good news. "Good work on the case so far," the submarine captain writes, "*pero su aventura* might have to be cut short. There's a big storm headed this way. It should hit *Isla de Providencia* in another three to four *días*, and it'll last for another *tres o cuatro*, at least. It won't be that severe—*la isla* should be fine. However, it will rough up the seas enough that we won't be able to surface for the rendezvous. If you want a ride off that *isla*, you'd better be ready to meet us by 23:00 hours three days from now."

"Great," mutters Stump. "How are we going to finish that quickly?"

"Work faster," you reply. "And if we're going to do that, we'll need our rest. *Buenas noches*, Stump."

The next morning, after a light breakfast, you ponder the clue from Bárbara. "The oldest of those who live at the sea's whim…," you mumble.

"Hey! Fishermen!" Stump exclaims.

You grin. "Good thinking, Stump! If we want to find fishermen, the best place to start looking is the wharf."

The two of you bike to the wharf as quickly as you can. However, when you get there, you don't see a single person. The fishermen left before dawn, and the recreational boaters haven't come yet.

"Well, we can keep a good watch for him from here," you say, sitting down on a wooden dock. "Let's study some Spanish while we wait for him."

In this section you will:

→ Increase reading comprehension.

→ Understand new vocabulary from context.

→ Use pronouns in correct word order with infinitive verbs.

→ Give and understand directions.

→ Read for meaning.

→ Learn new vocabulary from a story and then retell it.

Disc **3**   Track **1**

ACTIVITY 43

DiglotWeave™: Mi Primera Visita a México, Parte I

In this activity you will:

→ Increase reading comprehension.

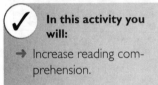

Disc **3** Track **2**

Argentina Culture Overview

Social and economic standing is generally important to the people of Argentina, as reflected by their frequent use of titles such as *señor, señora,* and *doctor.* Argentines, following the traditions of Italy and Spain, show great respect for women and the elderly. Roughly 90 percent of Argentines belong to the Roman Catholic church, but most of these people are not actively involved with their church. Religious freedom is guaranteed because church and state are officially separate.

A DiglotWeave™ Story

INSTRUCTIONS As you listen and read through this story, you must guess at the meaning of the Spanish from context inferencing—the natural method children employ so successfully in picking up a language, and one that adults must cultivate to succeed in mastering a language. Don't expect to get it all the first time. Don't even be concerned with learning a lot of Spanish from it. Just enjoy the story to the extent you can follow it, and notice how in repeated go-throughs, you understand more and more. Learn vocabulary through a story based in English with Spanish words added.

Parte Uno

As I passed *la frontera,* I was excited by the prospect of *mi primera visita a México,* but I felt shaky, *un poco* unsure of myself in this new *ambiente.* Having lived in California for the greater *parte* of *mi vida, y* having long had *un interés* in «*nuestros vecinos*» to the south, I had absorbed (*por ósmosis*) *un poco de español* through the years *pero* had never had *suficiente tiempo para realmente estudiar el idioma.*

I wanted to kick myself, *pero* now it was rather late—*sí, era un poco tarde* for that. I was comforted *muy poco* by my purchase of a *diccionario español-inglés en Tijuana.* But I determined to *practicar mi español* to the *límite.* I even made the *decisión* to write (I mean *escribir*) *mi diario en español* as much as *posible.*

I had no *misión oficial en México.* I was going there *estrictamente as un turista,* mostly out of *curiosidad y un deseo* to enjoy *una experiencia diferente de lo usual.*

Having been a soccer player *toda mi vida*—that is, *un jugador de fútbol* since I was a small *muchacho,* I looked forward to *la oportunidad* to attend *un partido de fútbol* on *domingo.* An *amigo* had given me *una lista de palabras de alta frecuencia* as a going-away *regalo* only a few *días* before. I appreciated his *regalo*, *y* I had *diligentemente* tried to *memorizar* some of *los términos más comunes y útiles.*

After *unas horas de viaje*, I came to a small *pueblo y* made a *decisión* to stop and look around *un poco*. There was a lot of heat, *sí, mucho calor*, just as I had expected *en México, y también*, as expected, *el pueblo* was *absolutamente tranquilo*. The ancient *proverbio* came to mind: *«EL SILENCIO ES ORO.»* It was *la hora de la siesta.*

Performance Challenge

Read through the first DiglotWeave™ story segment one more time, focusing on meaning. Then write down, in English, what you understood. Don't worry about direct translation, just do your best.

DiglotWeave™: Mi Primera Visita a México, Parte 2

In this activity you will:

→ Understand new vocabulary from context.

Disc **3**   Track **3**

Parte Dos

🔊

As I walked around *la plaza*, I almost expected to see *un Mexicano* propped up against *las* prickly *espinas de un cacto*, his *sombrero* pulled down over his *cara*. I even conjured up *la aparición de un bandido*, his *machete, pistolas, y bandolero* under his *poncho* ready for *uso inmediato*.

Actually I saw *ni una persona, sólo un* mangy old *perro*, taking a *siesta en la* cool *sombra de un árbol, y una vaca tranquilamente masticando su* cud. Then suddenly a *radio* came on. *La locutora* opened *el programa* with these *palabras*:

«*Saludos, amigos, y muy buenas tardes. Este es radio México, uno-dos-tres-cuatro. Amigo, amiga, tome Coca-Cola, el refresco más popular del mundo. Sí, amigos, ¡tomen Coca-Cola! ¡La Coca-Cola mexicana es excelente…magnífica… fantástica…indispensable! ¡Viva la Coca-Cola! ¡Viva México!*»

She paused *por un momento*, then *continuó*:

«*Y ahora «La Hora de Meditación,» un programa de meditación con música y lectura de las Sagradas Escrituras del Nuevo Testamento de nuestro señor Jesucristo. Este programa es bajo la dirección del evangelista David Gómez, pastor de la iglesia bautista de Sonora, México. Aquí con ustedes está el hermano Gómez:*»

«*Buenas tardes, hermanos y hermanas, amigos y amigas. El título de mi sermón para hoy es: El Señor es mi Pastor. En la Biblia (en el Antiguo Testamento), en el libro de Salmos, capítulo 23, versículo 1, se encuentra el famoso pasaje: «El Señor es mi Pastor, nada me faltará.» ¿Qué significa David, el salmista, con estas palabras?*»

From here *el evangelista* made *un comentario* on *el simbolismo poético de Salmo 23. Yo* was *muy impresionado* by the fact *que yo* was able to *comprender la mayor parte del sermón. El* short *sermón* was followed by *una selección de himnos* sung by *un coro. Generalmente no me gusta* to hear *himnos o música religiosa por radio* even *en* inglés, pero en esta ocasión, ¡Ay, qué bonito! Me gustó mucho. Me impresionó muchísimo.

After enjoying *la música por unos minutos, yo* walked through *la plaza,* crossed—*crucé—la calle central y entré en un restaurante* next to *El Hotel Casa Blanca.* I sat down at *una mesa y* was *admirando* the vase *de flores en medio de la mesa* when I heard *una voz* behind me which asked, *«¿Un menú, señor?»*

It was *realmente la voz de un ángel! Yo* looked *y* saw *una señorita muy bonita, una princesa encantadora. «No, gracias,»* I responded. *«Chile con carne, por favor, y papas fritas.»*

—*¿Una botella de vino, quizás? ¿O un vaso de leche pasteurizada?*

—*No, muchas gracias, señorita. Sólo agua purificada.*

—*Perdón, señor, no tenemos agua purificada. Tenemos agua filtrada. ¿Está bien?*

—*Sí, está bien. Un vaso de agua filtrada, por favor.*

—*Bueno, chile con carne, papas fritas, y un vaso de agua. ¿Sólo eso?*

—*Sólo eso, gracias.*

La señorita was *muy simpática.* She must've been eighteen *años* of age. Then I noticed that on the walls of *el restaurante* there were dozens—*docenas* —*de fotos de personas famosas, por ejemplo, presidentes de la república de México (Benito Juarez y otros), líderes del gobierno (senadores, ministros, y otros), futbolistas (como Pelé) y otros atletas, revolucionarios (como Pancho Villa), personajes del cine y del teatro (como Cantinflas) y otros. Muy interesante,* I thought, *y muy raro* that *tantas personas famosas* had *visitado aquí.* Just then *la señorita* came with *mi orden, y otra vez* I heard *la voz de un angel, «Señor, su chile con carne, papas fritas, y un vaso de agua filtrada.»*

—*Gracias, señorita. Mmm, deliciosa. Comida deliciosa, rica.*

—*¿Música, señor?*

—*¿Cómo?*

—*¿Quiere usted música?*

—*¿Por qué no?*

—*¿Qué clase de música prefiere usted?*

—*Me gusta muchísimo la música clásica. Especialmente Chopin.*

I expected her to tell me they *sólo* had *música mexicana, pero* instead she smiled *y* sat down at *el piano. Yo* listened *como en un trance* as *la princesa encantadora* played *la famosa* impromptu *de Chopin, mi pieza favorita. Y nunca* had I heard it played *tan expresivamente y expertamente.*

Who could she be? *¿Quién será esta princesa encantadora?* I wanted to know more about her, but *mi español era extremadamente limitado*. When she finished playing *el impromptu*, I asked, hopefully, «*¿Habla usted inglés, señorita?*»

—*No, señor, lamentablemente. Sólo español.*

—*¡Que lástima! ¿Su nombre?*

—*María Martínez, para servirle.*

—*¿Es usted de aquí?*

—*De aquí, no. Soy de la capital, de la Ciudad de México. Estoy aquí sólo durante el mes de agosto con mi tía que es la dueña del hotel. En septiembre regreso a mi casa en la capital. Y usted, señor, ¿está usted en México por primera vez?*

—*Sí, por primera vez.*

—*Usted comprende muy bien. Usted sabe mucho español.*

—*No, no mucho. En realidad muy poco. El español es difícil para mí. ¡Soy muy tonto!*

—*No, no, señor. Usted no es tonto. Yo no hablo inglés, pero no soy tonta.*

¡Qué lástima! I thought. Yes, what a pity! *Aquí estoy en mi primera visita a México con mi primera oportunidad de hablar con una señorita—una princesa—mexicana, y yo* was at a loss for *palabras para expresarme*.

INSTRUCTIONS   Here's a partial *lista de palabras* you've met in the story so far. Go through each column and see how many *palabras* you remember from the story. Place a checkmark by each one you are unsure of, and before you listen a second time, note which words are checked.

Checklist		
○ la frontera	○ muy raro	○ experiencia
○ la decisión	○ muy poco	○ unas horas
○ evangelista	○ comprender	○ un poncho
○ sombrero	○ sí	○ especialmente
○ la voz de un angel	○ actividad	○ versión
○ silencio	○ locutor(a)	○ vida
○ para expresar	○ la república	○ turista
○ diccionario	○ proverbio	○ primera visita
○ diligentemente	○ famoso	○ un perro
○ la plaza	○ los vecinos	○ por ejemplo

Checklist *(cont.)*

○ una sorpresa	○ mi deseo	○ pero
○ ¿Por qué no?	○ modo de aprender	○ mi
○ mucho calor	○ sombra	○ amigo
○ realmente	○ los líderes	○ no mucho
○ domingo	○ machete	○ restaurante
○ espinas	○ parte	○ docenas de fotos
○ unos minutos	○ estrictamente	○ me gusta
○ un vaso de leche	○ familiarizado	○ una lista de palabras
○ practicar	○ uso inmediato	○ tarde
○ idioma	○ agua purificada	○ Sagradas Escrituras
○ memorizar	○ usted	○ la siesta
○ pistola	○ visita	○ una breve digresión
○ ¿Qué clase?	○ diario	○ ¿Por qué?
○ alta frecuencia	○ favorita	○ curiosidad
○ México, mexicano	○ masticando	○ tiempo
○ ambiente	○ agua filtrada	○ servicios
○ misión oficial	○ interés	○ tranquilo
○ recomendar	○ yo	○ saludos
○ bandido	○ límite	○ estúpida (tonta)
○ simpática	○ en mi opinión	○ también
○ oro	○ teatro	○ pueblo
○ primera	○ personajes	○ diferente
○ escribir	○ ¿cómo?	○ cacto
○ Biblia	○ la respuesta	○ buenas tardes
○ vista	○ suficiente	○ personas
○ muy bonita	○ una oportunidad	○ estudiar
○ iglesia	○ absolutamente	○ nuestro
○ una botella de vino	○ el programa	○ un regalo
○ inglés	○ deliciosa (rica)	○ himno

Checklist *(cont.)*

○ *día*	○ *posible*	○ *encantadora*
○ *una vaca*	○ *español*	○ *sólo*

(To be continued)

Performance Challenge

Using Spanish words from this activity, try to retell the story in your own words.

Focus on the Language 11-12

INSTRUCTIONS Read through the following grammar exercise.

Focus 11

Lo, La, Los, Las

The normal order of sentence parts in Spanish is the same as in English:

Subject	Verb	Object
She	speaks	Chinese
Ella	habla	chino

However, to say "She speaks it" (where the object is a pronoun), the Spanish sentence order changes to:

Subject	Object	Verb
She	it	speaks
Ella	lo	habla

English	Spanish
She speaks Chinese.	*Ella habla chino.*
She speaks it.	*Ella lo habla* (NOT *Ella habla lo*).
He doesn't speak it.	*El no lo habla* (NOT *El lo no habla*).
She speaks Chinese and Spanish.	*Ella habla chino y español.*
She speaks them.	*Ella los habla* (NOT *Ella habla los*).

> **In this activity you will:**
> → Use pronouns in correct word order with infinitive verbs.

Facts and Figures on Argentina

- Spanish is the official language of Argentina, but many people speak some English, French, German, or Italian. Argentine Spanish contains many phrases and terms not used in other Spanish-speaking countries.
- The population of Argentina is about 34.4 million and is growing at 1.1 percent annually.
- Argentines eat more beef per capita than any other people in the world, including people in the United States.
- Soccer is the national sport, but Argentines also enjoy horse racing, rugby, ice hockey, tennis, polo, and basketball.
- A president, a vice president, and a cabinet make up the executive branch of the Argentine government. The national congress has two houses, and the judicial branch is independent.

Translate Orally From and Into Spanish

English	Spanish
They sing a funeral song.	*Ellos cantan un canto fúnebre.*
They sing it more or less well.	*Lo cantan más o menos bien.*
They sing hymns, too.	*Cantan himnos también.*
They sing them very well.	*Los cantan muy bien.*
She drinks milk.	*Ella toma leche.*
She drinks it a lot.	*La toma mucho.*
He doesn't speak Chinese.	*El no habla chino.*
No, he doesn't speak it.	*No, no lo habla.*

Focus 12

Lo, La, Los, Las with a Verb in the Infinitive

When you use the "to-form" (the infinitive form) of the verb (*tomar / hablar / cantar* etc.), the order of sentence parts is the same in Spanish and English, even when the object is a pronoun. However, in this case (where the object is a pronoun), the verb and object are combined in one word.

Verb	Object
To drink	the juice
Tomar	*el jugo*
To drink	it
Tomar	*lo* (but the verb and object are combined to make: *Tomarlo*)

English	Spanish
To drink the juice.	*Tomar el jugo.*
To drink it.	*Tomarlo* (NOT *Lo tomar*).
To drink the milk.	*Tomar la leche.*
To drink it.	*Tomarla* (NOT *La tomar*).
To speak Spanish and Chinese.	*Hablar español y chino.*
To speak them.	*Hablarlos* (NOT *Los hablar*).

Translate Orally From and Into Spanish

English	Spanish
What is it that he drinks?	*¿Qué es lo que él toma?*
He drinks milk. He drinks it a lot.	*El toma leche. La toma mucho.*
He likes to drink it.	*Le gusta tomarla.*
It's prohibited to drink it here.	*Está prohibido tomarla aquí.*
She doesn't eat the meat.	*Ella no come la carne.*
She doesn't like to eat it.	*No le gusta comerla.*
She speaks French.	*Ella habla francés.*
It's prohibited to speak it in the palace.	*Está prohibido hablarlo en el palacio.*
She likes to speak it with the prince.	*Le gusta hablarlo con el príncipe.*

Performance Challenge

This activity teaches you about some useful Spanish pronouns and how to use them correctly. Using the grammar from this activity and vocabulary from previous activities, write or say five sentences of your own that use the pronouns you just learned.

ACTIVITY

46

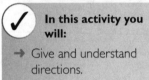

In this activity you will:

→ Give and understand directions.

Greetings in Argentina

Greetings are a little more formal in Argentina than the United States. When needing directions or help from a policeman or official, always greet them before asking the directions. Also, you should never call out when greeting someone, since raising a hand or smiling is more appropriate. When meeting or saying good-bye to a group of people, it is appropriate to greet each person individually and not as an entire group.

Self Quiz

Matching

INSTRUCTIONS   Match the lettered Spanish with the numbered English. Check your answers in Appendix A, on page 458.

	English		Spanish
1. _____	how many?	A.	*más que*
2. _____	who?	B.	*¿quién?*
3. _____	how?	C.	*aquella*
4. _____	which one?	D.	*mejor que*
5. _____	fewer than	E.	*¿cuántos?*
6. _____	that one (f)	F.	*¿cuál?*
7. _____	better than	G.	*¿dónde?*
8. _____	worse than	H.	*aquel*
9. _____	more than	I.	*menos que*
10. _____	right?	J.	*peor que*
11. _____	what?	K.	*¿verdad?*
12. _____	why?	L.	*¿por qué?*
		M.	*¿qué?*
		N.	*¿cómo?*
13. _____	not anymore	A.	*un poco*
14. _____	not also	B.	*también*
15. _____	a lot	C.	*ni…ni*
16. _____	neither…nor	D.	*todavía no*
17. _____	but rather	E.	*sino*
18. _____	a little	F.	*tampoco*
19. _____	and…and	G.	*pero*
20. _____	also	H.	*solamente*

	English (cont.)		Spanish
21. _____	either...or	I.	*nunca*
22. _____	not yet	J.	*y...y*
23. _____	there is	K.	*ahora*
24. _____	never	L.	*o...o*
		M.	*hay*
		N.	*mucho*
		O.	*ya no*

Error Detection

INSTRUCTIONS Of the following sentences, sixteen contain errors in translation. Identify them with C (correct) or I (incorrect). Check your answers in Appendix A, on page 458.

	English	Spanish
1. _____	The one (m) who used to play cries.	*Aquel que tocaba llora.*
2. _____	He used to either sing or play.	*Él o cantaba o tocaba.*
3. _____	The king that used to play now sings.	*El rey que tocaba ahora canta.*
4. _____	The king that used to sing is playing the drum.	*El rey que canta está tocando el tambor.*
5. _____	He is drinking milk.	*Él está toma leche.*
6. _____	She sings and he plays the piano.	*Él canta y ella toca el piano.*
7. _____	That queen doesn't sing.	*Aquella reina no está cantando.*
8. _____	The prince and princess play piano.	*La príncipe y el princesa tocan el piano.*
9. _____	The princesses already sing.	*Las princesas ya cantan.*
10. _____	The princess already sings.	*La princesa todavía canta.*
11. _____	The king no longer sings.	*El rey ya no canta.*
12. _____	They don't drink, and they don't eat either.	*Ellos no toman, y tampoco comen.*
13. _____	They're not playing but singing.	*No están tocando sino cantando.*

		English *(cont.)*	Spanish
14.	_____	Neither the king nor the queen plays well.	*Ni el rey ni la reina tocan bien.*
15.	_____	Who does the queen sing with?	*¿Con quién llora la reina?*
16.	_____	Who sings better, the princess or the duchess?	*¿Quién canta mejor, la princesa o la duquesa?*
17.	_____	They are singing and playing.	*Están cantando y tocando.*
18.	_____	Which princess used to cry?	*¿Cuál princesa lloraba?*
19.	_____	Does the cat sing in the tower?	*¿Canta el perro en el baño?*
20.	_____	Is she crying or singing?	*¿Están llorando o cantando ella?*
21.	_____	Do the king and the queen cry?	*¿Lloran el rey y la reina?*
22.	_____	Did the prince and the king used to sing better?	*¿Cantaba mejor el príncipe o el rey?*
23.	_____	Does the dog sing well too?	*¿Cantaba bien el perro también?*
24.	_____	Where does the queen cry?	*¿Cómo canta la reina?*
25.	_____	The one (f) who cries sings.	*Aquella que llora canta.*
26.	_____	This queen isn't crying.	*La reina no está llorando.*
27.	_____	The king doesn't drink; the duke doesn't either.	*El rey no toma; el duque tampoco.*

Reading Comprehension

INSTRUCTIONS   Read the following story about four animals and prepare to answer the questions below. Check your answers in Appendix A, on page 459.

En esta historia hay cuatro animales: un perro, un gato, un lobo, un cochinito (oink!). El perro toca himnos en la guitarra. Pero ahora no está tocando la guitarra. Ahora está cantando. Está cantando con el gato. Está cantando himnos con el gato en la iglesia. No. Eso no es correcto. El gato está tocando la guitarra y el perro está cantando solo. El perro canta mejor que el gato, pero el gato toca la guitarra mejor que el perro.

El lobo y el cochinito también cantan. Ellos cantan con el perro y el gato. Y ahora los cuatro están cantando himnos en la iglesia. O no, el gato está tocando la guitarra y los otros tres están cantando. Ellos no cantan muy bien, pero cantan. El cochinito canta peor que el gato. El lobo peor que el cochinito. El lobo toma mucho pero no fuma. El toma cuando está cantando (o canta cuando está tomando). El cochinito fuma, pero fuma solamente cuando el lobo está tomando.

INSTRUCTIONS   Mark the correct response to these questions. Try for a minimum of 9 correct answers out of 12.

1. *¿Dónde está cantando el perro? En*
   A. *la iglesia*
   B. *la cantina*
   C. *ni a ni b*
   D. *no se sabe* (= not known)

2. *¿El lobo y el cochinito cantan?*
   A. *sí*
   B. *no*
   C. *no se sabe*

3. *¿El cochinito canta peor que el lobo?*
   A. *sí*
   B. *no*
   C. *no se sabe*

4. *¿Cuál de los dos canta mejor?*
   A. *el cochinito*
   B. *el perro*
   C. *no se sabe*

5. *¿Qué está haciendo el gato ahora?*
   A. *está tocando la guitarra*
   B. *está cantando y tocando la guitarra*

6. *El lobo toma, ¿verdad?*
   A. *sí*
   B. *no*
   C. *no se sabe*

7. *¿Cuándo toma el lobo?*
   A. *sólo cuando el cochinito toma*
   B. *sólo cuando está cantando*
   C. *no se sabe*

8. *¿Cuál de los animales fuma?*
   A. *el lobo*
   B. *el cochinito*

9. **¿El perro toca la guitarra?**

   A. sí

   B. no

   C. no se sabe

10. **¿El gato toca mejor que el perro?**

    A. sí

    B. no

    C. no se sabe

11. **¿Qué clase de cantos cantan los animales?**

    A. cantos fúnebres

    B. himnos

    C. no se sabe

12. **¿Cuántos animales hay en ésta historia?**

    A. dos

    B. tres

    C. cuatro

Puntos, Líneas, y Figuras

Points, Lines, and Figures

INSTRUCTIONS   Study the scatter chart. When you have fully learned the contents of the chart, proceed to the next section.

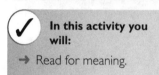

✓ **In this activity you will:**
→ Read for meaning.

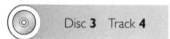

Disc **3**   Track **4**

A. Scatter Chart

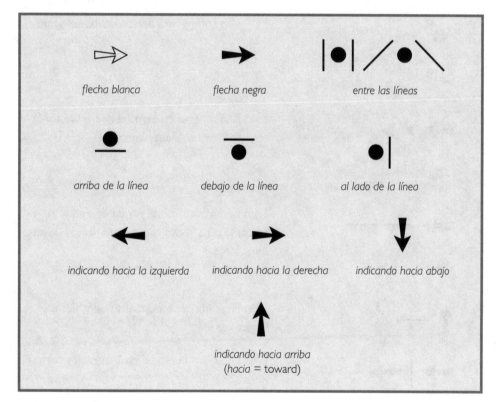

flecha blanca   flecha negra   entre las líneas

arriba de la línea   debajo de la línea   al lado de la línea

indicando hacia la izquierda   indicando hacia la derecha   indicando hacia abajo

indicando hacia arriba
(hacia = toward)

B. Look and Listen

Points, Lines, and Figures	Spanish
1. ⇨ ➡	Aquí hay una flecha blanca y una flecha negra.
2. ➡ ⇨	La flecha negra está arriba de la flecha blanca.
3. ⇨ ➡	La flecha negra está debajo de la flecha blanca.
4. ● ⇨	La flecha blanca está debajo del punto grande.
5. ➡ ➡ ● —	Una flecha negra está arriba de un punto; la otra está arriba de una línea.
6. ⇨ — — ⇨	Una flecha blanca está arriba de una línea corta; la otra flecha blanca está debajo de una línea larga.
7. ↑ — ↑	Una línea horizontal está entre dos flechas negras.
8. ➡ | ➡	Una línea corta vertical está entre dos flechas negras.
9. ↑ ↓	Una flecha indicando hacia arriba; la otra indicando hacia abajo.
10. ⇨ ◀	La flecha blanca a la izquierda indica hacia la derecha; la flecha negra a la derecha indica hacia la izquierda.

Points, Lines, and Figures *(cont.)*	Spanish
11.	*Esta flecha indica hacia la izquierda. La otra indica también hacia la izquierda.*
12.	*Estas cuatro flechas no indican hacia arriba. Estas cuatro tampoco.*

C. Listen and Look

INSTRUCTIONS   Listen to the audio follow along with the figures.

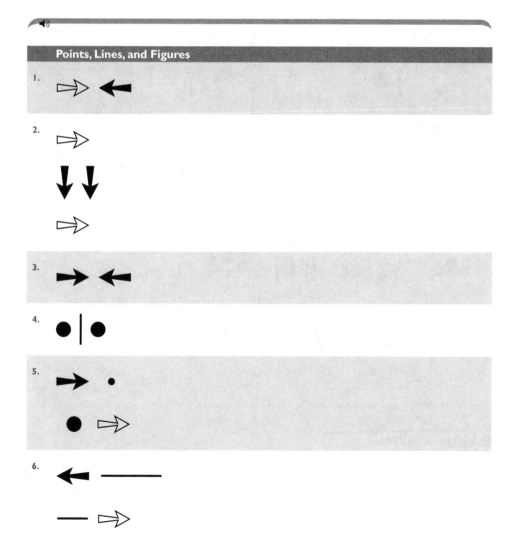

Points, Lines, and Figures
1.
2.
3.
4.
5.
6.

ACTIVITY 47

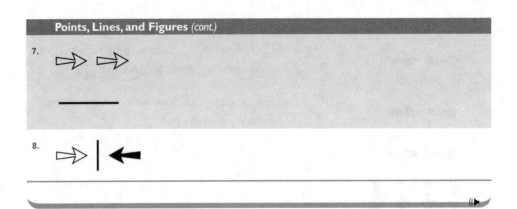

D. Multiple-Choice Frames

INSTRUCTIONS   Listen to the audio and choose the correct frame. Check your answers in Appendix A, on page 459.

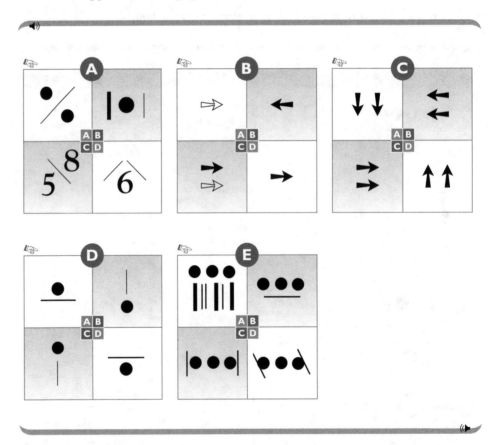

E. Listen and Draw

INSTRUCTIONS   Listen and draw what you hear. Pause the audio if the pace is too fast. Check your answers in Appendix A, on page 459.

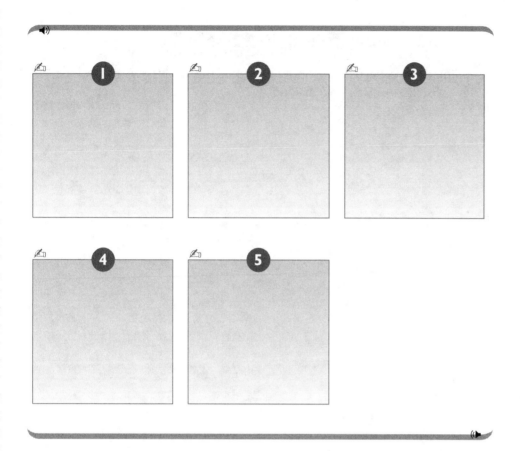

F. Read for Meaning

INSTRUCTIONS   Read the following sentences aiming to understand the meaning. Check the translations in Appendix A, on page 460.

1. *Dos flechas: una apuntando hacia arriba y la otra hacia abajo.*

2. *Una flecha blanca apuntando hacia un punto pequeño y una flecha negra apuntando hacia un punto grande.*

3. *Una línea larga horizontal al lado de una línea corta vertical.*

4. *Dos líneas: una línea larga, gruesa, y horizontal; y una línea corta, delgada, y vertical.*

5. *La línea horizontal está al lado de la línea vertical.*

6. *Un número y un punto pequeño entre dos líneas diagonales.*

7. *El número cinco y dos puntos grandes entre dos líneas verticales.*

8. *Una flecha blanca apuntando hacia la derecha y una flecha negra apuntando hacia la izquierda.*

9. *El punto está al lado derecho de la línea vertical.*

10. *Dos puntos están al lado izquierdo de la línea diagonal.*

Performance Challenge

Using the vocabulary and phrases presented in this activity, say out loud five sentences of your own making.

The Keys of Rome

ACTIVITY

48

ACTIVITY 48

✓ **In this activity you will:**

→ Learn new vocabulary from a story and then re-tell it.

 Disc **3**   Track **5**

Las Llaves de Roma

INSTRUCTIONS   Learn new vocabulary from this story, then learn to tell it yourself.

English	Spanish
Here are the keys of Rome.	*Estas son las llaves de Roma.*
Take them!	*¡Tómalas!*
In Rome there is a plaza.	*En Roma hay una plaza.*
In the plaza there is a street.	*En la plaza hay una calle.*
In the street there is a house.	*En la calle hay una casa.*
In the house there is a bed.	*En la casa hay una cama.*
In the bed there is a lady.	*En la cama hay una dama.*

Argentine Spanish

Argentine Spanish differs slightly from the Spanish spoken in other areas. For example, the *ll* usually makes a "y" sound, but in Argentina it makes a "zh" sound (like the "s" in "measure" or the "z" in "azure"). As a result, a word like *llave*—key—which is usually pronounced "yah-veh," would be pronounced "zhah-veh" in Argentina.

Argentines also use *vos* instead of the far more common *tú* as the second-person familiar subjective pronoun. Although *vos* is used elsewhere as an alternative to *tú*, it basically replaces *tú* in everyday speech in Argentina among people of all classes and education levels.

English *(cont.)*	Spanish
At the lady's feet there is a parrot.	*A los pies de la dama hay un perico.*
And the parrot says,	*Y el perico dice,*
"DON'T TELL LIES!"	*«¡NO DIGAS MENTIRAS!»*
The lady isn't in the bed.	*La dama no está en la cama.*
The bed isn't in the house.	*La cama no está en la casa.*
The house isn't in the street.	*La casa no está en la calle.*
The street isn't in the plaza.	*La calle no está en la plaza.*
The plaza isn't in Rome.	*La plaza no está en Roma.*
And these keys are not the keys of Rome.	*Y éstas llaves no son las llaves de Roma.*

INSTRUCTIONS Listen again, following this illustration. Then invest some time in learning to tell this story as if to a child sitting on your lap.

Performance Challenge

Practice telling this story in your own words, then tell it to someone else. Also, look for real situations in which you can use the vocabulary you've practiced.

You have completed all the activities for

Section 2.1.1
Day Three, 23:30 Hours

and are now ready to take the section quiz. Before continuing, be sure you have learned the objectives for each activity in this section.

Section Quiz

INSTRUCTIONS   Select the most correct answer for the following questions. Check your answers on the "Grading Sheet" found on the last page of the book.

1. **¿Por qué visita México el muchacho?**

    A. *tiene familia en México*

    B. *es un turista*

    C. *tiene una misión oficial*

    D. *es un jugador de fútbol*

2. **¿Qué programa está en la radio?**

    A. *un drama*

    B. *un programa romántico*

    C. *un programa espiritual*

    D. *un programa de música rock*

3. **¿Quién es María Martinez?**

    A. *su mamá*

    B. *una señorita que toca el piano*

    C. *una princesa*

    D. *una jugadora de fútbol*

INSTRUCTIONS   Choose the correct Spanish translation of the underlined English word or phrase.

4. **El come papas fritas. El <u>eats them</u>.**

   A. *come las*

   B. *las come*

   C. *los come*

   D. *come los*

5. **Ellos toman la leche. Ellos <u>drink it</u>.**

   A. *la toman*

   B. *toman lo*

   C. *toman la*

   D. *lo toman*

6. **He likes to play soccer. A *él le gusta* <u>to play it</u>.**

   A. *la jugar*

   B. *jugarla*

   C. *lo jugar*

   D. *jugarlo*

INSTRUCTIONS   Choose the correct response.

7. ● ╱ ● **Hay una línea ....**

   A. *entre dos puntos*

   B. *debajo de dos puntos*

   C. *arriba de dos puntos*

   D. *indicando dos puntos*

INSTRUCTIONS   Choose the correct Spanish translation of the underlined English word or phrase.

8. **En el pueblo <u>there is</u> una plaza.**

   A. *está*

   B. *hay*

   C. *es*

   D. *entre*

INSTRUCTIONS   Choose the answer that best completes the following sentences.

9. ➡ ➡   *Las flechas indican hacia ....*

A. *la izquierda*

B. *arriba*

C. *abajo*

D. *la derecha*

10. *El lápiz no ... en la mesa.*

A. *es*

B. *hay*

C. *está*

D. *entre*

Isla de Providencia

Day Four, 10:00 Hours

Sixty Hours to Rendezvous

You look up from the Spanish activities and notice that, while you were studying, someone else has joined you on the dock—an elderly man, with thin, curly white hair and skin browned and wrinkled by many decades in the sun. He sits only a few feet away, repairing an old-fashioned fishing net. He looks up from his work and grins.

"*¡Buenos días!*" you greet him. He returns your greeting and introduces himself as *Esteban Basso*. *Esteban*, as it turns out, spent his life as a sailor and traveled all over the world. His native language is Spanish, but in his travels he has learned some English. Between his English and your Spanish, you're able to communicate very well.

You ask him if he's the one *Bárbara* told you to find. He confirms that he is, and goes on to confirm your suspicions that you'll need to learn more Spanish if you want his clue. While you and Stump get back to work, *Esteban* starts telling you about one of his favorite countries, Argentina.

When you finish the exercises *Esteban* asked you to complete, he hands you a puzzle. Hoping that maybe you will have time to find two clues today, you get right to work.

"*El siguiente* contact is *un amigo* of mine," *Esteban* tells you when you've successfully completed the puzzle. "When you meet him, you'll be able to tell."

In this section you will:

→ Increase vocabulary in geography.
→ Retain vocabulary through songs and rhythm.
→ Understand instructional order.
→ Understand commands.
→ Use past, present, and future tense.
→ Understand spelling cognates.
→ Say numbers 100-900 using plural form.
→ Understand a joke in Spanish.

 Disc **3**   Track **6**

Puzzle

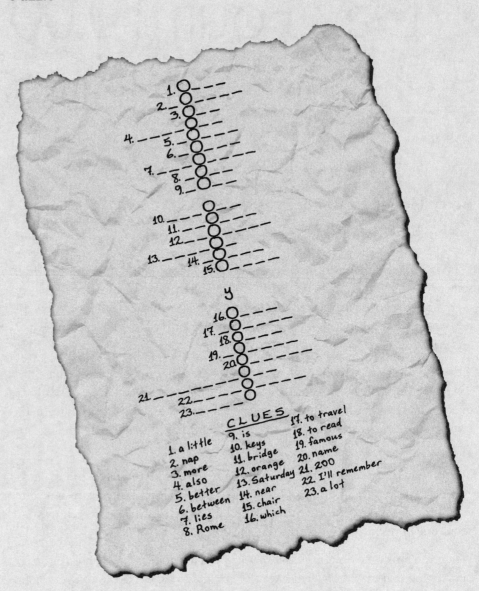

After working the puzzle out yourself, check the answers in Appendix A, on page 464.

Una Lección de Geografía

A Geography Lesson

INSTRUCTIONS In this lesson, you will build fluency in some basic geography vocabulary like: the directions North, South, East and West, capital cities, and oceans. Listen to the Spanish, following the text in the left column. Then compare the Spanish and English. Finally, listen to the Spanish again.

In this activity you will:

→ Increase vocabulary in geography.

Disc **3**   Track **7**

English	Spanish
Between South America and North America lies Central America.	*Entre Sudamérica y Norteamérica, se encuentra Centroamérica.*
Panama is here.	*Panamá está aquí.*
In Panama there is a canal that links the Atlantic and Pacific Oceans.	*En Panamá encontramos un canal que une los océanos Atlántico y Pacífico.*
The canal is a bridge between east and west.	*El canal es un puente entre el este y el oeste.*
Farther north lies Mexico.	*Más hacia el norte está México.*
Its capital is Mexico City.	*Su capital es la Ciudad de México.*
It is destined to become the world's largest city.	*Está destinada a ser la ciudad más grande del mundo.*
North of Mexico is the United States.	*Al norte de México están los Estados Unidos.*
The United States lies between the Pacific and Atlantic oceans.	*Los Estados Unidos están entre los océanos Pacífico y Atlántico.*
The east coast touches the Atlantic.	*La costa este toca el Atlántico.*
The west coast touches the Pacific.	*La costa oeste toca el Pacífico.*
The south coast touches the Gulf of Mexico.	*La costa sur toca el Golfo de México.*

Family Life in Argentina

The Argentine people, as well as most Hispanic people, have well defined the role of men and women. The wife has the primary responsibility for raising the children and managing household finances, while men tend to be more occupied with their work. Families tend to be smaller than most Hispanic countries, averaging only 2 children per family, but these children are central to the family and receive a lot of attention.

English (cont.)	Spanish
The capital, Washington, is on the east coast.	*Su capital, Washington, está en la costa este.*
The largest city, New York, is there, too.	*La ciudad más grande, Nueva York, está ahí también.*
On the west coast is California.	*En la costa oeste está California.*
San Francisco is here, in California.	*San Francisco está aquí en California.*
Los Angeles is here.	*Los Angeles está aquí.*
In San Francisco and Los Angeles there are many people who speak Spanish.	*En San Francisco y Los Angeles hay muchas personas que hablan español.*
The state of Utah is one of fifty states in the United States (U.S.).	*El estado de Utah es uno de los cincuenta estados de los Estados Unidos (E.U.).*
It is neither the biggest nor the smallest state.	*No es ni el más grande ni el más pequeño de los estados.*
It is located in the western part, but it is far from the west coast.	*Está en la parte oeste, pero está lejos de la costa oeste.*
Utah is famous for its salt lake and also for its beautiful parks.	*Utah es famoso por el lago salado y también por sus bellos parques.*

Performance Challenge

The vocabulary in this activity will help you keep up to date on current events. Get online or go to your local library and see if you can find information on the places mentioned in this activity.

Spanish Ditties

INSTRUCTIONS   Now relax and enjoy a couple of silly ditties in Spanish.

«Hoy es Sábado»

English	Spanish
Today is Saturday,	Hoy es sábado,
Today is Saturday,	Hoy es sábado,
"Saturday" in English,	«Saturday» en inglés,
"Saturday" in English,	«Saturday» en inglés,
And the whole time I am at home,	Y todo el tiempo estoy en mi casa,
And the whole time I am at home,	Y todo el tiempo estoy en mi casa,
And I sing again.	Y canto otra vez.

(The song repeats once more.)

«Manzana para Eva»

English	Spanish
Apple for Eva,	Manzana para Eva,
An orange for thee,	Naranja para ti,
Pineapple for the little girl,	Piña para la niña,
And grape for me.	Y uva para mí.
One for Eva,	Una para Eva,
One for thee,	Una para ti,

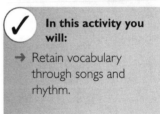

In this activity you will:

→ Retain vocabulary through songs and rhythm.

Disc **3**   Track **8**

English (cont.)	Spanish
One for the little girl,	*Una para la niña,*
And one for me.	*Y una para mí.*

«No tenemos dinero»

English	Spanish
We don't have money.	*No tenemos dinero.*
We don't have whereby	*No tenemos con qué*
we would buy food,	*compraríamos comida,*
And we do not know why.	*No sabemos por qué.*
We don't have beans.	*No tenemos frijoles.*
We don't even have salt.	*No tenemos ni sal.*
Money is lacking,	*Hace falta dinero,*
But it's not so bad.	*Pero no está tan mal.*
We are poor folks, they tell us;	*Somos pobres, nos dicen,*
We are poor folks, oh yes.	*Somos pobres, pues sí.*
But little we suffer	*Pero poco sufrimos*
For we always have thee.	*pues tenemos a ti.*

Performance Challenge

Look for real situations where you can use the vocabulary these ditties teach you.

Una Lección de Español

A Spanish Lesson

INSTRUCTIONS In this lesson, you will build fluency with some colors, order of instruction (i.e. first I do this, then I do this) and the commanding (imperative) voice (i.e. Look! Take! Select! etc.). Notice how parts of the lesson describe past, present, and future events.

In this activity you will:

→ Understand instructional order.

→ Understand commands.

→ Use past, present, and future tense.

  Disc **3** Track **9**

English	Spanish
On the table there's a black pencil, and on the chair there's a red one.	*En la mesa hay un lápiz negro, y en la silla hay uno rojo.*
They are both yours.	*Ambos son tuyos.*
I have here two other pencils, one black and one red.	*Aquí tengo otros dos lápices, uno negro y uno rojo.*
Both are mine.	*Ambos son míos.*
I will take one of mine, the red one, and stand it on the table.	*Tomaré uno de los míos, el rojo, y lo pararé en la mesa.*
I will stand it near yours, near that black one of yours.	*Lo voy a parar cerca del tuyo, cerca del negro tuyo.*
Now I will take the other, my black one, and lay it on this chair.	*Ahora voy a tomar el otro, el negro mío, y lo voy a acostar en esta silla.*
I will lay it at the side of yours.	*Lo voy a poner al lado del tuyo.*
Look, I first took my red pencil and stood it on the table near your black one.	*Mira, primero tomé mi lápiz rojo y lo paré en la mesa cerca del negro tuyo.*
Then I took my black one and laid it on this chair next to (at the side of) yours.	*Después tomé el negro mío y lo acosté en la silla al lado del tuyo.*
Now, do as I tell you.	*Ahora, haz lo que yo te diga.*

Argentina's Cultural Background

While most Hispanic countries have a large percentage of *Mestizos* (Spanish and Indian mix) there is only a small percent of *Mestizos* in Argentina. 85% of Argentines are descendents of Spanish and Italian immigrants.

English (cont.)	Spanish
Select one of your two pencils, either the black one that's on the table or the red one that's on the chair.	Selecciona uno de tus dos lápices, o el negro que está en la mesa o el rojo que está en la silla.
Lay it on top of this book.	Acuéstalo encima de este libro.
Now take the other pencil of yours and stand it on the table.	Ahora toma tu otro lápiz y páralo en la mesa.
Now, tell me what you did with your two pencils.	Ahora, dime qué es lo que hiciste con tus dos lápices.
What was the first thing you did?	¿Cuál fue la primera cosa que hiciste?
First you took one of the two, that black one, and laid it on this book here.	Primero tomaste uno de los dos, el negro, y lo acostaste encima de este libro aquí.
Then you took another pencil, the red one, and stood it on the table.	Después tomaste otro lápiz, el rojo, y lo paraste en la mesa.
Now what is the situation of the four pencils, mine and yours?	Ahora, ¿cuál es la situación de los cuatro lápices, los míos y los tuyos?
There are two standing on the table, one red one of yours and one red one of mine.	Hay dos parados en la mesa, un rojo tuyo y un rojo mío.
The other two, the black ones, are lying down, one on the book and one on the chair.	Los otros dos, los negros, están acostados, sobre un libro y uno en la silla.
Look, one of mine is standing, specifically the red one; and the other one, the black one, is lying down.	Mira, uno de los míos está parado, específicamente el rojo; y el otro, el negro, está acostado.
One of yours is also standing, and another one lying down.	Uno de los tuyos también está parado, y otro acostado.
How is the red one of yours?	¿Cómo está el rojo tuyo?
Standing or lying down?	¿Parado o acostado?
Whose pencil is it that is lying on the book?	¿De quién es el lápiz que está acostado en el libro?
Yours or mine? Yours, right?	¿Tuyo o mío? Tuyo, ¿No?
Who put it there, you or me?	¿Quién lo puso ahí?, ¿Tú o yo?
Who told you to put it there?	¿Quién te dijo que lo pusieras ahí?
I told you to put it there, right?	Yo te dije que lo pusieras ahí, ¿No?

English *(cont.)*	Spanish
Who stood my red pencil on the table?	*¿Quién paró mi lápiz rojo en la mesa?*
I did it, right?	*Yo lo hice, ¿No?*
Who told me to stand it on the table?	*¿Quién me dijo que lo parara en la mesa?*
No one.	*Nadie.*

Performance Challenge

Gather black and red pencils, a chair, and a table. Then listen to this activity again and try to use the items as they are outlined in the lesson.

A Continuación— Mi Primera Visita a México

ACTIVITY 52

In this activity you will:

→ Understand spelling cognates.

 Disc **3** Track **10**

Preparation

INSTRUCTIONS   Listen to the last part of the DiglotWeave™ story, and see how much vocabulary you can learn from it.

La «princesa encantadora» continua hablando conmigo.

A week before I left, a friend had given me *una lista de palabras de alta frecuencia.* "You'll be amazed at what *estas palabras* can do for you *en México*," he said. "Learn them by heart." I took his suggestion and kept *la lista* in my shirt pocket, taking it out to review *las palabras* at intervals. Here is that *lista de palabras:*

Spanish Infinitive	Spanish Verb Base Form	English Infinitive	English Verb Base Form	Memory Aids
leer	*lee*	to read	reads	as in "legible"
aprender	*aprende*	to learn	learns	compare "apprehend"
suponer	*supone*	to suppose	supposes	
creer	*cree*	to believe	believes	as in "credo"
saber	*sabe*	to know	knows	as in "savvy"
comer	*come*	to eat	eats	"come 'er" to eat
viajar	*viaja*	to travel	travels	related to "voyage," "via"
trabajar	*trabaja*	to work	works	compare "travail"
gastar	*gasta*	to spend	spends	compare "waste"

Eating in Argentina

Beef is a very important part of the Argentine diet because of the vast plains, or *pampas*, where cattle are raised. Argentine people eat more beef per capita than any other people in the world. It is not uncommon to see construction workers carry portable grills to cook meat on for lunch. *Mate* is a very popular hot tea that is drunk out of a silver cup and straw that often may be handed from one person to another. Because the straw is a silver alloy, the germs are not spread.

Spanish Infinitive (cont.)	Spanish Verb Base Form	English Infinitive	English Verb Base Form	Memory Aids
andar	anda	to walk	walks	compare "andante" in music
estar	está	to be	is	
tomar	toma	to take	takes	also means "drinks"
hablar	habla	to speak	speaks	
esperar	espera	to hope	hopes	despair is absence of hope
pensar	piensa	to think	thinks	as in "pensive"
vivir	vive	to live	lives	as in "revive"
escribir	escribe	to write	writes	as in "scribe"
decir	dice	to say	says	"dice will decide what to say"
tener	tiene	to have	has	"tenacious," "tenable"
soler	suele	to do at times	does at times	
entender	entiende	to understand	understands	intend to…
querer	quiere	to want	wants	
poder	puede	to be able	she's / he's able	

Spanish	English	Memory Aids
veneno	poison	venom
comida	food	a form of comer "to eat"
dinero	money	money for "dinnero"
feo	ugly	"Oh, Faye is feo"
perezoso	lazy	Mr. Perez is oh so perezoso!"
miedo	fear	
extraño	strange	"ex-strange-o"

If you will spend just *cinco minutos* with the *lista de palabras de alta frecuencia,* you'll be able to understand most of my conversation with *la «princesa encantadora»*. (I'll help you with a *palabra* here or there, but mostly you can guess the meanings.)

Parte Tres

🔊

—*Usted, señor, ¿de dónde es?*

—*Ahora de Boston.*

—*O, Boston es una ciudad muy grande, ¿verdad?*

—*Sí. Pero yo soy de una ciudad suburbana.*

—*Sí? ¿Conoce usted a la familia Kennedy?*

—(Do I know the Kennedy family?) *Creo que no. ¿Es una familia en Boston?*

—*Sí. John Kennedy.*

—*¿El es amigo de usted?*

—*No exactamente. El nombre John Kennedy es famoso.*

—*¿Famoso?*

—*Sí. El era presidente.*

—*¿Presidente?* (I was leading her on.)

—*Sí, un presidente, como George Washington o Abraham Lincoln, pero John Kennedy era un presidente moderno, un presidente de nuestro tiempo.*

Esto es increíble, I thought. *Esta princesa mexicana tan bonita y tan encantadora y con tantos talentos sabe del presidente Kennedy. «¿Cómo sabe usted del presidente Kennedy?»* I asked.

—*Yo trabajo con los voluntarios del cuerpo de paz. Fue el presidente Kennedy quien hizo el cuerpo de paz.*

Her *voz* was *dulce y sincera. Yo inmediatamente* told her *que* I'd like to *saber más.* Then she told me about some of the *proyectos* they were working on. *Yo* listened *muy atentamente.* It was like *ella* herself *era un ángel de paz.*

Just then *entró otra persona—un mexicano, obviamente, pero un hombre impresionante. El me habló en español, «Buenas tardes, señor. ¿Cómo está usted?»*

—*Muy bien, gracias. ¿Y usted?*

—*Bien, gracias.*

«¿Habla usted inglés?» I asked.

—*Un poco. Con varios compañeros norte-americanos.*

—*¿Compañeros norte-americanos?*

He smiled, *y la encantadora* laughed. Her laugh *era como una* fresh *brisa* from the seashore. «*El está hablando de su proyecto.*»

—She says I talk about my project.

«*El está hablando de los compañeros que tenía en su proyecto,*» she *continuó.*

«*Yo trabajaba con el cuerpo de paz,*» he explained.

—Oh, *¿Ustedes son hermano y hermana?*

She asked him something *que yo* didn't catch. I was afraid *que ella* was going to leave, so I thought of inviting them to have *una copa de café.* «*Permítanme comprarles algo para tomar. ¿Qué toman ustedes?*»

—*Agua, leche, jugos…*

—*¿Jugos? ¿Qué es eso?*

—*Jugo de tomate, jugo de piña, jugo de naranja … jugo de frutas.*

—*Ah, ahora entiendo:* juices. *Permítanme ofrecerles un vaso de leche o de jugo de fruta.*

—*Gracias, usted es muy simpático.*

While we were drinking our *jugos, la puerta* opened, and in came *dos jóvenes norte-americanos* en blue jeans. *La encantadora dijo,* «*Estos son nuestros amigos. Pero perdónenos. Nosotros vamos al Ballet Folklórico. Tenemos que ir ahora.*»

—Oh, you're going to *el Ballet Folklórico.*

«*Sí, pero nuestros amigos aquí pueden explicar todo,*» she said, gesturing to the two *jóvenes en camisas para trabajar y* blue jeans.

And with that, *mi ángel desapareció* with her *amigo.* I turned to *los dos jóvenes* when *uno de ellos dijo,* «*¿Qué sabe Ud. de fútbol?*»

Bonus: Familiar Words

English words of Latin derivation share many endings with Spanish words. The following words are spelled the same in English and Spanish, but their pronunciation differs between the two languages.

Words That End in -al			
vertical	horizontal	accidental	total
moral	continental	final	normal

Words That End in -al (cont.)

fundamental	formal	plural	mental
local	habitual	personal	postal
social	cultural	tropical	diagonal
criminal	celestial	capital	universal
principal	liberal	terminal	gradual
habitual	glacial	judicial	naval
imperial	canal	hospital	legal
manual	ideal	natural	radical
universal	general	actual	natal
central	individual	total	visual

Words That End in -or

humor	tenor	labor	rumor
favor	clamor	actor	motor
superior	editor	error	inspector
posterior	horror	color	mentor
pastor	interior	rigor	reflector
exterior	anterior	tractor	director
ulterior	candor	factor	valor
elector	honor	tutor	interior

Words That End in -ar

regular	insular	particular	solar
vulgar	peninsular	circular	peculiar
triangular	similar	vernacular	lunar
perpendicular	familiar	molecular	nuclear
popular	altar	secular	angular

Performance Challenge

Concentrate on comprehending as much Spanish as you can. Read through this final section of the story and write down as much as you can understand.

ACTIVITY 53

✓ **In this activity you will:**

→ Say numbers 100-900 using plural form.

 Disc **3**   Track **11**

Culture, Adventure, and Numbers

INSTRUCTIONS   Learn more Spanish numbers.

The "Century" Numbers: 100–900

🔊

You have learned virtually all of the elements of the Spanish numeric system, including the word *cien* for 100 with its alternate *ciento*. To say "hundreds and hundreds" you would say "*cientos y cientos*," using the plural form of *ciento*.

The one element you will now add is the plural form *cientos*, which is used in forming 200 to 900.

Listen and repeat: 200, 300, 400, *500, 600, *700, 800, *900.

The starred items above require the dependent form before the *-cientos*.

- Not *nueve-cientos*, but *nove-cientos*.
- Not *siete-cientos*, but *sete-cientos*.
- Not *cinco-cientos* and not *quin-cientos*, but *quin-ientos*.

(This last one would be *quincientos*, but the initial "c" of *cientos* is deleted.)

Say the hundreds from 900 downward: *nove-_____, ocho-_____, sete-_____, seis-_____, quin-_____, cuatro-_____, tres-_____, dos-_____.*

🔊

Listen and repeat: *500, 800, 400, *900, *700, 300, 600, 200, *500, *900.

Look off into space. Let these numbers drift through your mind.

INSTRUCTIONS Listen and point to the number pronounced on audio:

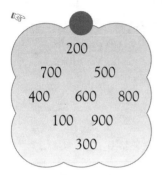

200
700   500
400   600   800
100   900
300

INSTRUCTIONS Listen to and point to the number pronounced:

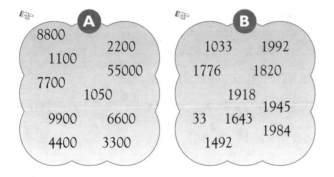

A
8800
1100   2200
7700   55000
        1050
9900   6600
4400   3300

B
1033   1992
1776   1820
    1918
        1945
33   1643
        1984
1492

The "Tens": 20-90

INSTRUCTIONS Now you will learn the last major elements of the Spanish numeric system— the numbers 20-90. Pay careful attention, and repeat each number several times, keeping the meaning in mind.

Number	Spanish
20	*veinte*
30	*treinta*
40	*cuarenta*
50	*cincuenta*
60	*sesenta*
70	*setenta*

Number *(cont.)*	Spanish
80	*ochenta*
90	*noventa*

Compound numbers are formed with *y*—the word "and". For example, 35 would be said *treinta y cinco*. The twenties, however, are a noteworthy exception. Numbers in the twenties are formed with *i* rather than *y*, and the two parts of the number are combined into one word. For example, 23 would be said *veintitres*.

Review

1. Read the following numbers and give the English equivalent.

Spanish Written Numbers		
cien	*doscientos*	*ochocientos*
seiscientos	*trescientos*	*cuatrocientos*
setecientos	*quinientos*	*novecientos*

2. Say these numbers in Spanish (across columns then down rows).

Spanish Numbers	
800	8000
900	9000
600	6000
770	7770
400	4000
500	5500
300	3300
200	2200

INSTRUCTIONS Close your eyes and imagine one number at a time from 100 to 900, giving the Spanish name for each number.

Performance Challenge

Some of the prefixes will change for the "hundreds" numbers, so take a few minutes and give those numbers some extra practice. Can you express the current year in Spanish?

A Joke in Spanish

INSTRUCTIONS   Listen to and read the following joke.

Knock, knock! Who's there?

Will you remember me in a day?

Yes, of course I'll remember you in a day.

Will you remember me in a week?

Why, yes. For sure I'll remember you in a week.

And will you remember me in a month?

Yes, of course I'll remember you in a month.

I won't forget you.

Will you remember me in a year?

Yes, yes. I'll never forget you.

Knock, knock!

Who's there?

Why, you forgot me already!

✓ In this activity you will:

→ Understand a joke in Spanish.

◎ Disc **3**   Track **12**

Argentina's Holidays

Argentina, which literally means silvery, is the eighth largest country in the world and is laced with rivers. Holidays or fiestas are great opportunities for families to spend time together. Most holidays are celebrated with fireworks. One holiday that Argentines celebrate that is different than most Hispanic countries is the death of *General José de San Martín*, who is known as the Liberator of Argentina, Chile, and Peru, from Spain. The holiday is August 17.

Performance Challenge

Practice telling this joke until you feel confident enough to tell it to someone else. Then, even if you have to tell both parts yourself, go ahead and tell the joke to someone else.

You have completed all the activities for

**Section 2.1.2
Day Four, 10:00 Hours**

and are now ready to take the section quiz. Before continuing, be sure you have learned the objectives for each activity in this section.

Section Quiz

INSTRUCTIONS   Choose the correct response. Check your answers on the "Grading Sheet" found on the last page of the book.

1. *¿Qué está al oeste de los Estados Unidos?*

    A. *el océano Pacífico*

    B. *México*

    C. *Nueva York*

    D. *el océano Atlántico*

2. *¿Cómo se dice 'apple' en español?*

    A. *manzana*

    B. *naranja*

    C. *fruta*

    D. *piña*

3. *¿Qué quiere decir frijoles en ingles?*

    A. beans

    B. food

    C. salt

    D. tortillas

INSTRUCTIONS   Choose the correct Spanish translation of the underlined English word or phrase.

4. *El lápiz es* <u>mine</u>.

    A. *mi*

    B. *mío*

    C. *tuyo*

    D. *suyo*

5. *Hay dos cosas en la silla; una* <u>mine</u> *y una* <u>yours</u>.

    A. *mío / tuyo*

    B. *mi / tu*

    C. *mi / ti*

    D. *mía / tuya*

INSTRUCTIONS   Choose the correct response.

6. **Which verb is NOT an infinitive?**

    A. *escribir*

    B. *pensar*

    C. *toma*

    D. *saber*

7. **Which of the following words is NOT spelled the same in both English and Spanish?**

    A. camel

    B. poison

    C. normal

    D. center

8. **Which of the following is NOT a common ending for Latin roots in English and Spanish?**

    A. *-al*

    B. *-or*

    C. *-ar*

    D. *-er*

9. **¿Cómo se dice 500 en español?**

   A. *cinco cientos*

   B. *cincuenta*

   C. *quinientos*

   D. *cinco*

10. *mil ochocientos noventa y siete =*

    A. *1897*

    B. *1987*

    C. *896*

    D. *886*

You have completed all the sections for

Module 2.1

and are now ready to take the module test. Before continuing, be sure you have learned the objectives for each activity in this module.

Module Test

INSTRUCTIONS   True or False: the following phrases or sentences are correct translations of each other. Check your answers on the "Grading Sheet" found on the last page of the book.

1. *El o cantaba o toca.* = He used to either sing or play.

   A. True

   B. False

2. *El rey que tocaba ahora canta.* = The king that used to play now sings.

   A. True

   B. False

3. *El rey que canta está tocando el tambor.* = The king that used to sing is playing the drum.

   A. True

   B. False

4. *El está toma leche.* = He is drinking milk.

   A. True

   B. False

5. *El y ella está tomando jugo.* = He and she are drinking juice.

   A. True

   B. False

6. *El canta y ella toca el piano.* = He sings and she plays the piano.

   A. True

   B. False

7. *Aquella reina no está cantando.* = That queen doesn't sing.

   A. True

   B. False

8. *La príncipe y el princesa tocan piano.* = The prince and the princess play the piano.

   A. True

   B. False

9. *Ahora los dos está cantando.* = Now both are singing.

   A. True

   B. False

10. *Las princesas ya cantan.* = The princesses already sing.

    A. True

    B. False

11. *La princesa todavía canta.* = The princess already sings.

    A. True

    B. False

12. *El rey ya no canta.* = The king no longer sings.

    A. True

    B. False

13. *No están tocando sino cantando.* = They're not playing but singing.

    A. True

    B. False

14. *¿Con quién llora la reina?* = Who does the queen sing with?

    A. True

    B. False

15. *Están cantando y tocando.* = They are singing and playing.

    A. True

    B. False

INSTRUCTIONS   Read the following sentences and do the math to find the answer.

16. **dos x ciento =**

A. mil cien

B. doscientos

C. dieciséis

D. dosentos

17. **tres x ciento =**

A. trescientos

B. treinta

C. tresento

D. tres cincuenta

18. **cinco x ciento =**

A. cincuentas

B. cincocientos

C. quincento

D. quinientos

19. **ocho x ciento =**

A. ochocientos

B. ochenta

C. ochosenta

D. dieciocho

20. **nueve x ciento =**

A. nuevecientos

B. novecientos

C. nueventa

D. novesentos

21. **quince x diez =**

A. quinientos

B. dieciquince

C. ciento cincuenta

D. quinces

22. **once x cien =**

A. *oncecientos*

B. *mil*

C. *mil cien*

D. *oncetos*

23. **catorce x cien =**

A. *catorcentos*

B. *cuatrocientos*

C. *mil cuatrocientos*

D. *mil catorce*

24. **diecisiete x cien =**

A. *ciento diecisiete*

B. *mil setecientos*

C. *setecientos*

D. *sietecentos*

25. **mil - cuatrocientos =**

A. *cuatrocientos*

B. *sesenta*

C. *seiscientos*

D. *cuatrocientos*

Module 2.2

Throughout this module we'll be learning about the cultures of El Salvador and Ecuador.

Keep these tips in mind as you progress through this module:

1. Read instructions carefully.

2. Repeat aloud all the Spanish words you hear on the audio CDs.

3. Go at your own pace.

4. Have fun with the activities and practice your new language skills with others.

5. Record yourself speaking Spanish on tape so you can evaluate your own speaking progress.

Isla de Providencia

Day Four, 14:00 Hours

Fifty-Six Hours to Rendezvous

You tell Esteban *muchas gracias* for his time and help. Then, with your new clue in hand, you and Stump get back on your borrowed bicycles and race to the southeast side of town, where the map indicates your fifth contact will be.

You follow the map closely, and about an hour later, you find yourself standing in front of the largest of the small island's very few apartment complexes. You and Stump squint up at the broad, flat-roofed, four-story structure.

"*¿Cómo* are we going to find Esteban's *amigo* in this place?" Stump asks.

"We look," you answer confidently.

You walk along one wall toward the main entrance. Before you reach it, though, a sudden shower of water splashes onto your shoulders. You look up. A man with a watering can leans over a second floor balcony. "*Lo siento,*" he calls down to you. "*Lo siento mucho.*"

"*Está bien,*" you reply. You take a closer look at his balcony. He has several healthy, exotic-looking shrubs growing on it. A few of their delicate fronds are visible through the balcony's open metalwork. The shrubs aren't what catch your attention, though—it's what's draped over them to protect them from birds. It's an old-fashioned fishing net that looks exactly like the one Esteban was repairing this morning.

"*¿Es usted un amigo de Esteban?*" you ask.

"*Sí, yo soy,*" he answers. "*¿Y ustedes?*"

"*Sí, nosotros también,*" you answer. "In fact, he told us to look for you."

"Really!" the man exclaims. "I wonder what the old rascal's up to this time. Wait there, I'll let you in."

Just a couple minutes later, you're safely settled in the man's living room. He introduces himself as Ricardo Hurtado and tells you he made friends with Esteban after moving here from El Salvador several years ago.

In this section you will:

→ Use demonstrative pronouns alone and with various tenses.

→ Use the various forms of the "to be" verbs.

→ Recognize how much you understand in Spanish.

→ Use explanations.

→ Create your own story using perception and plots.

→ Learn and retain action verbs.

→ Listen to a question and anticipate the correct response.

→ Understand the main points of a story.

→ Ask simple questions and understand the answer.

 Disc **3** Track **13**

Like Esteban, Ricardo asks you to do several more Spanish activities and hands you a puzzle with the code for your next clue when the activities are completed.

Puzzle

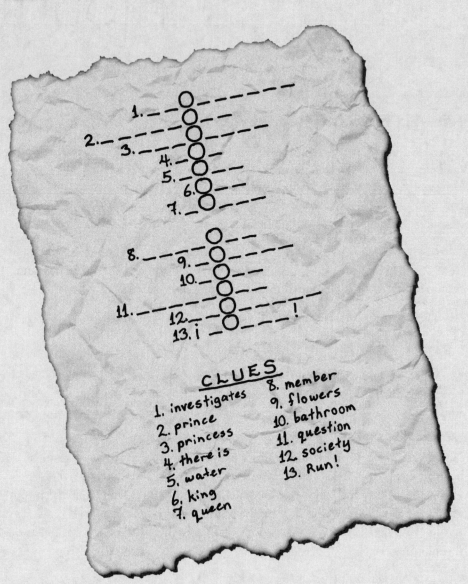

After working the puzzle out yourself, check the answers in Appendix A, on page 464.

Chatter at a Royal Ball

INSTRUCTIONS Use this activity to master the use of *hay, había, esta, ésta / éste,* and *éstas / éstes.*

English	Spanish
there is / there are	*hay*
there was / there were	*había / habían*
this (f) / this (m)	*ésta / éste*
these (f) / these (m)	*éstas / éstos*

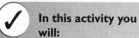

In this activity you will:

→ Use demonstrative pronouns alone and with various tenses.

Disc **3** Track **14**

English	Spanish
There's a king. This is the king .	*Hay un rey. Éste es el rey* *.*
There was a king. This was the king	*Había un rey. Éste era el rey* *.*
There's a queen. This is the queen	*Hay una reina. Ésta [es] la reina* *.*
There was a queen. This was the queen .	*Había una reina. Ésta era la reina* *.*
There's a princess. This is the princess	*Hay una princesa. Ésta es la princesa* *.*

El Salvador Culture Overview

Salvadorans are famous for their hospitality. After enduring a twelve-year civil war during the late seventies and the eighties, Salvadorans look forward to a future of peace and democracy. El Salvador is about 75 percent Roman Catholic, and food in El Salvador tends to be less spicy than that of other Central American nations. Some people have nicknamed El Salvador the sports capital of Central America. Soccer and basketball are the favorite sports of El Salvador.

ACTIVITY 55

English *(cont.)*	Spanish
There's a prince. This is the prince ![crowned face].	*Hay un príncipe. Éste es el príncipe* ![crowned face]*.*
There are animals. These are animals ![dog][cat].	*Hay animales. Éstos son animales* ![dog] ![cat]*.*
There's this dog ![dog] and this cat ![cat].	*Hay este perro* ![dog] *y este gato* ![cat]*.*
Which ones sing?	*¿Cuáles cantan?*
These (m) sing. These (f) don't.	*Éstos cantan. Éstas no.*

Focus on the Language 13-14

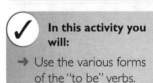

Enfoque sobre la Lengua

INSTRUCTIONS   Complete this exercise to learn more about Spanish usage. You are already familiar with the sentences in this reference, since they (or similar sentences) have been used in previous exercises.

In Spanish, the verb "to be" (is, was, are, were, will be) changes just as it does in English. The verb "to be" changes with the tense (past, present, future) and the number of nouns that go with it (singular or plural).

✓ **In this activity you will:**

→ Use the various forms of the "to be" verbs.

Focus 13

es: era, son: eran

English	Spanish
He is king. He was king.	*Él es rey. Él era rey.*
They are dukes. They were dukes.	*Ellos son duques. Ellos eran duques.*

Translate Orally From and Into Spanish

English	Spanish
She is queen. She was queen.	*Ella es reina. Ella era reina.*
They are princesses. They were princesses.	*Ellas son princesas. Ellas eran princesas.*

Focus 14

hay 'there is, there are' and *había / habían* 'there was, there were'

Note that in formal, written Spanish there is no plural form of *hay* and *había*; however, many Spanish speakers use *habían* when speaking. So, if you are writing or taking a test, don't use *habían*. On the other hand, if you're talking to someone, you can use it all you want.

English	Spanish
There is a king. There was a king.	*Hay un rey. Había un rey.*
There are dukes. There were dukes.	*Hay duques. Habían duques.*

Translate Orally From and Into Spanish

English	Spanish
There is a queen. There was a queen.	*Hay una reina. Había una reina.*
There are princesses. There were princesses.	*Hay princesas. Había princesas.*

★

Performance Challenge

Write sentences of your own to practice the verb forms you just learned.

Sentences

....

....

....

....

....

....

....

....

....

....

Wrap-Up Activities

Speak Spanish Before You Know It!

INSTRUCTIONS Complete these activities to test your understanding of Spanish. See how much Spanish you have learned. This simple story combines many different aspects of Spanish that you have learned up to this point. The questions that follow will help to build your comprehension of the story.

In this activity you will:

→ Recognize how much you understand in Spanish.
→ Use explanations.

Resumen

En este cuento hay un rey, un rey que no toma y no fuma. Es el rey que tocaba el tambor. Tocaba cantos fúnebres. Pero ahora no está tocando el tambor. Ahora está cantando. Está cantando con la reina, ¿verdad? Está cantando cantos fúnebres con la reina en la torre. El rey canta mejor. Sí, él canta mejor que ella…mejor que la reina. Ella canta más o menos bien…no muy bien. Pero ella toca bien el tambor.

En la historia hay un perro también y un gato que cantan con el rey y la reina. Sí, y ahora el perro y el gato están cantando. Están cantando con el rey y la reina en la torre. Imagínese. Un perro y un gato que cantan…que cantan cantos fúnebres. No cantan bien, pero cantan. El perro toma leche, pero no toma agua; el gato toma agua pero no toma leche. El perro también toma jugo, pero sólo toma cuando está cantando…o sólo canta cuando está tomando. ¡Muy extraño! ¡Increíble! ¡Absolutamente increíble!

La reina está en la torre ahora con el rey. Ambos están cantando, pero sólo la reina está tocando el tambor. Ella no toma. El rey tampoco. Interesante, ¿no?

Facts and Figures on El Salvador

- The population of El Salvador is about 6 million and is growing by 2% annually.
- El Salvador has nearly 200 extinct volcanoes and still has frequent earthquakes.
- El Salvador's federal government consists of the National Legislative Assembly and a president who serves one five-year term.
- El Salvador is the smallest country in Central America.
- The official language of El Salvador is Spanish, but many people also speak Nahua.

Reading Comprehension Questions

INSTRUCTIONS Write the answers to the following questions.

1. *¿Cantan el perro y el gato?*

   ....

2. *¿Con quiénes cantan?*

   ....

3. *¿Dónde cantan?*

....

4. *¿Cantan bien el rey y la reina?*

....

5. *¿Cantan bien el perro y el gato?*

....

6. *¿Cuál canta mejor, el rey o la reina?*

....

7. *¿Qué clase de canto están cantando?*

....

8. *El perro toma agua, ¿no?*

....

9. *¿Cuándo toma?*

....

10. *¿Cuál canta, el perro o el gato?*

....

11. *¿Cuándo canta el gato?*

....

Some Explanations

These examples will help you learn the formal explanations.

English	Spanish
Why does the king sing?	*¿Por qué canta el rey?*
The king sings because he loves the queen.	*El rey canta porque él ama a la reina.*
Why does the queen sing?	*¿Por qué canta la reina?*
The queen sings because she loves the king.	*La reina canta porque ella ama al rey.*
Why do they love each other?	*¿Por qué se aman?*
Who knows?	*¿Quién sabe?*
Why do kings and queens love each other?	*¿Por qué se aman los reyes y las reinas?*

English (cont.)	Spanish
When does the king sing?	¿Cuándo canta el rey?
The king sings when the queen is content.	El rey canta cuando la reina está contenta.
When does the queen sing?	¿Cuándo canta la reina?
The queen sings when the king is content.	La reina canta cuando el rey está contento.
They sing together when they both are content.	Ellos cantan cuando ambos están contentos.
And when are they content?	¿Y cuándo están contentos ellos?
They are content when they're singing.	Están contentos cuando están cantando.

Generating Sentences

INSTRUCTIONS   From this framework made up of different parts of Spanish, you can create numerous sentences and stories. Follow the directions at the end of this list and you will gain more confident with these words.

Function	Spanish
Actor-nouns	príncipe, reina, princesa, duque, duquesa, perro, gato
Modifier	el, la, un, una, este, esta (los, las, este, estas)
Pronouns	él, ella (ellos, ellas), los dos
Location	el bar / la cantina, la torre, el baño, la sala de bailar, aquí, allí, allá
Action-verb stems	cant-, llor-, toc-, fum-, tom-, habl-
Action-verb endings	-a(n), -aba(n), -ando
Auxiliary verb	está(n)
Complements	(habl-) español, chino
Manner	mejor / peor (que); (muy) bien, mal
Information-question words	¿Qué? ¿Cuál? ¿Dónde? ¿Cómo? ¿Cuánto? ¿Cuál? ¿Por qué? ¿Cuándo?
Attestation preface	él sabe que, él piensa que, él dice que, él lee que, él observa que
Quantity information	mucho, un poco

Function *(cont.)*	Spanish
Conjunctions and other words	*pero, ni…ni, y…y, también, todavía*
Rejoinders / answers	*Sí, no, imagínese, finalmente, es todo, por supuesto, de veras, es verdad, formidable, terrible, de acuerdo, creo que sí, cuán extraño, exactamente, probablemente, que lástima, imagínate*

Performance Challenge

After carefully studying and working through this activity, use the action verbs and actor nouns you learned and create your own sentences. Challenge yourself and see how many different sentences you can write.

....

....

....

....

....

....

....

....

....

....

....

....

....

....

Creating Your Own Mini-Story Plots

INSTRUCTIONS Take some time now to create more mini-story plots. Write them out and tell them orally. This will greatly enhance your fluency in Spanish and it will build your confidence in Spanish. Limit yourself to words you know, along with the additional words given below. Samples of mini-story plots are given at the end of this lesson.

✓ **In this activity you will:**

→ Create your own story using perception and plots.

English	Spanish
The court poet…	El poeta de la corte…
composes a poem.	compone un poema.
reads his poem to the queen.	lee su poema a la reina.
The member of the cabinet…	El miembro del gabinete…
considers the situation.	considera la situación.
observes the action.	observa la acción.
The attractive secretary…	La secretaria atractiva…
listens with much interest.	escucha con mucho interés.
works with enthusiasm.	trabaja con entusiasmo.
copies the document.	copia el documento.
has the key.	tiene la llave.
The humble gardener…	El jardinero humilde…
has an idea.	tiene una idea.
hides the flowers in the garden.	esconde las flores en el jardín.
hides himself among the flowers.	se esconde entre las flores.

Rebuilding El Salvador

El Salvador was devastated in the 1980's by civil war and again in 2001 by a massive earthquake, but the people of El Salvador are, with the help of various international volunteer organizations, rebuilding their country.

English (cont.)	Spanish
The malicious thief…	El ladrón malicioso…
hides himself in the garden.	se esconde en el jardín.
enters the treasury.	entra en el tesorería.
steals the jewels.	roba las joyas.
The inspector…	El inspector…
investigates the crime.	investiga el crimen.
finds the jewels in the bathroom.	halla las joyas en el baño.
encounters the thief.	encuentra al ladrón.
The impartial judge…	El juez imparcial…
denounces the crime.	denuncia el crimen.
pardons the gardener.	perdona al jardinero.
condemns the thief.	condena al ladrón.
The court magician…	El mago de la corte…
invents a formula.	inventa una fórmula.
still insists the formula is good.	todavía insiste que la fórmula es buena.
The vice-president…	El vicepresidente…
proposes a plan.	propone un plan.
contests the decision of the judge.	contesta la decisión del juez.
accuses the president.	acusa al presidente.
The innocent child…	El niño inocente…
responds to the question.	responde a la pregunta.
declares the truth.	declara la verdad.
The young engineer…	El ingeniero joven…
identifies the problem.	identifica el problema.
explains the problem.	explica el problema.
solves the problem.	soluciona el problema.
The intrepid driver…	El chofer intrépido…
divulges the secret.	divulga el secreto.
adopts the duchess' plan.	adopta el plan de la duquesa.
provokes an argument.	provoca una disputa.

English *(cont.)*	Spanish
The suspicious policeman…	*El policía sospechoso…*
suspects the poet is culpable.	*sospecha que el poeta es culpable.*
argues with the judge.	*disputa con el juez.*
insults the secretary.	*insulta a la secretaria.*
The leader of the society…	*El líder de la sociedad…*
refutes the argument.	*refuta el argumento.*
admits her mistake.	*admite su error.*
pardons the secretary.	*perdona a la secretaria.*
The leader of the union of matadors…	*El líder de la unión de matadores…*
provokes an argument.	*provoca una disputa.*
denies (negates) the accusation.	*niega la acusación.*
disobeys the order.	*desobedece el orden.*
The lawyer (advocate)…	*El abogado…*
contests the decision.	*contesta la decisión.*
presents incontestable evidence.	*presenta evidencia incontestable.*
The minister of finances…	*El ministro de finanzas…*
believes the poet is guilty.	*cree que el poeta es culpable.*
speaks with the chief by phone.	*habla con el jefe por teléfono.*
The vice-president…	*El vicepresidente…*
makes the soup.	*hace la sopa.*
insists that the soup is good.	*insiste que la sopa es buena.*

Perception

Some of the sentences of your mini-story plots may involve expressions such as "The policeman insults the lady." Many learners of Spanish overlook a certain detail in sentences where a PERSON is "acted upon." If you haven't noticed it before, a quick look at the following should help you see how native speakers handle this.

Observe these three paired Spanish sentences and note how 1A, 2A, and 3Aparallel their English equivalents word for word, but 1B, 2B, and 3B contain an extra piece in Spanish.

		English	Spanish
1.	A.	He (looks for) his book.	*Él busca su libro.*
	B.	He (looks for) * the queen.	*Él busca a la reina.*
2.	A.	He receives packages.	*Él recibe paquetes.*
	B.	He receives * the princesses.	*Él recibe a las princesas.*
3.	A.	He pardons the crime.	*Él perdona el crimen.*
	B.	He pardons * the criminal.	*Él perdona al criminal.*

Each pair of sentences shows the same contrast. In 1A, 2A, and 3A something is done to some THING. In 1B, 2B, and 3B something is done to some PERSON. The * in these three English sentences marks the place where the Spanish equivalent has an extra piece. If English had the same structure, when we spoke of something being done to a person, we would have to say: "He looks for TO the queen," "He pardons TO the criminal," "He receives TO the princesses."

About the Structure of Stories

Stories generally follow a more or less predictable story line that consists of several parts:

1. Introduction: Setting the story and its character(s) in time and place: "Once there was a king who lived in a tower…"

2. Further characterization: "This king was wicked, but he had a wife who was kind…"

3. Rise in suspense or anticipation of conflict: "She liked to sing, but he didn't like to hear her sing…"

4. Conflict: "He said to her: 'Don't sing or I'll get angry.'"

5. Climax: "But she sang anyway, and he got so angry he had a heart attack."

6. Conclusion or resolution of conflict: "Everyone felt relieved that the wicked king was dead."

Sample Plot

INSTRUCTIONS   Observe this structure in the following story plots. Translate the sentences into English. Check your answers in Appendix A, on page 460.

1. *En este cuento hay un palacio.*

2. *El rey está en el palacio.*

....

3. *El rey tiene un tesoro.*

....

4. *El tiene joyas.*

....

5. *El adora sus joyas.*

....

6. *Es un secreto dónde el tiene las joyas.*

....

7. *Pero la secretaria sabe el secreto.*

....

8. *Y el duque también sabe dónde el rey tiene las joyas.*

....

9. *En esta historia hay un ladrón.*

....

10. *El ladrón está también en el palacio.*

....

11. *El no sabe dónde están las joyas.*

....

12. *Pero él piensa que están en el baño.*

....

13. *El entra en el baño.*

....

14. *El busca y busca, pero no halla nada. No halla las joyas.*

....

15. *El piensa que las joyas están en la torre.*

....

16. *El sube la torre*

....

17. *El busca y busca, pero no halla las joyas. No halla nada.*

....

18. *El piensa que las joyas están en el cuarto de la reina.*

....

19. *El entra en el cuarto de la reina.*

....

20. *El busca y busca y finalmente halla las joyas.*

....

Here is a sentence-generation chart you can use to practice generating some typical story beginnings.

Había / habían	un	príncipe	que	era	pobre.
There was	a	prince	who	was	poor.

Había	dos	duques	que	eran	ricos.
There were	two	dukes	who	were	rich.

Practice generating some story beginnings from the chart. Most important is to understand what your sentences mean, but of course you should give attention to certain details of grammatical correctness: matching singular noun with singular verb form and plural noun with plural verb-form; and keeping the tense consistent: present with present, past with past (There is a king who is vs. There was a king who was).

Now create your own mini-story plots. Plan them out, using words you have used before plus new expressions taken from the material in this lesson. Write some stories out and practice presenting them orally (without reading). Do not start by writing out a story in English and then trying to find words and structures to translate it. Do not try to go beyond the words supplied. Practice telling them until you can tell them fluently from only an outline or from a sequence of the pictographs you have drawn on cards. Fluency is your aim, hesitation your enemy.

Performance Challenge

Formulate your own ideas into a story plot. Write a rough draft of your story. Read it to make sure all the elements of a proper story are there, and revise it if you need to. Then tell other people your story to give yourself plenty of speaking practice.

Focus on Action

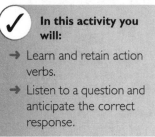

Enfoque Sobre la Acción

INSTRUCTIONS   In the *Enfoque Sobre la Acción* lesson, pictographs represent various actions. In the scatter chart (A) you are given the pictographs' English equivalent, then you are quizzed in (B) to make sure you know the pictographs' meanings. Then follow the now familiar multiple-choice frames (C) where you are presented with fifteen listening-comprehension tasks.

✓ **In this activity you will:**
→ Learn and retain action verbs.
→ Listen to a question and anticipate the correct response.

◎ Disc **3**   Track **15**

A. Scatter Chart

B. Self Quiz

INSTRUCTIONS   Can you "read" these pictographs in English? Check your answers in Appendix A, on page 460.

Accident-Prone San Salvador

Despite having been founded in 1546, El Salvador's capital city, San Salvador, has no old buildings for visitors to view. In its long history, the city has been destroyed by earthquakes in 1854 and 1873 (and badly damaged again in 2001), by the San Salvador volcano in 1917, and by floods in 1934. Each time, the city's citizens have rebuilt, on the same site as before.

Focus on Spelling

The pictographs are matched with the written Spanish.

¡póngase de pie!   ¡siéntese!   ¡coma!   ¡beba!   ¡lea!

¡escriba!   ¡camine!   ¡corra!   ¡hable!   ¡cante!

C. Multiple-Choice Frames

INSTRUCTIONS   Listen and identify which part of the frame contains the action or series of *acciones* described on the audio. Then listen for the correct response. Check your answers in Appendix A, on page 460.

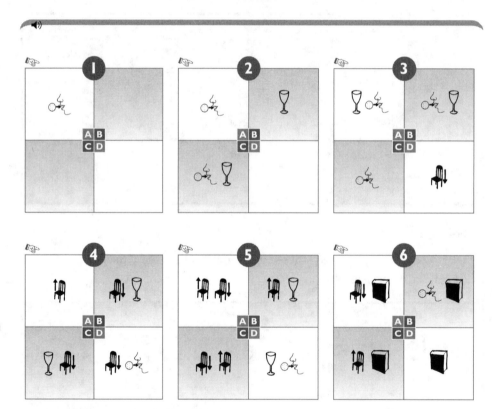

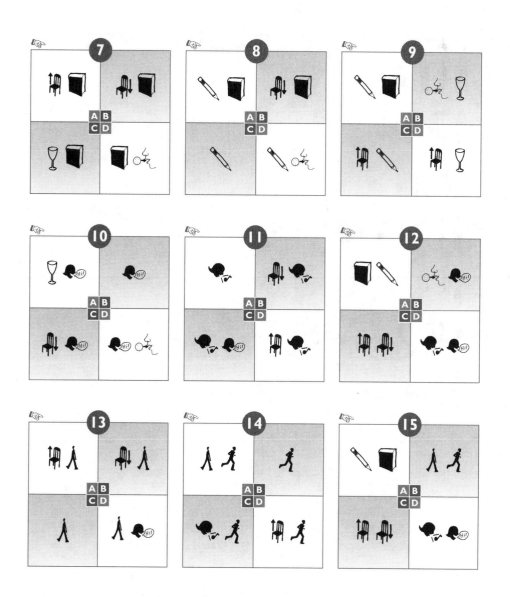

D. Listen and Anticipate the Response

INSTRUCTIONS   You'll hear, for example, (1) "What is this man doing?" "*¿Qué hace este hombre?*" followed by a short pause while you anticipate the response: "He eats." "*Él come.*" Check your answers in Appendix A, on page 461.

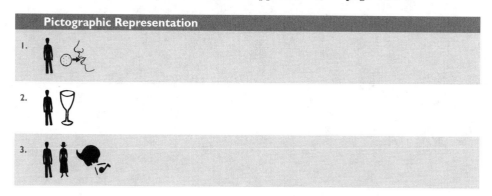

Pictographic Representation

4.

5.

6.

7.

8.

9.

10.

E. Act Out or Pantomime What You Hear

Script		
¡Póngase de pie!	¡Beba!	¡Siéntese y coma!
¡Lea y escriba!	¡Póngase de pie y camine!	¡Cante y hable!
¡Siéntese y escriba!	¡Lea y hable!	¡Póngase de pie, camine, y corra!
¡Siéntese!		

F. Read and Perform the *Acción*

Póngase de pie. Siéntese. Coma. Beba. Lea. Escriba. Camine. Corra. Hable. Cante. Siéntese y lea. Póngase de pie y cante. Siéntese y coma. Póngase de pie y hable. Siéntese, beba, coma, y hable. Póngase de pie, escriba, lea, cante, hable, y siéntese.

G. Look and Review

INSTRUCTIONS   Look back at the set of pictographs in (B) and see how many of them you can say in Spanish.

> ## Performance Challenge
>
> Copy the new pictographs onto note cards. Use these new cards, with ones you've made before, to create sentences and mini-stories of your own.

ACTIVITY

60

A Mother Talks With Her Baby

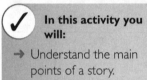

In this activity you will:

→ Understand the main points of a story.

Disc **3**   Track **16**

Una Madre Habla a Su Niñito

INSTRUCTIONS   This activity approximates how a mother interacts with her child. Children learn a tremendous amount of language in the early years with their parents. By mimicking the type of language a child is exposed to, you emulate a natural learning method employed by children. Listen to this story with your full attention.

English	Spanish
Here is your little girl dolly.	Ésta es tu muñequita.
Her name is Anita.	Ella se llama Anita.
Anita has hands and feet.	Anita tiene manos y pies.
Her hands and feet are like yours.	Sus manos y sus pies son como los tuyos.
But they are very little. Look.	Pero son chiquitos. Mira.
Look how little they are.	Mira cuán chiquitos que son.
Two tiny hands.	Dos manos chiquititas.
Two tiny little feet.	Dos pies chiquititos.
Here is Pinocchio.	Éste es Pinocho.
He is Anita's big brother.	Él es el hermano mayor de Anita.
Does Pinocchio have hands and feet?	¿Tiene Pinocho manos y pies?
He has hands and feet like Anita's.	Él tiene manos y pies como los de Anita.
He has hands and feet just like yours.	Él tiene manos y pies exactamente como los tuyos.
Look, his hands and feet are like yours.	Mira, sus manos y sus pies son como los tuyos.
Does Pinocchio have a nose?	¿Tiene Pinocho una nariz?

English (cont.)	Spanish
Yes, look at his nose.	Sí, mira su nariz.
He has a large nose.	Él tiene una nariz larga.
Is his nose like Anita's nose?	¿Es su nariz como la de Anita?
No, Pinocchio's nose is long.	No, la nariz de Pinocho es larga.
Look how large his nose is.	Mira qué larga que [es] su nariz.
Where is your nose?	¿Dónde está tu nariz?
Here it is. Here is your nose.	Aquí está. Aquí está tu nariz.
Is it large like Pinocchio's?	¿Es larga, como la de Pinocho?
No, it's not a large nose.	No ésta no es una nariz larga.
You don't have a large nose like Pinocchio.	Tú no tienes una nariz larga como Pinocho.
You have a little nose.	Tú tienes una nariz pequeña.
Look at Anita's face.	Mira la cara de Anita.
She has a pretty face, doesn't she?	Ella tiene una cara bonita, ¿no es cierto?
Where are Anita's eyes?	¿Dónde están los ojos de Anita?
Here are her eyes.	Éstos son sus ojos.
Her eyes are pretty, aren't they?	Sus ojos son bonitos ¿no?
Two pretty eyes.	Dos ojos bonitos.
Anita is a pretty dolly.	Anita es una muñeca bonita.
Where are Pinocchio's ears?	¿Dónde están las orejas de Pinocho?
Here they are. Here are his ears.	Aquí están. Aquí están sus orejas.
He has two ears and two eyes.	Él tiene dos ojos y dos orejas.
How many eyes do you have?	¿Cuántos ojos tienes tú?
You have two eyes, of course.	Tienes dos ojos, por supuesto.
And how many ears? Two.	¿Y cuántas orejas? Dos.
You have two ears and two eyes.	Tú tienes dos orejas y dos ojos.
Two ears to hear with.	Dos orejas para oír.
Two eyes to see with.	Dos ojos para ver.

Performance Challenge

Remember that translations between Spanish and English are not always literal. Read through this activity again and see how many differences you can spot.

Questions of a Child

Preguntas de un Niño

INSTRUCTIONS Read and listen to this conversation between a father and a child. You will learn many tenses of the verb "to live" in a simple manner.

English	Spanish
Daddy, where do giraffes live?	*¿Papa dónde viven las jirafas?*
Giraffes live in Africa.	*Las jirafas viven en África.*
Do I live in Africa?	*¿Vivo yo en África?*
No, you don't live in Africa.	*No, tú no vives en África.*
You and mama, do you live in Africa?	*Tú y mamá ¿viven ustedes en África?*
No, we don't live in Africa.	*No, no vivimos en África.*
Why?	*¿Por qué?*
Because we're not giraffes.	*Porque no somos jirafas.*

In this activity you will:

→ Ask simple questions and understand the answer.

 Disc **3** Track **17**

A Brief History of El Salvador

In Pre-Columbian times, El Salvador was inhabited by Olmec, Maya, Chorti, Lenca, and Pok'omame cultures. They operated a maize-based economy and independently developed such cultural complexities as hieroglyphic writing, astronomy, and mathematics. In 1525, Pedro de Alvarado claimed the land for Spain. The Spanish government went on to cultivate plantations of cotton, balsam, and indigo. Agriculture boomed through the 1700s, but its profits remained concentrated in the hands of only 14 elite European families, while the nation's natives remained poor or enslaved. Independence came in 1821 and has since, despite sizable setbacks, been striving for equality and justice in its society, economy, and government.

Performance Challenge

Take some time and see how many questions you can think of on your own. If you know someone who speaks Spanish, ask him or her the questions you created.

You have completed all the activities for

Section 2.2.1
Day Four, 14:00 Hours

and are now ready to take the section quiz. Before continuing, be sure you have learned the objectives for each activity in this section.

Section Quiz

INSTRUCTIONS Choose the correct Spanish translation of the underlined English word or phrase. Check your answers on the "Grading Sheet" found on the last page of the book.

1. <u>There is</u> *una reina.*
   A. *Hay*
   B. *Había*
   C. *Esto*
   D. *Esta*

2. *Hay* <u>this</u> *reina y* <u>this</u> *rey.*
   A. *ésta / éste*
   B. *esta / este*
   C. *éste / ésta*
   D. *este / esta*

3. *Cuando yo* <u>was</u> *niña, yo jugaba básket.*
   A. *soy*
   B. *es*
   C. *era*
   D. *eran*

4. <u>There were</u> *tres perros y dos gatos.*
   A. *Habían*
   B. *Había*
   C. *Hay*
   D. *Son*

5. ¿<u>When</u> canta la reina?

   A. Dónde

   B. Por qué

   C. Cuándo

   D. Quién

....

INSTRUCTIONS Choose the correct Spanish translation of the English sentence.

6. **He greets the girl.**

   A. El saluda la muchacha.

   B. El saluda a la muchacha.

7. **Stand up and walk!**

   A. ¡Siéntese y corra!

   B. ¡Póngase de pie y beba!

   C. ¡Siéntese y escriba!

   D. ¡Póngase de pie y camine!

....

INSTRUCTIONS Choose the correct Spanish translation of the underlined English word or phrase.

8. **Mira <u>the nose</u> de Pinocho.**

   A. la nariz

   B. los ojos

   C. las orejas

   D. la boca

9. **Yo <u>live</u> en Nicaragua.**

   A. vives

   B. viven

   C. vivo

   D. vivimos

10. **Ellos <u>live</u> en Colombia.**

    A. vives

    B. viven

    C. vivo

    D. vivimos

Isla de Providencia

Day Four, 19:00 Hours

Fifty-one Hours to Rendezvous

Very pleased with yourselves for earning two clues in one day, you and Stump return to the *Quintana* residence for a late dinner of *pupusas*, a traditional food of El Salvador, and a good night's sleep. You wake early the next morning, eager to continue your Spanish learning adventure. You and Stump pedal your bicycles to the sixth location marked on the map. It turns out to be a dance studio.

"Please tell me we won't have to dance for our next clue," Stump groans.

"I doubt it," you reassure him. You're more concerned with the sign on the studio's door, which informs you that the studio won't open until *las tres de la tarde*—three o'clock this afternoon. You point this out to Stump.

"Well, there's a café across the street," Stump points out. "We can at least be comfortable while we wait."

Over a couple of nice, cold *tazas de limonada*, you and Stump discuss your case so far. Given the clues you've gotten, you're quite confident that you're looking for some sort of recipe, but what? And why on earth would your supervisors send you so far for a recipe?

Not long after noon, though, Stump taps your arm and points to the dance studio across the street. Sure enough, a slender woman about your age, who carries herself with the elegant poise of a classically trained dancer but walks with the aid of a cane, is approaching the studio. She stops in front of it, unlocks the door, and lets herself in.

You and Stump hastily pay for your *limonadas* and follow her into the studio. She introduces herself as Ana Hernandez and informs you that she'd actually come in early, because her friend Ricardo had told her you might be waiting. She shows you to a wooden bench running along one wall of the empty studio, then shows you which activities you'll need to complete to solve her clue. While you work, Ana tells you a bit about her native country, Ecuador.

By the time you finish the activities, students are starting to trickle into the studio for Ana's first afternoon class. Silently, she hands you the puzzle you must

In this section you will:

→ Use various verb conjugations.
→ Problem solve with geometrical shapes.
→ Expand listening and reading comprehension.
→ Build fluency using imperatives.
→ Use pronouns as objects in a sentence.
→ Improve spelling.
→ Understand a conversation without pictographs.
→ Read a DiglotWeave™ and comprehend the information.
→ Increase verb structures.
→ Understand a Spanish geography lesson and master the vocabulary related to Europe.

Disc **4**   Track **1**

SECTION **2.2.2**

solve for her clues, then goes to look after her students. At the bottom of the puzzle is a brief note in Ana's flowing handwriting: *"La última persona que deben buscar viene de un país sudamericano que comienza con la letra c."*

Recipe: *Pupusas*

Dough

- 2 cups flour
- 2 cups *masa harina* (specially prepared cornmeal, available in most supermarkets)
- 1/2 teaspoon salt
- 1/2 teaspoon cumin
- 1/2 cup shortening
- cold water as needed (add about 2 tablespoons at a time)

Chicharrón Filling

- 1 cup bacon, chopped into bite-sized pieces
- 1 teaspoon garlic salt
- 4 tomatoes, finely chopped and drained
- 1 green pepper, finely chopped
- salt to taste

Directions Stir together flour, *masa harina*, salt, and cumin. Cut in shortening until mixture resembles fine crumbs. Add cold water a little at a time until mixture makes a stiff dough. Set aside.

Cook bacon with garlic salt, and drain off the bacon grease. Mix in tomatoes, green pepper, and salt. (If possible, grind together. At least mix very thoroughly.)

With your hands, roll two tablespoons of dough into a ball. Carefully flatten the ball out between your hands until it forms a round tortilla about 1/8" thick. Continue making tortillas this way until the dough is used up. Cover prepared tortillas with waxed paper or a towel so they don't dry out. Take one tortilla, put one heaping tablespoon of filling on top of it, spread the filling out to within 1/2" of the tortilla edge, and top it with another tortilla. Press the edges of the two tortillas together, making sure they stick well. (Moisten the tortilla edges with a little water, if needed, to make the tortillas stick together.) Repeat with remaining tortillas and filling. Cook pupusas on a slightly greased griddle over low-medium heat (325 to 350 degrees), turning about halfway through cooking. Depending on the thickness of the tortilla, each side will need about 4 minutes to cook completely. Top with pickled cabbage and tomato sauce, and serve warm. For variety, *pupusas* can also be filled with refried beans and/or cheese.

Puzzle

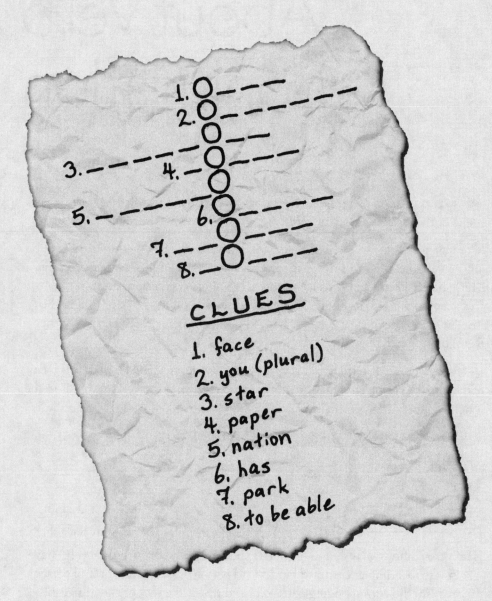

CLUES

1. face
2. you (plural)
3. star
4. paper
5. nation
6. has
7. park
8. to be able

After working the puzzle out yourself, check the answers in Appendix A, on page 464.

About Verb Conjugation

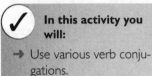

In this activity you will:

➔ Use various verb conjugations.

Poetry and Song in El Salvador

Poetry and song are popular methods of self-expression in El Salvador. Some musicians use a type of song called *canción popular* to comment on current events in their turbulent nation.

INSTRUCTIONS Complete the following activity. This activity will help you review some of the different types of verb conjugations you have learned.

Conjugation Review: Verbs change form depending on who performs that action of the verb, i.e. *canto* (I sing—1st person) *cantas*, (you sing—2nd person) *canta* (he / she / it sings—3rd person) *cantamos* (we sing—1st person) and whether the verb is past, present, or future, i.e. *cantaba* (he / she / it used to sing) *canta* (he / she / it sings) *cantará* (he / she / it will sing). Picking the proper version of the verb, or proper verb ending, is called conjugation.

A few centuries back, the English verb system was more complex than it is today. Compare the conjugation pattern of the present tense of the verb "to bind" in the English of today and of then.

	Today's English	Early English
1st person:	I bind	I bind-e
2nd person:	you bind	thou bind-est
3rd person:	he bind-s	he bind-eth

The verb endings -e, -est, and -eth (1st, 2nd, and 3rd person, respectively) have given way to a simpler contrast: bind-s (3rd person) vs. bind (1st or 2nd person). In Spanish, the corresponding pattern of endings is like that of early English, a different ending tied to (i.e. conjugated with) each "person."

	Spanish	Early English
1st person:	*yo tom-o*	I take
2nd person:	*tú tom-as*	thou takest
3rd person:	*él tom-a*	he taketh

There are two verb classes, called (because of their "thematic" vowels) -ar verbs (Class 1) and -er or -ir verbs (Class 2). The -er and -ir verbs are so much alike they are each viewed as submembers of Class 2.

1. Verbs with thematic vowel A are called "-ar verbs" (*tomar, cantar*)

2. Verbs with thematic vowel E are called "*-er* verbs" (*comer*, *comprender*)

3. Verbs with thematic vowel I are called "*-ir* verbs" (*recibir*, *vivir*)

Present Tense *-ar* Verbs

Example: to take

Singular	Plural	Singular	Plural	Isolated	Ending
I take	we take	*yo* tom-*o*	*nosotros* tom-amos	-o	-amos
you take	you take	*tú* tom-*as*	*ustedes* tom-an	-as	-an
he takes	they take	*él / ella* tom-*a*	*ellos* tom-an	-a	-an

Present Tense *-er* Verbs

Example: to receive

Singular	Plural	Singular	Plural	Isolated	Ending
I receive	we receive	*yo* comprend-*o*	*nosotros (-as)* comprend-emos	-o	-emos
you receive	you receive	*tú* comprend-es	*ustedes* comprend-en	-es	-en
he takes	they receive	*él / ella* comprend-*e*	*ellos (-as)* comprend-en	-e	-en

Present Tense *-ir* Verbs

Example: to live

Singular	Plural	Singular	Plural	Isolated	Ending
I live	we live	*yo* viv-*o*	*nosotros* viv-imos	-o	-imos
you live	you live	*tú* viv-es	*ustedes* viv-en	-es	-en
he lives	they live	*el / ella* viv-e	*ellos / ellas* viv-en	-e	-en

The Verb *ser* 'to be' is Irregular

Example: to be

Singular	Plural	Singular	Plural
I am	we are	*yo soy*	*nosotros somos*
you are	you are	*tú eres*	*ustedes son*
she / he is	they are	*él / ella es*	*ellos son*

★

Performance Challenge

The irregular verbs in Spanish can be difficult to remember. Give yourself more practice by using the ones in this activity in your own sentences.

Points, Lines, and Figures

Puntos, Líneas, y Figuras

A. Scatter Chart

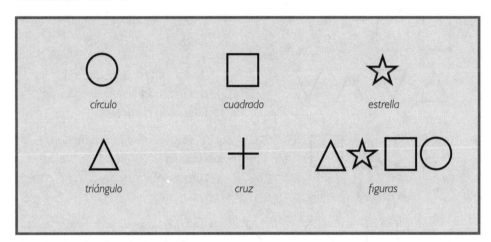

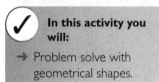

In this activity you will:

→ Problem solve with geometrical shapes.

Disc **4**   Track **2**

B. Look, Listen and Read

INSTRUCTIONS   Listen to the audio and read through the Spanish and pictographic representations.

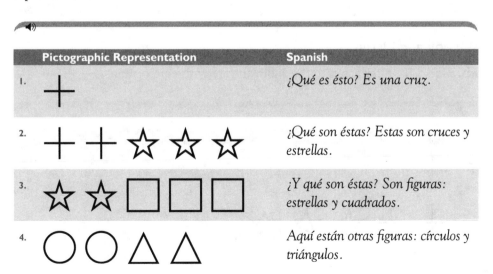

Geography of El Salvador

In terms of size, El Salvador is about the size of Massachusetts. El Salvador is bordered by Guatemala to the west, Honduras to the north and east, and the Pacific Ocean to the south. Most of the country is lush and green, though less than 6% of it is still forested. Coffee is the crop of choice in the highlands, while sugarcane takes its place in the lowlands. More than 25 extinct volcanoes dot the landscape of this small country.

	Pictographic Representation *(cont.)*	Spanish
5.	○ △ □ ☆ ○ △ □ ☆	Los círculos, los triángulos, los cuadrados y las estrellas, todas éstas son figuras.
6.	○	¿Qué tipo de figura es éste? Es un círculo. Y también es la letra o.
7.	▬▬▬	¿Cuál tipo de línea es éste? Es una línea horizontal, larga, y gruesa.
8.	—	¿Cuál tipo de línea es éste? Es una línea horizontal, corta, y delgada.
9.	□ □	¿Estas figuras son triángulos o cuadrados? Son cuadrados.
10.	△ ▽ △ ▽	Todas estas figuras son triángulos, dos indicando hacia arriba y dos indicando hacia abajo.
11.	□ □ △ □ ▽ □ □	Varios cuadrados y triángulos. Los cuadrados son grandes y pequeños, pero todos los triángulos son grandes.
12.	— ‖‖‖ \ \ / ⁄	Todas éstas son líneas rectas: líneas horizontales, líneas verticales y líneas diagonales.

C. Look and Listen

INSTRUCTIONS Now listen to the audio and study the pictographs.

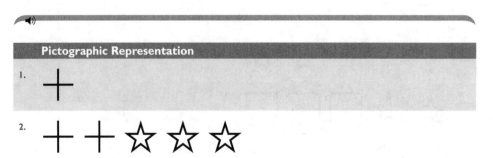

	Pictographic Representation
1.	✛
2.	✛ ✛ ☆ ☆ ☆

Pictographic Representation (cont.)

3.
4.
5.
6.
7.
8.
9.
10.
11.
12.

D. Multiple-Choice Frames

INSTRUCTIONS   Listen to the audio and choose the correct frame. Check your answers in Appendix A, on page 461.

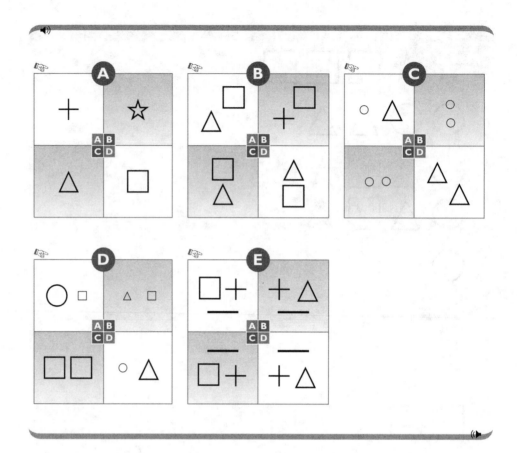

E. Listen and Draw

INSTRUCTIONS   Pause the audio if the pace is too fast. Check your answers in Appendix A, on page 461.

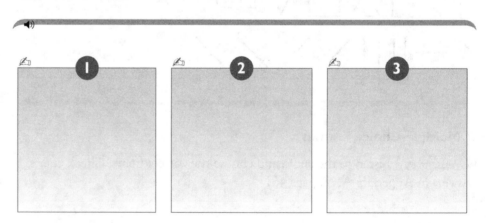

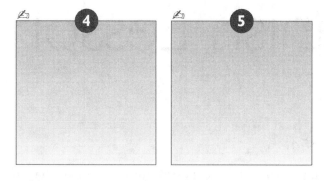

F. Read for Meaning

INSTRUCTIONS   See if you can understand the following sentences. You don't need to know every word to understand the general meaning of the sentence! Check your translations in Appendix A, on page 462.

1. *¿Qué letra es ésta? ¿Es la letra D o la letra O? Es una D.*

2. *¿Qué tipo de figura es ésta? ¿Es un círculo o un cuadrado?*

3. *Todos estos triángulos apuntan hacia arriba y todas estas flechas apuntan hacia abajo.*

4. *Estas dos figuras están entre dos líneas verticales.*

5. *¿Qué tipo de figura precede la letra F?*

6. *¿Qué tipo de figura sigue a la letra F?*

7. *¿Qué letra está después del triángulo grande, y cuál precede el círculo grande?*

8. *¿No sigue el triángulo grande de la letra B?*

ACTIVITY 64

A Spanish Lesson

Una Lección de Español

INSTRUCTIONS In this lesson, you will build fluency with the commanding imperative) voice (i.e. Write! Take! Put! etc.) and with pronouns as objects (i.e. put it here, cross it out, take it etc.). Notice how the lesson describes both past and present events. Listen to this lesson in Spanish. See how much you can understand without reading the English.

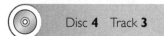

In this activity you will:

→ Expand listening and reading comprehension.

Disc **4** Track **3**

★ Quito

ECUADOR
Guayaquil

Iquitos

Piura

Ecuador Culture Overview

Because attitudes vary widely from one group to another, it is difficult to make overall statements. However, generally, Ecuadorians are proud of their country and history. Ecuador is inhabited by three main groups: the *Serranos* (people from mountain highlands, including Quito), the *Costeños* (people who live in the coastal regions), and the Native American groups from the Amazon region who maintain their own customs.

English	Spanish
Write your name on this paper.	*Escriba su nombre en este papel.*
(You're writing your name.)	*(Ud. está escribiendo su nombre.)*
Very well. You wrote your name.	*Muy bien. Ud. escribió su nombre.*
Now cross it out.	*Ahora táchelo.*
(You're crossing out your name.)	*(Ud. está tachando su nombre.)*
Very well. You wrote your name, and then you crossed it out.	*Muy bien. Ud. escribió su nombre, y luego lo tachó.*
Write the name of your father or mother.	*Escriba el nombre de su padre o madre.*
(You're writing your father's name.)	*(Ud. está escribiendo el nombre de su padre.)*
Very well. You wrote your father's name, right?	*Muy bien. Ud. escribió el nombre de su padre, ¿verdad?*
Now write your mother's name.	*Ahora escriba el nombre de su madre.*
Now cross out your father's name.	*Ahora tache el nombre de su padre.*
Very well. You wrote your own name and then crossed it out.	*Muy bien. Ud. escribió su propio nombre y luego lo tachó.*
Then you wrote your father's name and crossed it out.	*Luego escribió Ud. el nombre de su padre y lo tachó.*
And then you wrote your mother's name and crossed it out.	*Y luego escribió el nombre de su madre y lo tachó.*

English *(cont.)*	Spanish
Now write my name and then cross it out.	*Ahora escriba el nombre mío y luego táchelo.*
Take your pencil. Take it.	*Tome su lápiz. Tómelo.*
Put your pencil here. Put it here.	*Ponga su lápiz aquí. Póngalo aquí.*
Take your white paper. Take it.	*Tome su papel blanco. Tómelo.*
Put your paper here. Put it here.	*Ponga su papel aquí. Póngalo aquí.*
Take my red pencil. Take it.	*Tome mi lápiz rojo. Tómelo.*
Put my pencil here. Put it here.	*Ponga mi lápiz aquí. Póngalo aquí.*
Take my red paper. Take it.	*Tome mi papel rojo. Tómelo.*
Put my paper here. Put it here.	*Ponga mi papel aquí. Póngalo aquí.*
Excellent!	*¡Magnífico!*
Sack. Box. There is or there are.	*Bolsa. Caja. Hay.*
Here there's a pencil.	*Aquí hay un lápiz.*
Here there are two pencils.	*Aquí hay dos lápices.*
How many pencils? Two.	*¿Cuántos lápices? Dos.*
Put this one in the box.	*Meta éste en la caja.*
Put it in.	*Métalo.*
Put these in the box too.	*Meta éstos en la caja también.*
Put them in.	*Métalos.*
Take a paper and put it in this box.	*Tome un papel y métalo en esta caja.*
Take another paper and put it in the same box.	*Tome otro papel y métalo en la misma caja.*
Take two pencils and put them in this sack.	*Tome dos lápices y métalos en esta bolsa.*
Take another pencil and put it in the same sack.	*Tome otro lápiz y métalo en la misma bolsa.*

Performance Challenge

Listen to this activity's audio track again. This time, gather all the materials you need and follow all the instructions in the activity.

Spanish Verbs

INSTRUCTIONS   Read the following explanations to learn about Spanish verbs.

Part I

Suppose that a Spanish speaker recognized the basic meaning of the English verb "speak," but did not know how it changed in different sentences (for instance we say "he is speaking," the king speaks quietly," "she spoke," "when he had spoken," etc.). For him or her, it would make sense to fit this word into Spanish patterns, making phrases like the following. We'll call his new language "Spanglish."

In this activity you will:

→ Build fluency using imperatives.

→ Use pronouns as objects in a sentence.

Spanglish Form	Parallel to Normal English	Technical Name
él SPEAK-a	he speaks	simple present
él SPEAK-ará	he will speak*	future
él SPEAK-aría	he would speak*	conditional
él SPEAK-aba	he spoke (at times)**	imperfective (unbounded / not closed)
él SPEAK-ó	he spoke (on a given occasion)**	preterite or perfective (bounded / closed)
SPEAK-a!	speak! (address to a familiar)***	familiar singular imperative
SPEAK-e!	speak! (formal address)****	formal singular imperative
SPEAK-en!	speak! (formal address)****	plural imperative
SPEAK-ar	to speak	infinitive form
SPEAK-ando	speak-ing	present participle form
SPEAK-ado	spok-en	past participle form
él ha SPEAK-ado	he has spok-en	present perfect
él había SPEAK-ado	he had spok-en	past perfect

Facts and Figures on Ecuador

- Ecuador's population is about 11.9 million and is growing by 2.2% annually.
- Spanish is Ecuador's official language, but *Quechua* is also widely spoken, and many of its words have been adopted into Ecuadorian Spanish.
- Ecuador is one of only two nations in South America that does not share a border with Brazil. (The other is Chile.)
- Soccer is Ecuador's most popular sport.
- Ecuador has a president, a unicameral legislature, and an independent judicial branch.

Spanglish Form *(cont.)*	Parallel to Normal English	Technical Name
él habrá SPEAK-ado	he will have spok-en	future perfect
él habría SPEAK-ado	he would have spok-en	conditional perfect

NOTE

* Note that Spanish uses suffixes to talk about the future; for instance, to say "he will speak" in Spanglish is "*él speak-ara*" whereas English uses a separate word "will" to talk about what would happen.

** Note that Spanish uses suffixes to talk about the conditional voice (talking about what would happen if certain conditions were met) whereas English uses separate words (such as would) to talk about what would happen.

*** Spanish is different than English in many ways, including that Spanish distinguishes between past actions that were ongoing and those that describe a single event. For example, you could say "When I was at college, I called home and spoke to my parents every week." In this instance where the action was ongoing, the Spanglish word is *speak-aba*. In contrast, you could say "Last week I called home and spoke to my parents for over an hour." In this instance where the action was a single event, the Spanish word is *speak-ó*.

**** Note the difference between familiar and formal address.

Part 2

Furthermore, as you can see from what you already know of Spanish verbs, this Spanish speaker would feel that the following ways of linking verb with pronoun makes perfect sense. In fact, because of the distinctive verb endings, he would feel comfortable speaking without the subject pronoun, if the context were clear.

Person	Singular English	Spanglish	Plural English	Spanglish
First	I speak	*yo SPEAK-o*	we speak	*nosotros SPEAK-amos*
Second	you speak	*tú SPEAK-as*	you speak	*ustedes SPEAK-an*
Third	he speaks	*él SPEAK-a*	they speak	*ellos SPEAK-an*
	she	*ella*		
	it			

Part 3

The auxiliary word of paramount importance for forming the "I have spoken" form of the verb is *haber.* Its conjugation is: *he, has, ha, hemos, han, han.*

English	Spanglish
I have spoken	*yo he SPEAK-ado*
you (sg) have spoken	*tú has SPEAK-ado*
he has spoken	*él / ella ha SPEAK-ado*
we have spoken	*nosotros hemos SPEAK-ado*
you (pl) have spoken	*ustedes han SPEAK-ado*
they have spoken	*ellos / ellas han SPEAK-ado*

Performance Challenge

Look up some verbs you've used in earlier activities. Using the patterns shown in this activity, try to put these earlier verbs into the different verb forms you studied today.

ACTIVITY

66

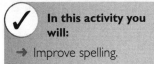

In this activity you will:

→ Improve spelling.

Familiar Words

Here are some Spanish cognates that you should recognize.)

-ABLE / -IBLE			
(im)posible	venerable	invencible	(in)tolerable
(in)visible	(in)variable	(in)corruptible	(in)discutible
perceptible	(in)separable	(ir)redimible	(im)perdonable
(in)corregible	(in)curable	(in)tangible	(ir)refutable
(im)permeable	(in)variable	(in)formidable	

-CION (Compare to English -tion, -sion)			
participación	variación	veneración	operación
inflexión	percepción	visión	opresión
obligación	corrección	refutación	omisión
federación	inspección	preparación	reflexión
nación	dirección	insolación	
invención	corrupción	elaboración	
formación	adición	misión	

Ecuador's Population

Although Ecuador's population was once concentrated in the Andes region, today it is almost equally distributed between the mountains and the coast. Due to migration to the cities, especially Quito and Guyaquil, almost half of Ecuador's population lives in urban areas. The Amazon region remains the most sparsely populated area, with just 3% of the country's population in its isolated villages.

Chatter at a Royal Ball

INSTRUCTIONS   Learn these words and the following conversation.

Getting Ready for *Conversación*

English	Spanish
to dance	*bailar*
to know, know how	*saber*
knows how to dance	*sabe bailar*
(she / he) has	*tiene*
to joke	*bromear*
I'm not joking.	*No estoy bromeando.*
I know	*(Yo) sé*
Listen!	*¡Escucha!*
Listen to!	*¡Escúchame!*
Can you beat that?	*¡Fíjese!*
in fact	*de hecho*
Don't tell me!	*¡No me digas!*

Conversation 8

	English	Spanish
•:	The king of France has a horse.	*El rey de Francia tiene un caballo.*
••:	Of course he has a horse. What king doesn't have a horse?	*Por supuesto que tiene un caballo. ¿Qué rey no tiene caballo?*
•:	And you know, his horse is white.	*Y, ¿sabes? su caballo es blanco.*

In this activity you will:

→ Understand a conversation without picto-graphs.

Disc **4**   Track **4**

Foods of Ecuador

Ecuador is well known for its tropical fruits, its top-notch seafood, and its wide variety of Andean potatoes. *Ají*, or hot sauce, accompanies almost every meal, and most households have their own special recipe. However, Ecuador's specialty food is soup. Most lunches and dinners have a first course of soup. One well-known soup of Ecuador is *locro* soup. Made with cheese, potatoes, and avocados, this soup may sound odd but is actually very tasty. *Chupe de pescado*, a fish and vegetable soup from coastal regions, is also popular.

English *(cont.)*	Spanish
●●: Of course I know. What king doesn't have a white horse?	*Claro que lo sé. ¿Qué rey no tiene un caballo blanco?*
●: Listen to me! His horse knows how to dance.	*¡Escúchame! Su caballo sabe bailar.*
●●: Whose horse knows how to dance?	*¿El caballo de quién sabe bailar?*
●: The horse of the king of France.	*El caballo del rey de Francia.*
●●: You are joking.	*Estás bromeando.*
●: I'm not joking. It's true. His horse knows how to do the cha-cha-cha.	*No estoy bromeando. Es la verdad. Su caballo sabe bailar el cha-cha-cha.*
●●: Can you beat that?!	*¡Fíjese!*
●: In fact, the horse and the dog and the cat dance together.	*De hecho, el caballo, el perro, y el gato bailan juntos.*
●●: Don't tell me! The white horse of the king of France dances with the dog and cat?	*¡No me digas! ¡El caballo blanco del rey de Francia baila con el perro y el gato?*
●: Precisely.	*Precisamente.*

Performance Challenge

Remember to look for real life situations where you can use the words and phrases you are learning.

DiglotWeave™: An Incident in a Park, Part I

In this activity you will:

→ Read a DiglotWeave™ and comprehend the information.

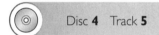

Disc **4**   Track **5**

Un Incidente en un Parque en Centro América

INSTRUCTIONS   Listen to this DiglotWeave™. See how much vocabulary you can learn from context!

Let me *contar* you *una historia*. Do you see this picture? It's a *dibujo* of a *parque* where people come to enjoy themselves. And it is *en este parque* that my *historia* takes place. *El incidente* that I'm going to *contar* about involved some soldiers, some *soldados* in this small *pueblo en Centro América*. Some of *los soldados* were *de Cuba, los otros* were *de Norteamérica, de los Estados Unidos de América*. Picture that: *soldados norte-americanos y soldados cubanos* en a nice little *parque…un parquecito…en* a nice little *pueblo…un pueblito…*somewhere *en Centro América.* Can you anticipate *que pasa?* I don't think so.

Look at *el dibujo.* In it you can see *el pueblito, y aquí en el pueblito* you can *ver el parquecito.* What do you suppose *que los soldados norteamericanos* were doing *en el parque?* Do you suppose *que* they *estaban* working…*trabajando?* No, *ellos* weren't *trabajando…no estaban trabajando.* If *los soldados norteamericanos no estaban trabajando en el parque, ¿qué estaban haciendo?* They were playing *béisbol…jugando béisbol,* that's what. *Ellos estaban jugando béisbol.*

(To be continued)

Performance Challenge

Listen to the audio track again and see how much you can comprehend without looking at your textbook. Write down what you think the story is saying, then listen to it one more time. See how much your comprehension increases each time you listen to the story.

Chatter at a Royal Ball

INSTRUCTIONS   Learn the words and the following conversation.

Getting Ready for *Conversación*

Words

INSTRUCTIONS   Learn the following list of words.

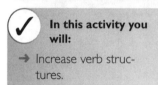

In this activity you will:

→ Increase verb structures.

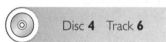

Disc **4**   Track **6**

English	Spanish
to assure	*asegurar*
to lie	*mentir*
to prove	*probar*
to be able, can	*poder*
to eat	*comer*
to say	*decir*
to cook	*cocinar*
to work	*trabajar*
to dance	*bailar*
owner	*propietario*
frankly	*francamente*
I can do it.	*Yo puedo hacerlo.*
when	*cuando*
once in a while	*de vez en cuando*
to swallow	*tragar*
to have oneself a swig	*tomarse un trago*
while	*mientras*

Sites to See in Quito

Ecuador's capital city is debatably one of the nicest in Latin America to visit. Just 22 kilometers south of the equator, it nonetheless maintains a pleasant, spring-like climate all year thanks to its high altitude. The old city center is preserved much as it was in centuries past and has been declared a World Cultural Heritage Site by UNESCO. North of this old city center, though, is a fully modernized city, with everything one would expect to see in a national capital. Some sites to see include the 16th century Monastery of San Francisco, Ecuador's oldest church; *La Ronda*, a beautifully preserved alley full of colonial-era buildings; and *El Panecillo*, a hill that offers excellent views of the city, complete with an open-air market at the foot of the hill. In the new part of town, *Avenida Amazonas* is the showcase of modern Quito and is an excellent spot to find a good meal and watch the rest of the world bustle past.

Phrases

INSTRUCTIONS Learn the following list of phrases.

English	Spanish
You're lying.	*Estás mintiendo.*
I don't lie.	*No miento.*
You're pulling my leg!	*¡Me estás tomando el pelo!*
I assure you it is so.	*Te aseguro que es así.*
I don't believe you.	*No te creo.*
I don't believe it.	*No lo creo.*
I can't believe it.	*No puedo creerlo.*
I can prove it.	*Puedo probarlo.*
That's fantastic!	*¡Eso es fantástico!*
It's no big thing.	*No es gran cosa.*
Don't tell me!	*¡No me digas!*
Who can believe it?	*¿Quién puede creerlo?*
How can I believe that?	*¿Cómo puedo creer eso?*
his (her / your / their) restaurant	*su restaurante*
The cook is in the kitchen cooking.	*El cocinero está en la cocina cocinando.*
You're not telling the truth.	*No dices la verdad.*
I'm telling the truth.	*Digo la verdad.*

Conversación 9

	English	Spanish
•:	Where do the duchess's dog and cat eat now?	*¿Dónde comen el perro y el gato de la duquesa ahora?*
••:	They always eat together in their restaurant.	*Siempre comen juntos en su restaurante.*
•:	Do the dog and the cat have a restaurant now?	*¿El perro y el gato ahora tienen un restaurante?*

English *(cont.)*	Spanish
••: Yeah, the dog is the owner and the cat is the cook…he works in the kitchen.	*Sí pues, el perro es el propietario y el gato es el cocinero…él trabaja en la cocina.*
•: Ha! That's fantastic!	*¡Ja! ¡Eso es fantástico!*
••: That is fantastic. And they say the cat dances while he cooks.	*Eso sí es fantástico. Y dicen que el gato baila mientras cocina.*
•: Don't tell me! I can't believe it!	*¡No me digas! ¡No puedo creerlo!*
••: I'm telling the truth.	*Digo la verdad.*
•: I don't believe you. You're lying. You're pulling my leg.	*No te creo. Estás mintiendo. Me estás tomando el pelo.*
••: I assure you it is so. I'm not lying. I can prove it.	*Te aseguro que es así. No miento. Puedo probarlo.*

Performance Challenge

See how many of these phrases you can incorporate into real life conversations. Be creative, and write down some conversations of your own.

A Geography Lesson

In this activity you will:

→ Understand a Spanish geography lesson and master the vocabulary related to Europe.

Disc **4**   Track **7**

Una Lección de Geografía

INSTRUCTIONS   The following reading is designed to help you master European geography vocabulary. Listen to and read the lesson.

English	Spanish
Last time, we discussed the general situation of our planet, the earth, in the solar system.	*La última vez hablamos sobre la situación general de nuestro planeta, la Tierra, en el sistema solar.*
We identified its geography and briefly discussed the United States.	*Identificamos su geografía y hablamos brevemente de los Estados Unidos.*
Today I would like to take you on a little trip around a beautiful part of our world; I would like us to visit Europe.	*Hoy quisiera llevarlos a un pequeño viaje a una parte muy bella de nuestro mundo; me gustaría que visitáramos Europa.*
Here is a map of Europe.	*Aquí tenemos un mapa de Europa.*
If you remember, Europe is situated in the northern hemisphere.	*Si se acuerdan, Europa está situada en el hemisferio norte.*
Let's start with these islands here.	*Comencemos con estas islas aquí.*
These are what we call the British Isles.	*Éstas son las que llamamos Las Islas Británicas.*
Here is an easy question for you:	*Aquí hay una pregunta fácil para ustedes:*
What language is spoken in England?	*¿Qué idioma se habla en Inglaterra?*
English, just like in the United States and many other countries.	*Inglés, tal como en los Estados Unidos y en muchos otros países.*
Just across the English Channel is France.	*Justo al otro lado del Canal de la Mancha está Francia.*
What is the capital of France?	*¿Cuál es la capital de Francia?*

English *(cont.)*	Spanish
Paris, of course! Everyone knows.	¡París, por supuesto! Todos lo saben.
And what do you know about Paris?	¿Y qué saben ustedes de París?
Right, that's where the Eiffel Tower is!	Bien, ¡Ahí es donde está la Torre Eiffel!
Look here, this is a peninsula.	Miren aquí, esto es una península.
On this peninsula, we find Spain and Portugal, homelands of the beautiful Spanish and Portuguese languages.	En esta península encontramos España y Portugal, hogar de los bellos idiomas español y portugués.
Do you know anyone who speaks Spanish or Portuguese?	¿Conocen a alguien que hable español o portugués?
This country in the shape of a boot is Italy.	Este país con forma de bota es Italia.
And this one that looks like a hand is Greece.	Y esta que parece mano es Grecia.
Wouldn't you like to live there and swim in the Mediterranean sea? I would!	¿No les gustaría vivir ahí y nadar en el Mar Mediterráneo? ¡A mí sí!
Right here in the middle is the tiny country of Switzerland.	Justo aquí en el centro está el pequeño país de Suiza.
An interesting characteristic of Switzerland is that in spite of its small size, it has three national languages: Italian, French, and German.	Una característica interesante de Suiza es que a pesar de su pequeño tamaño tiene tres idiomas nacionales: italiano, francés, y alemán.
In what other country is German spoken?	¿En qué otro país se habla alemán?
In Germany, of course, but also here in Austria.	En Alemania, por supuesto, pero también aquí en Austria.
There is another language that is closely related to German.	Hay otro idioma que está muy relacionado con el alemán.
It is called Dutch.	Se llama holandés.
Do you know where Dutch is spoken?	¿Saben dónde se habla holandés?
Yes, here in Holland.	Sí, en Holanda.
Next to Holland are Belgium and Luxemburg.	Al lado de Holanda están Bélgica y Luxemburgo.
These two countries are also French-speaking.	En estos dos países también se habla francés.

ACTIVITY 70

English *(cont.)*	Spanish
To the North here, we have what we call Scandinavia.	*Hacia el norte, aquí, tenemos lo que llamamos Escandinavia.*
Five countries are included in Scandinavia: Denmark, Finland, Sweden, Norway and way out here we have Iceland.	*Escandinavia incluye cinco países: Dinamarca, Finlandia, Suecia, Noruega y lejos, por allá, tenemos Islandia.*
All the countries we have talked about so far form Western Europe.	*Todos los países de los que hemos hablado hasta ahora forman la Europa Occidental.*
In Eastern Europe are found Poland, Czechoslovakia, Hungary, Bulgaria, Romania, and other countries.	*En la Europa Oriental se encuentran Polonia, Checoslovaquia, Hungría, Bulgaria, Rumania, y otros países.*
There's another important country in Eastern Europe.	*Hay otro país importante en Europa Oriental.*
Can you guess? It's Russia, of course.	*¿Puedes adivinarlo? Es Rusia, por supuesto.*
Part of Russia is included in Eastern Europe and the rest in Asia.	*Parte de Rusia está incluida en Europa Oriental y el resto en Asia.*
It is a very large country.	*Es un país muy grande.*
It stretches from Finland to Japan.	*Se extiende desde Finlandia hasta Japón.*
It is the largest country in the world.	*Es el país más grande del mundo.*
Well, we're out of time.	*Bueno, se nos acabó el tiempo.*
How did you like our little trip?	*¿Les gustó nuestro viaje?*
So many countries, so many languages, so many cultures.	*Tantos países, tantos idiomas, tantas culturas.*

INSTRUCTIONS Now go back and review, review, review!

Performance Challenge

Go online or visit your local library and find information on one of the places discussed in this lesson.

√ You have completed all the activities for

**Section 2.2.2
Day Four, 19:00 Hours**

and are now ready to take the section quiz. Before continuing, be sure you have learned the objectives for each activity in this section.

Section Quiz

INSTRUCTIONS Choose the correct response. Check your answers on the "Grading Sheet" found on the last page of the book.

1. **Which of the following verbs is not in the *él / ella* (3rd person singular) form?**

   A. *vive*

   B. *toma*

   C. *come*

   D. *bailo*

2. **Which of the following is NOT an example of an *-er* verb?**

   A. *comprender*

   B. *vivir*

   C. *comer*

   D. *leer*

INSTRUCTIONS Choose the correct Spanish translation of the underlined English word or phrase.

3. *Tú* <u>dance</u> *la salsa.*

   A. *bailo*

   B. *baila*

   C. *bailas*

   D. *bailamos*

....

INSTRUCTIONS   Choose the correct response.

4.   △ ☐ ☐   *¿Qué son estos?*

   A. *un triángulo y dos cuadrados*

   B. *un cuadrado y dos triángulos*

   C. *una cruz y dos círculos*

   D. *un triángulo y dos círculos*

....

INSTRUCTIONS   Choose the correct Spanish translation of the underlined English word or phrase.

5. *Escriba su nombre.* <u>Write it.</u>

   A. *Escríbalo.*

   B. *Lo escriba.*

   C. *Lo escribe.*

   D. *Escribirlo.*

6. *Tome un papel y <u>put it</u> aquí.*

   A. *tómelo*

   B. *póngalo*

   C. *lo tome*

   D. *lo ponga*

....

INSTRUCTIONS   Choose the answer that best completes the following sentences.

7. **He has eaten.** *El ... comido.*

   A. *he*

   B. *has*

   C. *ha*

   D. *han*

INSTRUCTIONS   Choose the correct response.

8. **What are the endings of the following cognate words?** *intoler___; invis___; inspec___*

   A. -ible; -able; -ción

   B. -able; -ible; -ción

   C. -ción; -ible; -able

   D. -able; -ción; -ible

INSTRUCTIONS   Choose the correct Spanish translation of the English sentence.

9. **I don't believe you.**

   A. *No te creo.*

   B. *No lo creo.*

   C. *No me digas!*

   D. *No miento.*

INSTRUCTIONS   Choose the correct response.

10. *¿Cuál NO es un país en Escandinavia?*

   A. *Dinamarca*

   B. *Noruega*

   C. *Suecia*

   D. *Alemania*

You have completed all the sections for

Module 2.2

and are now ready to take the module test. Before continuing, be sure you have learned the objectives for each activity in this module.

Module Test

INSTRUCTIONS Determine whether or not the following verb conjugation are correct. Check your answers on the "Grading Sheet" found on the last page of the book.

1. **yo tomo**

   A. True

   B. False

2. **tú tomas**

   A. True

   B. False

3. **el / ella tome**

   A. True

   B. False

4. **nosotros tomamos**

   A. True

   B. False

5. **ustedes toman**

   A. True

   B. False

6. **ellos / ellas toman**

   A. True

   B. False

MODULE 2.2

7. *yo come*

   A. True

   B. False

8. *tú comes*

   A. True

   B. False

9. *el / ella comen*

   A. True

   B. False

10. *nosotros comes*

    A. True

    B. False

11. *ustedes comen*

    A. True

    B. False

12. *ellos / ellas comen*

    A. True

    B. False

13. *yo reciba*

    A. True

    B. False

14. *tú recibes*

    A. True

    B. False

15. *el / ella reciben*

    A. True

    B. False

16. *nosotros recibimos*

    A. True

    B. False

17. *ustedes recibes*

   A. True

   B. False

18. *ellos / ellas reciben*

   A. True

   B. False

....

INSTRUCTIONS   True or False: the following words are correct translations of each other.

19. *preparación* = **preparation**

   A. True

   B. False

20. *elaboración* = **elevation**

   A. True

   B. False

21. *invariable* = **invariable**

   A. True

   B. False

22. *curable* = **curable**

   A. True

   B. False

23. *refutación* = **reputation**

   A. True

   B. False

24. *insulación* = **insulation**

   A. True

   B. False

25. *venerable* = **venerable**

   A. True

   B. False

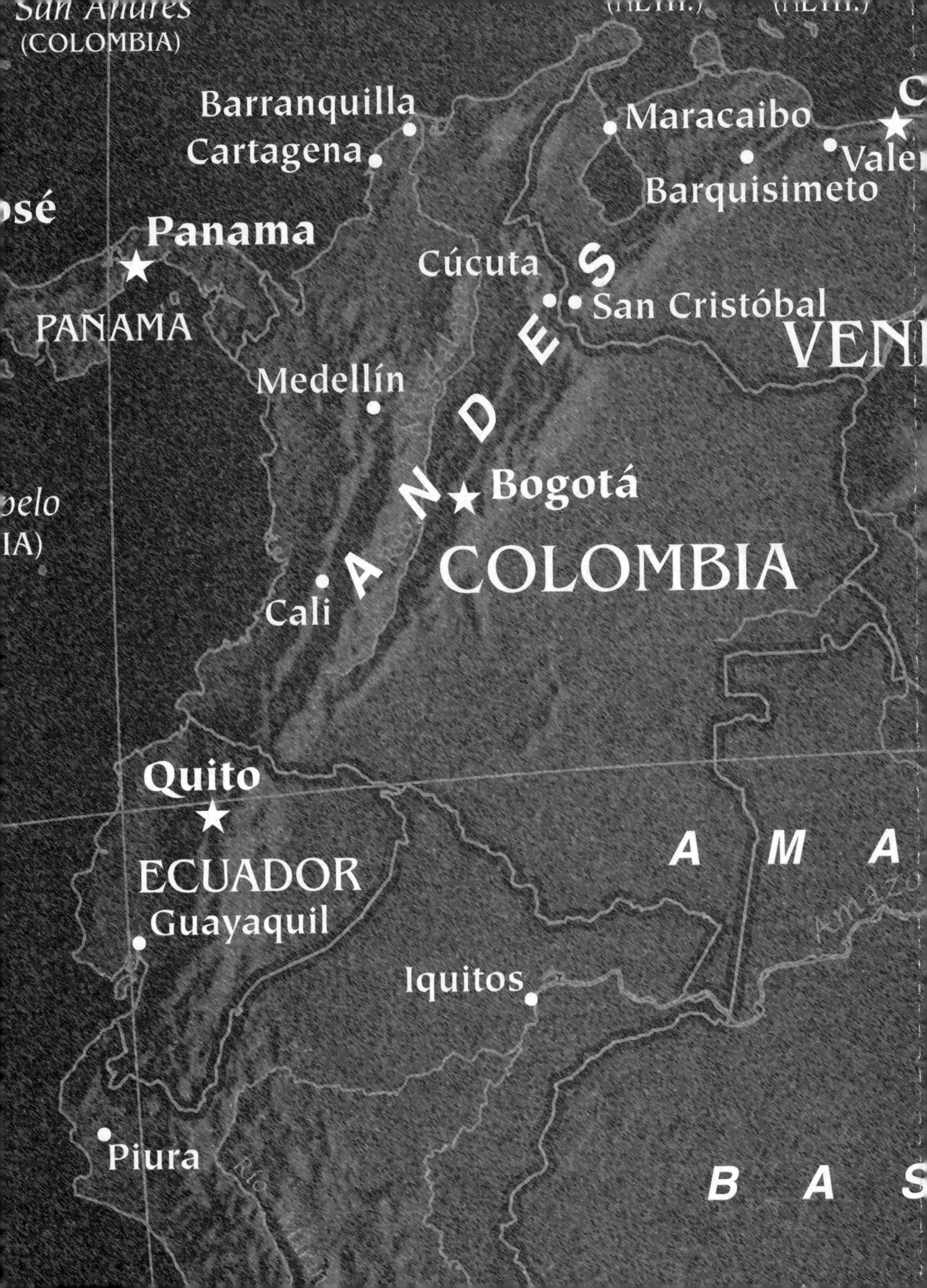
(COLOMBIA)
Barranquilla
Cartagena
Maracaibo
Barquisimeto
Panama
PANAMA
Cúcuta
San Cristóbal
Medellín
A N D E S
Bogotá
COLOMBIA
Cali
Quito
ECUADOR
Guayaquil
Iquitos
Piura

Module 2.3

Throughout this module we'll be learning about the culture of Colombia.

Keep these tips in mind as you progress through this module:

1. Read instructions carefully.
2. Repeat aloud all the Spanish words you hear on the audio CDs.
3. Go at your own pace.
4. Have fun with the activities and practice your new language skills with others.
5. Record yourself speaking Spanish on tape so you can evaluate your own speaking progress.

San Andrés
(COLOMBIA)

osé

pelo
(A)

N

Lago de
Reflejos

Avenida Las Palomas

Parque San
Cristobal

Playa Negra

Río de Plata

El Volcán

Playa Roja

Laguna
del Oro

Isla de Providencia

Day Five, 16:00 Hours

Thirty Hours to Rendezvous

"One more clue to go!" Stump exclaims. "We're going to make it after all!"

You and Stump eagerly race to the final destination marked on the map. By the time you reach it, though, it's dark—inside the building as well as outside. Your last clue is in the island's elementary school, and everyone has gone home for the day. Whomever you're supposed to find here, you obviously aren't going to find him or her tonight.

Reluctantly, you and Stump return to the Quintana residence, where Chiquita has *flan de legumbres*, a vegetable soufflé made in Ecuador, waiting for you.

In this section you will:

→ Comprehend a Spanish story and re-tell it in your own words.
→ Read and answer questions in Spanish.
→ Learn new vocabulary through Spanish poems and jingles.
→ Learn new action verbs.
→ Act out what you've read.
→ Compose new sentences orally and in writing.
→ Compare and contrast different objects.
→ Comprehend new vocabulary in context.
→ Understand irregular verbs.

 Disc **4**   Track **8**

Recipe: *Flan de Legumbres*

- 6 slices bacon, cut into bite-sized pieces
- 1 cup bread crumbs
- 1/2 cup milk
- 4 tablespoons tomato sauce
- 1 cup chicken broth
- 2 tablespoons melted butter
- 1 tablespoon parsley
- 1/2 teaspoon garlic salt
- pepper to taste
- 2 cups chopped mixed vegetables, already cooked
- 3 eggs, well-beaten

Directions   Preheat the oven to 350 degrees. In a medium skillet, cook bacon over medium heat until crisp. Remove from heat and drain on paper towels. In a large bowl, combine bacon, bread crumbs, milk, tomato sauce, broth, melted butter, parsley, garlic salt, and pepper. Fold in the mixed vegetables, then gently fold in the eggs. Butter a 1 1/2 quart casserole or soufflé dish, and pour the soufflé mixture into the buttered dish. Cook for one hour, or until knife inserted into the center of the soufflé comes out clean.

Seventeen Hours to Rendezvous

You and Stump get an early start the next morning and pedal to the elementary school as fast as you can. Most of the teachers are there when you arrive, but it will be another half hour before classes start.

"Where should we start?" Stump asks you.

"With the secretary," you reply, pointing to the school's main office. "The secretary should know everyone."

The secretary, in fact, does know just about everyone at the small school, but she doesn't know who comes from a country that starts with the letter c, especially since you can't give her any sort of name. Reluctantly, she agrees to let you check with the teachers who are getting ready for their classes. However, she does ask you to leave before classes start.

You and Stump agree, then start wandering from one classroom to the next, looking for a teacher who can help you. Near the end of the main hallway, you find one *Miguel Gutierrez*, a fourth grade teacher who's taping a map of Colombia to his chalkboard. Information on the country is already written next to the map.

"Colombia…," Stump murmurs. "That's *un país sudamericano* that starts with c."

"*Perdóneme, Señor Gutierrez,*" you say, "*pero ¿viene usted de Colombia?*"

"*Sí,*" he replies. "*Ustedes tienen que ser los amigos de Ana.* She told me you'd be stopping by." He shows you some of the activities you'll need to work on to solve his clue, hands you a puzzle, then promises to meet you on the playground at lunchtime to discuss your case with you in greater depth.

You and Stump thank *Miguel* for his time, walk out of the school, and spend the rest of the morning seated under a tree on the playground working on *Miguel's* activities and puzzle.

Puzzle

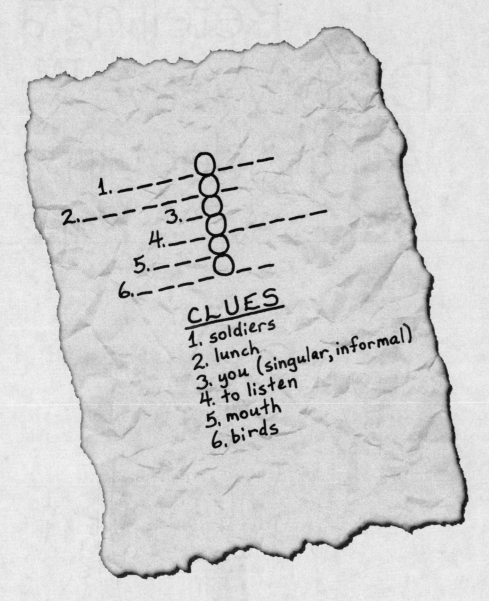

1. _ _ _ _ _ _ _

2. _ _ _ _ _ 3. _ _ _ _ _ _

4. _ _ _ _ _

5. _ _ _ _ _ _

6. _ _ _ _ _ _ _

<u>CLUES</u>

1. soldiers
2. lunch
3. you (singular, informal)
4. to listen
5. mouth
6. birds

After working the puzzle out yourself, check the answers in Appendix A, on page 464.

ACTIVITY 71

In this activity you will:

→ Comprehend a Spanish story and re-tell it in your own words.

→ Read and answer questions in Spanish.

Disc **4**   Track **9**

Colombia Culture Overview

Colombians generally value courtesy and proper etiquette more than punctuality. They are proud of their history of independence and democracy. Nearly 95 percent of Colombians are Roman Catholic, and traditional values still have tremendous influence in family relations.

Retelling a DiglotWeave™: An Incident in a Park

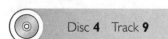

¿Y qué estaban haciendo los soldados cubanos? ¿Supone usted que estaban trabajando ellos? No, ellos no estaban trabajando. ¿Estaban jugando béisbol? No, no estaban jugando béisbol tampoco. Si los soldados cubanos no estaban trabajando y no estaban jugando béisbol, ¿qué era que ellos estaban haciendo? Ellos estaban eating their lunch *y listening to música en la radio. That's right, ellos estaban* seated at *una mesa comiendo* their *almuerzo y escuchando música. That is to say, ellos estaban* relax-

ing…*relajándose*. Do you like to *relajarse en un parque* sometimes *y* eat your *almuerzo y escuchar música?*

Look at *el dibujo* again. *El parque* is beautiful, *¿verdad? Hermoso. En el parque* there are *árboles…algunos árboles, no muchos. Aquí en el centro del dibujo* is *un árbol muy alto. Es una* palm tree, *una palmera. Este árbol es el árbol más alto en el parque. También en el parque* there are *muchas* fragrant *flores de varios colores: rojas, amarillas, azules, blancas…las flores son bonitas, ¿no?*

También en el parque hay mesas to eat on *y bancos* to sit on. *Aquí, sentado en este banco, hay un* dog, *un perro. ¿Ve usted el perro? Y aquí* on *el* same *banco* where *el perro está sentado, hay una radio. ¿Ve usted la radio? Usted puede ver la radio, pero no puede* hear *la radio…no puede oír la música en la radio. ¿Por qué no puede oír la música? Eso no es posible* because *este es un dibujo nada más ¿verdad?*

En la mesa hay tasty-looking *comida: frutas y sandwiches. ¿Puede usted* smell *la comida? No, no puede oler la comida…y no puede oler las flores tampoco. ¿Por qué no puede? Porque este es un dibujo nada más. Pero* surely *el perro y los soldados cubanos pueden oír la música y pueden oler la comida y las flores.*

The scene…*la escena*…is peaceful, *tranquila. Pero* something is about to happen. Will there be *conflicto entre los cubanos y los norteamericanos…un encuentro violento,* perhaps? Will *los cubanos* shout: "Go home, *yanquis!*" Or will *los cubanos y los yanquis* perhaps become *amigos?* Well, *esto es lo que pasó: uno de los norteamericanos* hit *la pelota* high *en el aire. Y dónde supone usted que la pelota* landed? *¿Supone que ella aterrizó en la mesa donde los soldados cubanos estaban sentados comiendo su almuerzo? No, la pelota no aterrizó en la mesa. ¿Supone usted que la pelota* got caught *en las* branches *del árbol, la palmera alta? Exactamente, eso es lo que pasó. La pelota* got caught *en las ramas de la palmera alta. Y uno de los soldados cubanos vio lo que pasó. Él vio que la pelota* was caught *en las ramas del árbol. Éste soldado* climbed up *el árbol, recojió la pelota y* threw it back to *los soldados norteamericanos.*

Then *¿qué hicieron los norteamericanos? Ellos* cheered. And when the *soldado cubano descendió del árbol, ellos* went over to him *y le dijeron: "Muchas gracias." Y el cubano dijo: "No hay por qué."* Then *los cubanos ofrecieron comida a los yanquis: sandwiches y frutas. Uno de los norteamericanos* went *y* brought *un cassette* de música americana y* gave it to *el soldado que* retrieved *la pelota. Este dijo: "Gracias, muchas gracias."* Then *los yanquis invitaron a los cubanos* to play *béisbol* and they had a good time together. Even *el perro* played *con ellos. So, as el incidente* turned out, *los yanquis y los cubanos se hicieron amigos.*

**Some say *una cassette*, others say *un cassette*.

Preparation for Retelling in Your Own Words

INSTRUCTIONS Preparing to retell the story in your own words (weaving Spanish with English to the extent you need), review new words and phrases you will want to use. After review, see how well you can recall the Spanish equivalents for the following checklist. Check off the phrases you understand.

Checklist		
○ the picture	○ an incident	○ town
○ nice little town	○ nice little park	○ park
○ soldier	○ North American	○ the United States
○ Cuban	○ working	○ playing baseball
○ What were they doing?	○ music on the radio	○ listening [to] the music
○ lunch	○ eating lunch	○ flowers of various colors
○ a tall tree	○ dog	○ palm tree
○ you can	○ the tallest tree	○ benches and tables
○ nothing more	○ you can't	○ that is not possible

Pronunciation and Key-Link Memory Aids

INSTRUCTIONS Use these memory aids to help your memorization of Spanish words.

English	Spanish	Memory Aids
to hear	*oír*	Oh-EAR
listening	*escuchando*	"Skootch" could be English slang for "listen"
relaxing	*relajándose*	Ray-La-HAN-Doe-Say
eating	*comiendo*	Co-Myen-Dough
lunch	*almuerzo*	All-muWEAR-so
they became	*se hicieron*	SAY EASY ARROWn --> SAY EASSY ARROWn

INSTRUCTIONS Review and see how well you can recall the Spanish for the following checklist. Check off phrases you understand.

Checklist	
○ the branches of a palm tree	○ he saw the ball
○ he came down from the tree	○ he said "thanks"

Checklist	
○ he said "you're welcome"	○ they became friends
○ they offer food	○ it's not possible
○ a tranquil scene	○ conflict between the Cubans and the Yankees

Reading Activity

INSTRUCTIONS Read the following sentences. Try to understand the main ideas while translating into English. Check your translations in Appendix A, on page 462.

1. *En este dibujo Ud. puede ver un parque.*

2. *Y en el parque puede ver algunas mesas y algunos bancos.*

3. *También en el parque hay soldados de dos países.*

4. *Éste es un soldado norteamericano.*

5. *Los otros son de Cuba.*

6. *Éstos son los soldados cubanos.*

7. *El parque está situado en un pueblo en un país de Centro América.*

8. *¿Qué estaban haciendo los cubanos en el parque, trabajando o relajándose?*

9. *Y los yanquis, ¿qué estaban haciendo ellos?*

10. *¿Trabajando o jugando?*

11. *¿Quiénes están escuchando música en la radio, los yanquis o los cubanos?*

Comprehension Questions

INSTRUCTIONS Answer the following questions. First, see if you can answer the questions in English. Then, try to answer the questions in Spanish. Check your translations in Appendix A, on page 462.

1. *¿Dónde sucedió este incidente? ¿En los Estados Unidos de América o en Centro América?*

2. *¿En qué país de Centro América? ¿En Nicaragua?*

3. *En el parque había dos grupos: un grupo era de norteamericanos. ¿Y el otro grupo?*

4. *¿Qué estaban jugando los norteamericanos?*

5. *¿Qué estaban haciendo los cubanos?*

6. *¿Qué estaban comiendo? ¿Pizza?*

7. *¿Quién subió el árbol y recogió la pelota? Uno de los cubanos o uno de los norteamericanos?*

8. *¿Quién dijo «No hay por qué»?*

ACTIVITY

71

9. *¿A quién se lo dijo ésto? ¿A uno de los norteamericanos o a uno de los cubanos?*

Preparing to Retell the Story in Your Own Words

INSTRUCTIONS In preparation for telling this story in your own DiglotWeave™, you may wish to review some of the key words and add a few more.

Checklist		
○ historia	○ soldado	○ ¿Qué supone Ud. que…?
○ incidente	○ las ramas del árbol	○ ¿Por qué?
○ dibujo	○ también	○ pueblo / pueblito
○ bancos y mesas	○ nada más	○ parque / parquecito
○ flores…colores	○ un árbol alto	○ comida
○ hermoso	○ los otros	○ palmera
○ tampoco	○ ¿Dónde supone Ud. que…?	

✶

Performance Challenge

Using as much Spanish as you can, retell this activity's story to a family member or friend.

Poems

Now here are some poems for you to enjoy. These poems are a refreshing break which will give you a knowledge of important words.

Only One Mouth	Sólo una Boca
Two eyes to see with,	Dos ojos con que ver,
Two ears to hear with,	Dos orejas con que oír,
Two hands to work and pray,	Dos manos con que trabajar y orar,
Two feet to walk with,	Dos pies con que caminar,
But only one mouth to eat	Pero solo una boca con que comer
and speak with.	y hablar.

Birds and Me	Los pájaros y Yo
At night birds sleep like this.	De noche los pájaros duermen así.
They hide their eyes and don't see me.	Esconden sus ojos y no ven a mí.
They pay no attention to the dark,	No se dan cuenta de la oscuridad,
They just fall asleep	Se duermen, se duermen
with tranquillity.	con tranquilidad.
By day birds fly like this.	De día los pájaros vuelan así,
They stretch their wings	Estiran sus alas
and fly about me.	y vuelan sobre mí.

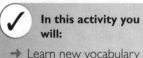

In this activity you will:

→ Learn new vocabulary through Spanish poems and jingles.

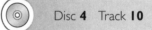

Disc **4**   Track **10**

Performance Challenge

Memorize one of these short poems, and tell it to a family member or friend.

Ditties

Now here are some ditties for you to enjoy. Ditties help you to easily remember the vocabulary you've learned. Sing these to your friends and they will learn Spanish, too!

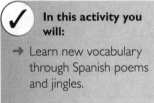

In this activity you will:

→ Learn new vocabulary through Spanish poems and jingles.

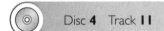

Disc **4** Track **11**

English	Spanish
Good evening,	*Buenas tardes,*
You, how're you?	*¿Tú qué tal?*
More or less good,	*Más o menos bien,*
And more or less bad.	*Y más o menos mal.*
G'morning,	*Buenos días,*
Mrs. Tren,	*Señora Tren,*
How have you been?	*¿Qué tal ha estado?*
Fine, fine, fine.	*Bien, bien, bien.*
Little boy,	*Muchachito,*
Well then,	*Bueno pues,*
How many years are you?	*¿Cuántos años tienes?*
Two or three.	*Dos o tres.*
Now I go,	*Ya me voy,*
He-he-he! Ho-ho-ho!	*Ji-ji-ji! Jo-jo-jo!*
Do you wanna go with me?	*¿Quieres ir conmigo?*
Oh, you bet!	*¡Cómo no!*
When're you coming?	*¿Cuándo vienes?*
I don't know,	*Yo no sé,*
Tell me it tomorrow?	*¿Mañana me lo dices?*
Yes, O.K.	*Sí, okey.*
See you later,	*Ya nos vemos,*

English *(cont.)*	Spanish
Eleanor, my sweetheart.	*Eleanor, mi amor.*
Wanna come with me?	*¿Quieres ir conmigo?*
No, señor. Please.	*No, señor. Por favor.*
We're going now,	*Ya nos vamos,*
So good-bye,	*Adiós,*
Come along with us,	*Vengan con nosotros,*
Two by two.	*Dos en dos.*

Performance Challenge

Look for chances to use the words and phrases these ditties taught you in a real conversation.

Focus on Action

Enfoque sobre la Acción

A. Scatter Chart

INSTRUCTIONS Study these eleven new action pictographs to help you in the following exercises.

Sleep! Wake up! Paint! Point! Jump! Lie down!

Get up! Count! Think! Close the eyes! Open the eyes!

B. Self Quiz

INSTRUCTIONS Without looking at the scatter chart, can you interpret the new action pictographs in English?

✓ In this activity you will:

→ Learn new action verbs.

→ Act out what you've read.

→ Compose new sentences orally and in writing.

Facts and Figures on Colombia

- Colombia's population is about 36.6 million and is growing by 2.1% annually.
- The official language of Colombia is Spanish.
- Catholicism is the state religion of Colombia.
- *Arroz con pollo*, chicken with rice, is a popular national dish.
- Soccer is the most popular sport in Colombia. People also enjoy dancing and music.
- Colombia's federal government consists of a bicameral congress and a president. The judicial branch is separate.

Review of Previously Presented Pictographs

¡póngase de pie!	¡siéntese!	¡coma!	¡beba!	¡lea!
¡escriba!	¡camine!	¡corra!	¡hable!	¡cante!

The Eleven Action Pictographs with Written Spanish

¡Duerma!	¡Despiértese!	¡Pinte!	¡Salte!	¡Acuéstese!	¡Levántese!
¡Muestre con el dedo!	¡Cuente!	¡Piense!	¡Cierre los ojos!	¡Abra los ojos!	

Read and Act out the Called-For Action

INSTRUCTIONS Read through the actions to cement your knowledge of them.

Called-For Action Sentences	
¡Pinte y cante!	¡Muestre con el dedo y hable!
¡Siéntese y coma!	¡Muestre con el dedo y pinte!
¡Acuéstese y hable!	¡Cierre los ojos y abra los ojos!
¡Cuente y cante!	¡Siéntese, cierre los ojos y hable!
¡Duerma y pinte!	¡Abra los ojos y cante!
¡Piense y escriba!	¡Siéntese, cierre los ojos, y duerma!
¡Acuéstese y lea!	¡Acuéstese, cierre los ojos, piense, y hable!
¡Póngase de pie y salte!	¡Acuéstese, cierre los ojos, y cuente!
¡Abre los ojos y lea!	¡Despiértese y muestre con el dedo y piense!
¡Levántese y siéntese!	¡Despiértese, abra los ojos, y levántese!
¡Levántese y ande!	

Sample Question and Responses Tied to a Pictographic Representation

INSTRUCTIONS First, read the Spanish sentences. Next, compose the sentences on your own, looking only at the pictographs.

	Pictographs	Question	Answer	Tense
ex.		¿Qué están haciendo estas personas?	Ellos están saltando.	Present
		What are these persons doing?	They are jumping.	
		¿Qué va a hacer estas personas?	Ellos van a saltar.	Imminent Future
		What are these persons going to do?	They are going to jump.	
1.		¿Qué está haciendo este hombre?	El está pintando.	Present
		¿Qué va a hacer este hombre?	El va a pintar.	Imminent Future
2.		¿Qué está haciendo esta mujer?	Ella está mostrando con el dedo.	Present
		¿Qué va a hacer ésta mujer?	Ella va a mostrar con el dedo.	Imminent Future
3.		¿Qué están haciendo estas personas?	Ellos están durmiendo.	Present
		¿Qué van a hacer estas personas?	Ellos van a dormir.	Imminent Future
4.		¿Qué están haciendo estas personas?	Todos están contando.	Present
		¿Qué van a hacer estas personas?	Todos van a contar.	Imminent Future
5.		¿Qué están haciendo estas personas?	Uno se está acostando y el otro se está levantando.	Present
		¿Qué van a hacer estas personas?	Uno va a acostarse y el otro va a levantarse.	Imminent Future

Pictographs (cont.)	Question	Answer	Tense
6.	¿Qué están haciendo estas personas?	Una está saltando y el otro está contando.	Present
	¿Qué van a hacer estas personas?	Uno va a saltar y el otro va a contar.	Imminent Future
7.	¿Qué está haciendo esta mujer?	Ella se está acostando, cerrando los ojos y pensando.	Present
	¿Qué va a hacer esta mujer?	Ella va a acostarse, cerrar los ojos y pensar.	Imminent Future

Performance Challenge

Copy this activity's pictographs onto note cards and use them with other pictograph note cards to form new sentences.

A Spanish Lesson

Una Lección de Español

INSTRUCTIONS See how much you can understand before reading the English. In this lesson, you will work with comparing and contrasting different objects.

In this activity you will:
→ Compare and contrast different objects.

Disc **4** Track **12**

English	Spanish
Look at these two objects I have.	*Mire estos dos objetos que tengo.*
Compare them.	*Compárelos.*
In what way are they the same?	*¿En qué forma son similares?*
Yes, both are blocks.	*Sí, ambos son bloques.*
Are they the same size?	*¿Son del mismo tamaño?*
Yes, they are both the same length.	*Sí, ambos son del mismo largo.*
Are they the same color?	*¿Son del mismo color?*
No, they are different colors.	*No, son de diferentes colores.*
One is black, the other is yellow.	*Uno es negro, el otro es amarillo.*
And in what other way are they different?	*¿En qué formas son diferentes?*
Are they the same weight?	*¿Pesan lo mismo?*
Pick them up (and weigh them).	*Tómalos y pésalos.*
This one is heavier than that one.	*Éste es más pesado que ése.*
That one is lighter than this one.	*Ése es más liviano que éste.*
Now close your eyes.	*Ahora cierra los ojos.*
I'll take the two blocks.	*Yo tomaré los dos bloques.*
Now open your eyes.	*Ahora abre los ojos y mira.*
Can you tell which is which?	*¿Puedes distinguir cuál es cuál?*

English *(cont.)*	Spanish
Which is relatively heavy, this one or that one?	*¿Cuál es relativamente pesado, éste o ése?*

Performance Challenge

Listen through this activity again. This time, cover all the English sentences so that you can practice thinking and comprehending in Spanish.

ACTIVITY
76

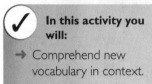
In this activity you will:
→ Comprehend new vocabulary in context.

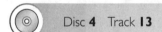
Disc **4**   Track **13**

A Mother Talks with Her Child

Una Madre Habla con Su Niño

INSTRUCTIONS   Learn vocabulary and sentence patterns from this activity.

🔊

English	Spanish
This man's name is Peter.	*El nombre de este hombre es Pedro.*
Peter has a long, black beard.	*Pedro tiene una barba larga y negra.*
But he doesn't have hair on top of his head.	*Pero no tiene pelo encima de la cabeza.*
You have hair on the top of your head, don't you?	*Tú tienes pelo encima de la cabeza, ¿no?*
Mama has hair on top of her head too.	*Mamá tiene pelo encima de la cabeza también.*
This is a baby, a little baby boy.	*Éste es un niño, un niñito.*
He has a mouth, but he doesn't have teeth yet.	*Él tiene la boca, pero todavía no tiene dientes.*
He doesn't have hair on his head yet.	*Y no tiene pelo encima de la cabeza.*
Does this little baby have a beard?	*¿Lleva este niñito barba?*
No, babies don't have beards.	*No, los niñitos no llevan barbas.*
Your mama doesn't have a beard either.	*Tu mamá no lleva barba tampoco.*
No, mamas don't have beards.	*No, las mamás no llevan barbas.*
This man is called Smee.	*Este hombre se llama Smi.*
Smee is a pirate.	*Smi es un pirata.*
Poor Smee!	*¡Pobre Smi!*
He has only one eye.	*El tiene solamente un ojo.*

English (cont.)	Spanish
And only one ear.	Y solamente una oreja.
And only one leg.	Y solamente una pierna.
He doesn't have a pretty face.	No tiene cara bonita.
But worse yet, he doesn't have friends.	Pero todavía peor, él no tiene amigos.
Here is another pirate, a well-known pirate.	He aquí otro pirata, un pirata bien conocido.
Do you recognize him?	¿Lo reconoces?
It's Captain Hook.	Es el capitán Gancho.
He has only one arm: his right arm.	El tiene solamente un brazo: su brazo derecho.
Do you know why he has only one arm?	¿Sabes por qué tiene solamente un brazo?
Do you know why he is missing his left arm?	¿Sabes por qué le falta el brazo izquierdo?
It's because a crocodile ate his other arm. Ah!	¡Ay! Es porque un cocodrilo se lo comió. ¡Ay!
Does Captain Hook have friends?	¿Tiene amigos el capitán Gancho?
No, he doesn't have even one friend.	No, él no tiene ni un amigo.
Imagine!	¡Fíjate!
But he still has his eyes and his ears.	Pero todavía tiene sus ojos y sus orejas.
He can see with his eyes.	Con sus ojos él puede ver.
He can hear with his ears.	Con sus orejas él puede oír.
He listens constantly to hear the tic-toc of a clock.	El escucha constantemente para oír el tic-toc de un reloj.
You know why, don't you?	Tú sabes por qué, ¿no?
Here is a person without eyes.	He aquí una persona sin ojos.
He is blind, poor fellow.	Es ciego, pobrecito.
He can't see. He can't see anything.	No puede ver. No puede ver nada.
Without eyes you can't see anything.	Sin ojos uno no puede ver nada.
Do you know a blind man?	¿Conoces a un hombre ciego?
Do you know a person with only one eye?	¿Conoces a una persona con solamente un ojo?

English *(cont.)*	Spanish
Here is a giant, a monster.	*He aquí un gigante, un monstruo.*
He was born with only one eye in the middle of his forehead.	*El nació con un solo ojo en medio de la frente.*
He can see. He is not blind.	*El puede ver. No es ciego.*
But he doesn't have friends.	*Pero él no tiene amigos.*
Why doesn't he have any friends?	*¿Por qué no tiene amigos?*
Because everybody is afraid of him.	*Porque todo el mundo le tiene miedo.*

Performance Challenge

Again, cover the English sentences and see how much you can understand just by listening to the Spanish.

Irregular Verbs

INSTRUCTIONS Read these explanations to learn more about irregular Spanish verbs. You are already familiar with the materials in this reference, since they (or similar materials) have been used in previous exercises.

There are quite a few verbs whose roots have alternate forms. For example, look at the forms of the verb *ten-Er* "to have."

Present (Indicative)		Present (Subjunctive	
teng-o	ten-Emos	teng-A	teng-Amos
tien-Es	tien-En	teng-As	teng-An
tien-E	tien-En	teng-A	teng-An

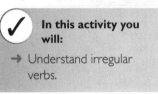

In this activity you will:

→ Understand irregular verbs.

Notice the peculiarity: In the infinitive *tener* the root is *ten-*, as it is also in *ten-Emos*. The root has the form *tien-* whenever it is stressed and when it precedes a front vowel (E or I). The root has the form *teng-* whenever it precedes a back vowel (O or A). So we have three roots: *ten-*, *tien-* and *teng-*. Look at an *-Ir* verb (*ven-Ir*, "come") that follows this same pattern. Identify the three root forms and account for their variation as in the explanation above.

Present Indicative		Present Subjunctive	
veng-o	ven-Imos	veng-A	veng-Amos
vien-Es	ven-Is	veng-As	veng-An
vien-E	vien-En	veng-A	veng-An

Here is an *-Ir* verb (*sal-Ir*, "leave") with two root forms.

Present Indicative		Present Subjunctive	
salg-o	sal-Imos	salg-A	salg-Amos
sal-Es	sal-Is	salg-As	salg-Ais
sal-E	sal-En	salg-A	salg-An

INSTRUCTIONS Compare the following verbs:

English	Spanish	
to put	poner	(pongo, pones…)
to value	valer	(valgo, vales…)

Colombian Arts

Modern Colombian arts, from crafts to literature, from sculpture to music, reflect much of Colombian culture and history. Influences from pre-Colombian Indian cultures are readily apparent in the stone sculptures, pottery, gold work, basketwork, and weaving, while influences from imported African cultures and colonial Spanish culture are more visible in Colombia's musical traditions.

English (cont.)	Spanish	
to fall	caer	(caigo, caes…)
to say	decir	(digo, dices…)
to bring	traer	(traigo, traes…)

Here is an -Er verb (volv-Er "return") with two root forms.

Present Indicative		Present Subjunctive	
vuelv-o	volv-Emos	vuelv-A	volv-Amos
vuelv-Es	volv-Eis	vuelv-As	volv-Ais
vuelv-E	vuelv-En	vuelv-A	vuelv-An

Notice that the root has the form *vuelv-* whenever it is stressed, otherwise it is *volv-*.

Performance Challenge

In this activity, you learned conjugations for some irregular Spanish verbs. To practice these new verbs, write ten sentences using these verbs as well as vocabulary from previous activities.

You have completed all the activities for

**Section 2.3.1
Day Five, 16:00 Hours**

and are now ready to take the section quiz. Before continuing, be sure you have learned the objectives for each activity in this section.

Section Quiz

INSTRUCTIONS Choose the correct response. Check your answers on the "Grading Sheet" found on the last page of the book.

1. *¿Qué estaban haciendo los soldados cubanos en el cuento?*

   A. *Estaban jugando béisbol.*

   B. *Estaban comiendo y escuchando música.*

   C. *Estaban trabajando.*

   D. *Estaban corriendo.*

INSTRUCTIONS Choose the correct Spanish translation of the English sentence.

2. **Two hands to work with.**

   A. *Dos manos trabajar con.*

   B. *Dos manos con que trabajar.*

   C. *Dos manos que trabajan.*

   D. *Trabajar con dos manos.*

INSTRUCTIONS Choose the correct response.

3. *¿Quieres ir conmigo?*

   A. *Bien, bien, bien.*

   B. *Adiós.*

   C. *¡Cómo no!*

   D. *Ya nos vemos.*

INSTRUCTIONS   Choose the correct Spanish translation of the English sentence.

4. **How old are you?**

    A. *¿Cuántos años tienes?*

    B. *¿Quieres ir conmigo?*

    C. *¿Qué tal?*

    D. *¿Cómo estás?*

INSTRUCTIONS   Choose the correct Spanish translation of the underlined English portion.

5. **¿Qué está haciendo este hombre? He is laying down and sleeping.**

    A. *El va a acostarse y dormir.*

    B. *El está acostándose y durmiendo.*

    C. *El está levantándose y pensando.*

    D. *El va a levantarse y pensar.*

INSTRUCTIONS   Choose the correct Spanish translation of the English sentence.

6. **They are going to think.**

    A. *Ellos están pensando.*

    B. *Ellos van a pensar.*

    C. *Ellos piensan.*

    D. *Ellos van a piensan.*

INSTRUCTIONS   Choose the correct Spanish translation of the underlined English word or phrase.

7. **Fútbol es el deporte most popular en Guatemala.**

    A. *menos*

    B. *mismo*

    C. *más*

    D. *ambos*

8. **Mis manos son del <u>same</u> tamaño como las de María.**

   A. *más*

   B. *menos*

   C. *mismo*

   D. *ambos*

9. **¿<u>Do you know</u> a un gigante?**

   A. Conoces

   B. Sabes

   C. Miras

   D. Tienes

10. **<u>I say</u> muchas cosas importantes en español.**

    A. Vengo

    B. Traigo

    C. Digo

    D. Pongo

N

Lago de
Reflejos

Avenida Las Palomas

Parque San
Cristóbal

Río de
Plata

o7

o6

o3

Playa Negra

o4

o2

El
Volcán

o5

Playa Roja

o1

Laguna
del Oro

Isla de Providencia

Day Six, 11:30 Hours

Eleven and a Half Hours to Rendezvous

The bell rings for lunchtime, and only a few minutes later, children start to flood the playground. You and Stump keep an eye out for Miguel while trying to look inconspicuous. He sees you and walks over, smiling.

"Ah, you've solved the first puzzle, I see," he says, as he methodically checks your work. "You are very near to achieving what you seek. However, since this is your final stop, I have to make things a bit more difficult. Here's another puzzle you'll have to solve for your final clue. If you solve it successfully, I will show you the object of your quest."

Miguel hands you another puzzle, then quickly goes to separate a couple of students who are arguing. You assume that you'll need to finish the last few activities in your notebooks to solve the puzzle. You and Stump get right to work.

As you work, you notice that the sky is growing steadily darker, though it's only mid-afternoon. You look up to see thick gray clouds pushing their way across the sky. It looks like the storm the submarine captain warned you about is almost here.

"Come on," Stump says, recalling you to the task at hand. "It looks like we'd better hurry."

Taking Stump's advice, you work swiftly but carefully through the few remaining activities. You smile as you work. In addition to the excitement of being so close to completing your mission successfully, you're thrilled with how much Spanish you've been able to learn during your adventure on *Isla de Providencia*.

In this section you will:

→ Expand listening and reading comprehension.

→ Use weights and measurements.

→ Use a verb phrase as a description.

→ Understand the different nuances between *saber* and *conocer*.

→ Create your own mini story.

→ Use placement terms.

→ Build fluency in past tense.

→ Ask and answer useful questions.

 Disc **4**   Track **14**

Puzzle

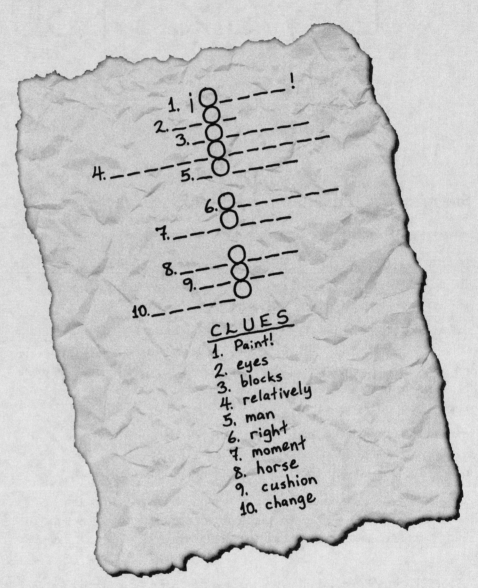

After working the puzzle out yourself, check the answers in Appendix A, on page 465.

A Spanish Lesson

Una Lección de Español

INSTRUCTIONS   Listen to this lesson in Spanish, and see how much you can understand. In this lesson, you will build fluency with line features.

English	Spanish
Compare these two lines.	*Compara estas dos líneas.*
In what way are they similar?	*¿De qué forma son similares?*
Both are long, thin lines, aren't they?	*Ambas son líneas largas y finas, ¿no?*
Now contrast these similar lines.	*Ahora contrasta estas líneas similares.*
What kind of line is this?	*¿Qué tipo de línea es ésta?*
Straight or curved?	*¿Derecha o curva?*
It's straight. It's a straight line.	*Es derecha. Es una línea derecha.*
With your finger, draw a straight line.	*Con tu dedo dibuja una línea derecha.*
Below it, draw a curved line.	*Debajo de ésta dibuja una línea curva.*
On top, draw another curved line.	*Encima dibuja otra línea curva.*
What kind of lines are these?	*¿Qué tipo de líneas son éstas?*
All are curved.	*Todas son curvas.*
Among them there is no straight line.	*Entre ellas no hay ninguna línea derecha.*
Now add a straight line.	*Ahora añade una línea derecha.*
All the lines except this one are curved.	*Todas las líneas excepto ésta son curvas.*
Only this line is straight.	*Sólo esta línea es derecha.*
Count from ten to twenty in Spanish.	*Cuenta de diez a veinte en español.*
Count from one to ten in English and again in Spanish.	*Cuenta de uno a diez en inglés y de nuevo en español.*
Make a dot. Draw a cluster of dots.	*Haz un punto. Haz un grupo de puntos.*

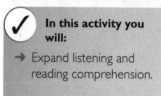

In this activity you will:
→ Expand listening and reading comprehension.

Disc **4**   Track **15**

English (cont.)	Spanish
A moment ago you drew a straight line with your finger.	*Hace un momento dibujaste una línea derecha con el dedo.*
After drawing that line, what line did you draw?	*Después de dibujar esa línea, ¿que línea dibujaste?*
Was it a straight line or a curved line?	*¿Fue una línea derecha o una línea curva?*
Was it the straight line or the curved that was on top? Do you remember?	*¿Era la línea derecha or la curva la que estaba encima? ¿Te acuerdas?*
The curved line was on top, wasn't it?	*La línea curva estaba encima, ¿no?*
Another curved one was below.	*Había una línea curva abajo.*
Draw another line and put a dot at the midpoint.	*Dibuja otra línea y ponle un punto en medio.*
Label the midpoint X.	*Nombra el punto de en medio X.*
Label the end C and the beginning D.	*Nombra el final C y el principio D.*
Under that line draw a broken line.	*Debajo de esta línea dibuja una línea quebrada.*
What's the difference between the two lines?	*¿Cuál es la diferencia entre las dos líneas?*
One is a solid line; the other is a broken line.	*Una es una línea sólida, y la otra es una línea quebrada.*
What's the difference between these two?	*¿Cuál es la diferencia entre éstas dos?*
One is a straight line; the other is a curved line.	*Una es una línea derecha, y la otra es una línea curva.*
What's the difference between these two?	*¿Cuál es la diferencia entre éstas dos?*
One is a curved line; the other is a wavy line.	*Una es una línea curva, y la otra es una línea ondeada.*
This crooked line looks like steps.	*Esta línea chueca parece unas escaleras.*
Here is another crooked line.	*Aquí hay otra línea chueca.*
Draw a line like this one.	*Dibuja una línea como ésta.*
Draw a broken line above it.	*Dibuja una línea quebrada sobre ella.*
At the side of this line draw a tall vertical line.	*Al lado de esta línea dibuje una línea vertical larga.*

English *(cont.)*	Spanish
Draw a short, thick horizontal line on top of the tall vertical line.	*Dibuja una línea horizontal corta y gruesa sobre la línea vertical larga.*
These lines intersect at point A.	*Estas líneas se intersecan en el punto A.*
These two lines touch, but don't intersect.	*Estas dos líneas se tocan, pero no se intersectan.*
These two lines are perpendicular.	*Estas líneas son perpendiculares.*
This is a right angle, therefore this is a right triangle.	*Éste es un ángulo recto; por lo tanto, éste es un triángulo recto.*

Performance Challenge

Listen to this activity again, this time following all the directions as though you were in a Spanish-speaking study group.

ACTIVITY 79

ACTIVITY
79

Questions of a Child

In this activity you will:

→ Use weights and measurements.

Disc **4**   Track **16**

Preguntas de un Niño

INSTRUCTIONS   Learn vocabulary and verb conjugation from this conversation.

English	Spanish
Mama, how much does a horse weigh?	Mamá, ¿cuánto pesa un caballo?
500 kilos more or less, I imagine.	Quinientos kilos, más o menos, me imagino.
Do I weigh 500 kilos?	¿Peso yo quinientos kilos?
No, son, you don't weigh that much.	No, hijito, tú no pesas tanto.
Do you weigh 500 kilos?	¿Pesas tú quinientos kilos?
No, I don't weigh that much.	No, yo no peso tanto.
Does Papa weigh 500 kilos?	¿Pesa papá quinientos kilos?
No, not even half (of that).	No, ni la mitad.
Why don't we weigh so much?	¿Por qué nosotros no pesamos tanto?
Well…because we're not horses, son.	Bueno…porque no somos caballos, hijito.

Conjugation of the Verb *pesar*, "to weigh"

Pesar			
yo	peso	nosotros	pesamos
tú	pesas	ustedes	pesan
Él / ella / Ud.	pesa	ellos / ellas	pesan

★

Performance Challenge

Formulate some questions similar to those you learned in this activity.
Look for chances to ask these questions.

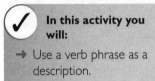

In this activity you will:

→ Use a verb phrase as a description.

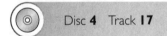

Disc **4**   Track **17**

Colombian Food

The main staples of Colombian cuisine are rice, beans, chicken, pork, potatoes, and soups. Colombia has an amazing array of tropical fruits and, naturally, world-renowned coffee.

Chatter at a Royal Ball

Getting Ready for *Conversación*

INSTRUCTIONS   Learn these vocabulary words for the following conversation.

English	Spanish
wrote poetry	*escribía poesías*
knew the lady	*conocía a la señora*
knew so many languages	*sabía tantas lenguas*
so that, so…	*así que…*
sends gifts	*manda regalos*
has begun to write	*ha comenzado a escribir*
lovely, beautiful	*bella*
long ago	*hace mucho tiempo*
young	*joven*
even more	*aún más*
has suffered a lot	*ha sufrido mucho*
would suffer even more	*sufriría aún más*
He fell in love with her.	*Se enamoró de ella.*
How did you know?	*¿Cómo sabía Ud.?*
How did you come to know?	*¿Cómo supo Ud.?*
How did you come to know?	*¿Cómo supiste tú?*
He knew Tarzan.	*Él conocía a Tarzán.*
He met Tarzan.	*Él conoció a Tarzán.*
He was learning Albanian.	*Él aprendía albanés.*
He learned Albanian.	*Él aprendió albanés.*

English *(cont.)*	Spanish
a famous love poem	*un famoso poema de amor*
She's thinking of living there.	*Ella piensa vivir allá.*
No (room for) doubt.	*No cabe duda.*
What's to become of her?	*¿Qué será de ella?*
to write	*escribir*
to know (someone)	*conocer*
to learn	*aprender*
to think	*pensar*
to send	*mandar*
to begin	*comenzar*
to live	*vivir*
to remember	*acordarse*
to suffer	*sufrir*
to fall in love	*enamorarse*

Conversación 10

INSTRUCTIONS   Learn the following conversation.

	English	Spanish
•:	And the lovely princess who knew so many languages and wrote poetry…you remember her, don't you?	*Y la bella princesa que sabía tantas lenguas y escribía poesías…te acuerdas de ella, ¿no?*
••:	The one who knew Tarzan and wrote the famous love poem?	*¿La que conocía a Tarzán y escribió el famoso poema de amor?*
•:	That one. What's become of her, do you know?	*Ésa misma. ¿Qué le ha pasado a ella, sabes?*
••:	Oh, not long ago she met a young Albanian prince…	*Oh, no hace mucho tiempo ella conoció a un joven príncipe Albanés…*
•:	…and fell in love with him, right?	*…y se enamoró de él, ¿verdad?*
••:	Right. So now she's learning Albanian and…	*Correcto. Así que ahora está aprendiendo albanés y…*

	English *(cont.)*	Spanish
•:	…and has already begun to write crazy things in Albanian to that prince, right?	…y ya ha comenzado a escribirle tonterías en albanés a ese príncipe, ¿verdad?
••:	Right. How did you know?	Correcto. ¿Cómo sabías?
•:	And he sends gifts to her.	Y él le manda regalos a ella.
••:	Exactly. Oh, you know about everything.	Exactamente. Oh, tú sabes de todo.
•:	So now what is the princess going to do?	Así que ahora, ¿qué va a hacer la princesa?
••:	She's thinking of living in Albania.	Ella piensa vivir en Albania.
•:	Oh, poor thing! She's suffered a lot, and there she'd suffer even more.	¡Ay, pobrecita! Ha sufrido mucho, y allá sufriría aún más.
••:	Indeed. There's no doubt.	Sí pues. No cabe duda.
•:	Ay! What is to become of her?	¡Ay! ¿Qué será de ella?

Performance Challenge

After listening to this activity a few times, try writing your own conversation to encourage spontaneous thoughts in Spanish.

Verbs: *Saber vs. Conocer*

INSTRUCTIONS   Read this explanation, then complete the practice exercises to learn the uses of *saber* and *conocer*. You are already familiar with these words, since they have been used in previous exercises.

Although both *saber* and *conocer* may be translated "know," *saber* means "know" in a different sense than *conocer*. *Saber* has reference to knowing things like facts. *Conocer* means "being acquainted with, being familiar with." One can "*conocer*" not only people, but also places (*El conoce México bien*) and works of art (*Ella conoce la Biblia, la música de Bach, las obras de Milton*).

✓ **In this activity you will:**

→ Understand the different nuances between *saber* and *conocer*.

English	Spanish
He knows things.	*Él sabe cosas.*
She knew a lot about politics.	*Ella sabía mucho de política.*
He knows that 2 + 2 = 4.	*Él sabe que 2 + 2 = 4.*
NOT:	**Ella conoce que 2 + 2 = 4*

English	Spanish
He knew Saint Francis.	*Él conocía a San Francisco.*
She knew San Francisco (the city)	*Ella conocía a San Francisco.*
NOT:	**Él sabía a San Francisco* or
	*Él sabía San Francisco.

Practice A

INSTRUCTIONS   Determine which verb is appropriate, *saber* or *conocer*. Write S for *saber* and C for *conocer*. Check your answers in Appendix A, on page 462.

1. _____ The prince knew the answer.

2. _____ The prince knew everyone.

3. _____ The king knew what happened.

4. _____ The queen knows the answer.

5. _____ Who knows the city best?

6. _____ Who knows who?

7. _____ Who knows who is singing?

8. _____ Who knows if John came?

9. _____ He knows Shakespeare's plays.

10. _____ He knows the judge is right.

Practice B

INSTRUCTIONS   Cover the English column and try to understand the Spanish. Then cover the Spanish column and translate the English into Spanish.

	English	Spanish
1.	Ana knows many things.	*Ana sabe muchas cosas.*
2.	Ana knows many queens.	*Ana conoce a muchas reinas.*
3.	Ana knows that the princess drinks milk.	*Ana sabe que la princesa toma leche.*
4.	She knows the princess well.	*Ella conoce bien a la princesa.*
5.	Yes, she knows her very well.	*Sí, la conoce muy bien.*
6.	She knows a lot about her.	*Ella sabe mucho de ella.*

Performance Challenge

The two verbs you explored in this activity are very similar in meaning but very different in usage. Write some sentences using each verb. Remember, be creative, but make sure other people can understand what you write!

Wrap-Up Activities

INSTRUCTIONS   Use these exercises to test your understanding of Spanish. Create your own mini-story plots.

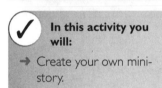

In this activity you will:
→ Create your own mini-story.

New Vocabulary

Persons and Samples of Associated Verbs

INSTRUCTIONS   Read the following phrases and learn the verbs within them.

English	Spanish
The fat-one…	*El gordo…*
eats the whole watermelon.	*come la sandía entera.*
The cook…	*La cocinera…*
prepares the food.	*prepara la comida.*
The parrot…	*El loro…*
tells the truth.	*dice la verdad.*
The doctor…	*El doctor…*
cures the ill-one (f).	*cura a la enferma.*
The baker…	*El panadero…*
eats the bread.	*come el pan.*
The sailor…	*El marinero…*
guards the ship.	*guarda la nave.*
The athlete…	*El atleta…*
jumps over the table.	*salta sobre la mesa.*
The fisherman…	*El pescador…*
eats the fish.	*come el pescado.*

English *(cont.)*	Spanish
The shepherd…	*El pastor de ovejas…*
counts the sheep.	*cuenta las ovejas.*
The fireman…	*El bombero…*
puts out the fire.	*apaga el fuego.*
The cowboy…	*El vaquero…*
loves the cows.	*ama las vacas.*

Places and Associated Verbs

INSTRUCTIONS   Learn the following place verbs.

English	Spanish
the kitchen	*la cocina*
works in the kitchen	*trabaja en la cocina*
the bridge	*el puente*
crosses the bridge	*cruza el puente*

Concrete Objects and Associated Verbs

INSTRUCTIONS   Study and learn the verbs below.

English	Spanish
watermelon	*sandía*
eats the whole watermelon	*come la sandía entera*
water	*agua*
pours water in the soup	*echa agua en la sopa*
juice	*jugo*
drinks the juice	*bebe el jugo*
hammer	*martillo*
uses his pistol	*usa su martillo*

Adverbs

INSTRUCTIONS   Learn the following adverbs.

English	Spanish
in fact	*de hecho*
In fact, he always speaks truth.	*De hecho, el siempre dice la verdad.*

Verbs and associated nouns

INSTRUCTIONS   Study and learn the following verbs and nouns.

English	Spanish
goes out of	*sale de* (think of "sallies forth from")
She leaves the kitchen.	*Ella sale de la cocina.*
contains	*contiene*
The soup contains poison.	*La sopa contiene veneno.*
crosses	*cruza* (compare *la cruz*, "the cross")
He crosses the bridge.	*El cruza el puente.*
listens	*escucha*
He listens but hears not.	*El escucha pero no oye.*
hears	*oye*
He hears something.	*El oye algo.*
dies	*muere*
The parrot dies.	*El loro muere.*
uses	*usa*
He uses his hammer.	*El usa su martillo.*
buys	*compra*
The baker buys the juice.	*El panadero compra el jugo.*

Sample Mini-Story Plot

INSTRUCTIONS   Translate the following sample story into English. Check your translation in Appendix A, on page 462.

Hay un loro. Es el loro de la princesa. El loro siempre dice la verdad. La princesa nunca dice la verdad. El loro dice que el rey viene. La princesa dice que el rey no viene. De hecho, el rey viene. El viene con la reina. La princesa detesta el loro porque el loro siempre dice la verdad. La princesa está en la cocina con la cocinera. La cocinera está preparando sopa de tomate para dar al loro. El agente secreto número cero cero siete ve que la princesa echa algo en la sopa. La princesa da un poco de la sopa al lora. ¿Piensa Ud. que el loro bebe la sopa? ¿Piensa Ud. que el agente secreto número cero cero siete viene?

....

....

....

....

....

....

....

....

....

....

....

....

....

....

....

....

....

....

....

....

....

....

....

....

Performance Challenge

Prepare a story of your own and tell someone your story. Write it down. If you're feeling artistic, you can even make illustrations to go with your story.

A Surprising Discovery

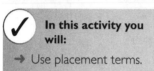

✓ **In this activity you will:**
→ Use placement terms.

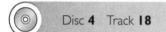

Disc **4**   Track **18**

Un Revelación Asombrosa

INSTRUCTIONS   Read and review this story to learn new vocabulary. By studying this poem, you will build fluency with the past tense and the Spanish placement terms for "under" and "on."

English	Spanish
One night when I was small,	*Una noche, cuando yo era chica,*
I looked through a keyhole,	*miré por la cerradura de una puerta,*
and this is what I saw:	*y esto es lo que ví:*
I saw a table,	*ví una mesa,*
I saw a chair,	*ví una silla,*
I saw a cushion,	*ví un cojín,*
and I saw a candle.	*y ví una vela.*
The table was on the floor,	*La mesa estaba sobre el piso,*
the chair was on the table,	*la silla estaba sobre la mesa,*
the cushion was on the chair,	*el cojín estaba sobre la silla,*

Troubles in Colombia

Despite its beautiful landscapes, rich cultural heritage, and beautiful architecture, Colombia is not a popular tourist destination. Guerilla warfare, political assassinations, and drug cartels have reached such massive proportions that the press has dubbed Colombia *"Locombia"*—the mad/crazy country.

English *(cont.)*	Spanish
and the candle lit up the room.	*y la vela iluminaba el cuarto.*
I blinked my eyes and looked again,	*Parpadeé mis ojos y miré de nuevo,*
and this is what I saw:	*y esto es lo que ví:*
I saw a candle,	*ví una vela,*
I saw a cushion,	*ví un cojín,*
I saw a chair,	*ví una silla,*
and I saw a table.	*y ví una mesa.*
The cushion was under the candle,	*El cojín estaba debajo de la vela,*
the chair was under the cushion,	*la silla estaba debajo del cojín,*
the table was under the chair,	*la mesa estaba debajo de la silla,*
the floor was under the table,	*el piso estaba debajo de la mesa,*
and you know, the same candle	*y ¿sabes?, la misma vela*
lit up the room.	*iluminaba el cuarto.*

Performance Challenge

This activity helped you practice prepositions, words that explain where things are located. Go back through this activity and underline each preposition you find.

What a Beautiful Sight!

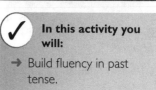

✓ **In this activity you will:**

→ Build fluency in past tense.

◉ Disc **4** Track **19**

!Que Hermosa Vista!

INSTRUCTIONS Read and review this story to learn new vocabulary. By studying this poem, you will build fluency with the past tense and the Spanish placement terms for "behind" and "in front".

◀))

English	Spanish
One day when I was small,	Un día, cuando yo era pequeño,
I looked out the window	miré por la ventana hacia afuera
and this is what I saw:	y esto es lo que ví:
I saw a bird,	ví un pájaro,
I saw a tree,	ví un árbol,
I saw a kite,	ví un cometa,
I saw an airplane,	ví un avión,
I saw a cloud,	ví una nube,
and I saw the sun.	y ví al sol.
And the sun lit up the sky.	Y el sol iluminaba el cielo.

English (cont.)	Spanish
The sun was behind the cloud,	El sol estaba detrás de la nube,
the cloud was behind the plane,	la nube estaba detrás del avión,
the plane was behind the kite,	el avión estaba detrás del cometa,
the kite was behind the tree,	el cometa estaba detrás del árbol,
and the tree was behind the bird,	el árbol estaba detrás del pájaro,
and I thought: what a beautiful sight!	y yo pensé: ¡qué hermosa vista!
I blinked my eyes and looked again,	Parpadeé mis ojos y miré otra vez,
and this is what I saw:	y esto es lo que ví:
I saw the same bird,	ví el mismo pájaro,
I saw the same tree,	ví el mismo árbol,
I saw the same kite,	ví el mismo cometa,
I saw the same plane,	ví el mismo avión,
I saw the same cloud,	ví la misma nube,
and I saw the same sun.	y ví el mismo sol.
But now…	Pero ahora…
the bird was in front of the tree,	el pájaro estaba enfrente del árbol,
the tree was in front of the kite,	el árbol estaba enfrente del cometa,
the kite was in front of the plane,	el cometa estaba enfrente del avión,
the plane was in front of the cloud,	el avión estaba enfrente de la nube,
and the cloud was in front of the sun,	la nube estaba enfrente del sol,
and the sun lit up the sky.	y el sol iluminaba el cielo.
And I thought again:	Y yo pensé de nuevo:
What a beautiful sight!	¡Qué hermosa vista!

Performance Challenge

This activity, too, helps you practice prepositions. To give yourself even more practice, try using each preposition that appears in this activity in sentences of your own.

Questions and Answers

Preguntas y Respuestas

INSTRUCTIONS Learn these useful questions and answers. By studying this activity, you will build valuable conversation skills. It is one thing to be able to answer "yes" or "no" or "maybe", but when you have learned to give more specific answers, you will have made great leaps forward in communicating in Spanish.

In this activity you will:

→ Ask and answer useful questions.

Disc **4**   Track **20**

English	Spanish
May I?	¿Puedo?
Yes, you may.	Sí, puede.
May I come in?	¿Puedo entrar?
Come in, please.	Adelante, por favor.
Understood?	¿Entendido?
Yes, understood.	Entendido.
What happened?	¿Qué pasó?
Nothing of importance.	Nada de importancia.
What's happening here?	¿Qué pasa aquí?
Nothing is happening.	No pasa nada.
What's new?	¿Qué hay de nuevo?
Nothing much.	No mucho.
What's new?	¿Qué hay de nuevo?
Nothing.	Nada especial.
Don't you believe it?	¿No lo crees?
No, I can't believe it.	No, no puedo creerlo.
May I come in?	¿Puedo entrar?

Colombian Geography

Colombia is the fourth largest country in South America. It's the only country in South America with borders on both the Pacific Ocean and the Caribbean Sea. It shares its borders with several countries, as well—Panama on the northwest, Venezuela on the east, Brazil on the southeast, Peru on the south, and Ecuador on the southwest. The western part of the country is very mountainous, while the eastern part consists of lowlands and tropical rain forests. Because the country lies very close to the equator, its temperature varies very little at different times of the year.

English (cont.)	Spanish
Surely. Please come in.	Sí, claro. Pase adelante.
Shall we go on?	¿Seguimos?
Of course. Go right ahead.	¿Cómo no? Siga, no más.
Can it be done?	¿Se puede?
It certainly can. Of course.	Sí se puede. Claro que sí.
How are you?	¿Cómo le va?
Very well, thanks, and you?	Muy bien, gracias, ¿y ud.?
Who is going to win?	¿Quién va a ganar?
Who knows?	¿Quién sabe?
What's happening?	¿Qué pasa?
Nothing is happening.	No pasa nada.
Where do you live?	¿Dónde vive usted?
Not far from here.	No lejos de aquí.
What is this?	¿Qué es esto?
I think it's a computer.	Creo que es una computadora.
By the way, have you any change?	A propósito, ¿tiene usted cambio?
Not a penny.	Ni un centavo.
Where is the entrance?	¿Dónde está la entrada?
Over there, next to the telephone.	Allá, al lado del teléfono.
Where is the exit?	¿Dónde está la salida?
Over there on the other side, do you see?	Allá al otro lado, ¿ve ud.?
Mom, are we having fun now?	Mamá, ¿ya estamos divirtiéndonos?
I suppose so, son.	Supongo que sí, hijito.
Are there cherubim in the world now?	¿Hay querubines en el mundo ahora?
Not that I know of.	Que yo sepa, no.
Don't you believe me?	¿No me cree ud.?
No way.	De ninguna manera.
Do you understand?	¿Entiende ud.?
Please speak louder. I don't hear well.	Por favor, hable más alto. No oigo bien.

English *(cont.)*	Spanish
Do you have any change?	*¿Tienes cambio?*
How much do you need?	*¿Cuánto necesitas?*
Do you want to come?	*¿Quiere venir ud.?*
You bet!	*¡Ya lo creo!*
Can it be done?	*¿Se puede hacer?*
Sure it can.	*Sí, se puede.*
Did you understand?	*¿Entendió ud.?*
No, I didn't understand. Please say it again.	*No, no entendí. Por favor, dígalo otra vez.*
What happened to you, man?	*¿Qué te pasó, hombre?*
Nothing. Nothing happened to me.	*Nada. No me pasó nada.*
Today or tomorrow?	*¿Hoy o mañana?*
Tomorrow. Tomorrow night will be best.	*Mañana. Mañana [la noche] será mejor.*

Performance Challenge

The questions and answers in this activity could really be useful. Practice them until you can say them fluently, then look for chances to use them in real life.

You have completed all the activities for

**Section 2.3.2
Day Six, 11:30 Hours**

and are now ready to take the section quiz. Before continuing, be sure you have learned the objectives for each activity in this section.

Section Quiz

INSTRUCTIONS   Choose the correct response. Check your answers on the "Grading Sheet" found on the last page of the book.

1. ... *¿Qué tipo de línea es ésta?* ——

    A. *Una línea ondeada.*

    B. *Una línea derecha.*

    C. *Una línea curva.*

    D. *Una línea chueca.*

2. **To ask Pablo how much Maria weighs, you would say, "*Pablo, cuánto ... María?*"**

    A. *peso*

    B. *pesas*

    C. *pesan*

    D. *pesa*

INSTRUCTIONS   Choose the correct Spanish translation of the underlined English word or phrase.

3. **Yo escribo poemas de amor y yo los <u>send</u> a la princesa.**

    A. *mando*

    B. *vivo*

    C. *conozco*

    D. *pienso*

4. **Marta <u>knows</u> a Ana.**

    A. conozco

    B. conoce

    C. sabe

    D. sé

5. **Ellos <u>know</u> muchas canciones de Venezuela.**

    A. conocen

    B. conocemos

    C. saben

    D. sabemos

6. **La <u>cook</u> trabaja en la cocina y prepara la comida.**

    A. trabajadora

    B. panadera

    C. cocinera

    D. pescadora

7. **Ellos <u>cross</u> el puente.**

    A. comen

    B. cruzan

    C. escuchan

    D. compran

8. **La mesa estaba <u>underneath</u> del plato.**

    A. encima

    B. sobre

    C. entre

    D. debajo

9. **Un día <u>I saw</u> un avión en el cielo.**

    A. vi

    B. escuché

    C. estaba

    D. pensé

10. **Hay muchos árboles <u>behind</u> de mi casa.**

   A. *detrás*

   B. *encima*

   C. *enfrente*

   D. *sobre*

N

osé

pelo
(IA)

Lago de
Reflejos

Avenida Las Palomas

Parque San
Cristobal

07

06

03

Río de Plata

Playa Negra

04

02

El Volcán

05

Playa Roja

01

Laguna
del Oro

Isla de Providencia

Day Six, 17:00 Hours

Seven Hours to Rendezvous

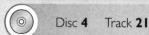

Disc **4**   Track **21**

Miguel stays late helping a couple of students with their complicated science project, but finally he rejoins you and Stump on the playground. "*¡Excelente!*" he exclaims, checking your work. "Follow me, please."

Without any explanation, he walks over to where his bicycle is parked. You and Stump bring your borrowed bicycles as well, and the three of you pedal north, through town, into the thick forest outside town. You're sure the beach can't be far away. Then you see lights up ahead.

The lights are coming from the windows of a small, red-roofed cottage. It looks like there's some sort of party inside. Miguel knocks on the door, and a very pleasant-looking old woman, with twinkling brown eyes and white hair tied in a neat bun, opens the door, introduces herself as Violeta, and invites all three of you to come in.

Inside, you see all the people you've met on your adventure. They greet you warmly and congratulate you on your success. A wonderful smell pervades the room, and it doesn't take you very long to figure out why. Violeta emerges from the kitchen carrying a platter of *tortilla* chips and a bowl of salsa that smells just wonderful. You sample it with the other guests. It tastes every bit as good as it smells.

"Wow," says Stump. "If this is what we're after, it really was worth the trip."

"*Sí*, this is what you're after," says Violeta. "*Éste es el tesoro de esta isla*. This is the ultimate salsa—not to spicy, not too mild, not too salty, nor too sweet. It's a very old recipe, that has been handed down through *mi familia* for many, many generations. However, I am the last. I needed to find someone to keep my salsa recipe, *mi receta de salsa*, in use. *Mis amigos* here on *la isla* offered to help me find people who would not only treasure my tasty *receta* but also the language *y cultura* from which it came.

"You have shown great promise in making it this far. If you can pass this one final test that I will give you, *mi receta* will be yours. There are many more *recetas* y *aventuras* to be found on *esta isla*, *pero* they are after *este* course. I hope that some-day you will return and explore those language *aventuras* as well."

You and Stump gladly accept her challenge.

Section Quiz

INSTRUCTIONS   Complete this quiz over the cultural material presented in this course. Feel free to consult Appendix C and the information in the course as needed. Check your answers on the "Grading Sheet" found on the last page of the book.

1. **What are two of the oldest and most important cultural bonds in Hispanic cultures?**
   A. the Spanish language and a fondness for spicy foods
   B. the Spanish language and the Roman Catholic faith
   C. the Roman Catholic faith and a fondness for spicy foods
   D. the Spanish language and the flamenco

2. **About how many Spanish speakers are there in the world?**
   A. 29.7 million
   B. 14 million
   C. 140 million
   D. 297 million

3. **Why do native Spanish speakers often have two last names?**
   A. One last name is never enough.
   B. It allows people to name their children after others in the family.
   C. Most Hispanics carry on the tradition of keeping the first surname of both the mother and the father.
   D. It's just tradition—no one's certain why.

4. **What is a very common greeting in Hispanic cultures?**
   A. *un abrazo*, a bear hug
   B. a kiss on the cheek
   C. a handshake
   D. waving both hands

5. **What are the four official languages of Spain?**

   A. Castilian Spanish, French, Catalan, and Basque

   B. Castilian Spanish, Catalan, Galician, and Portuguese

   C. Castilian Spanish, Catalan, Galician, and Basque

   D. Castilian Spanish, Galician, French, and Portuguese

6. **In Spain, what are *tunas*?**

   A. *Tunas* are a kind of fish, very tasty on sandwiches.

   B. *Tunas* are a kind of music, originally guitar and song but often including dance.

   C. *Tunas* are saltwater eels, considered a culinary delicacy in Spain.

   D. *Tunas* are groups of university students, similar to fraternities, who form music bands and perform at parties and restaurants.

7. **When do the people of Spain celebrate *el Día de los Reyes*?**

   A. January 6th

   B. January 17th

   C. July 6th

   D. July 17th

8. **Where is *La Meseta* located?**

   A. Northern Spain

   B. Central Spain

   C. Southern Spain

   D. Mexico

9. **About how many Indian languages are still spoken in Mexico?**

   A. as many as 100

   B. less than 50

   C. more than 100

   D. more than 200

10. **What are students required to wear in Mexico?**

    A. neckties

    B. black shoes

    C. hats

    D. uniforms

11. **Which of the following is one of Mexico's main agricultural products.**

    A. wool

    B. cotton

    C. indigo

    D. oats

12. **What three countries border Mexico?**

    A. Honduras, Guatemala, and Belize

    B. the USA, Guatemala, and Honduras

    C. the USA, Guatemala, and Belize

    D. Honduras, Guatemala, and El Salvador

13. **Why does Mexico celebrate two independence days?**

    A. Mexico achieved independence from Spain twice and celebrates both occasions.

    B. It celebrates its independence from Spain on May 5 and its independence from England on September 16.

    C. One day isn't enough for that much celebrating.

    D. It celebrates independence from Spain on September 16 and its independence from France on May 5.

14. **What has Guatemala been nicknamed?**

    A. "The Sports Capital of Central America"

    B. "The Land of the Eternal Spring"

    C. "The Land of Eternal Summer"

    D. "The Soccer Capital of Central America"

15. **Spanish is Argentina's official language, but what other languages are commonly spoken?**

    A. English, French, German, or Italian

    B. English, French, Portuguese, or Italian

    C. French, Portuguese, German, or Italian

    D. German, Italian, French, or Quechua

16. **Argentines eat more of this per capita than people of any other country on Earth. What is it?**

    A. onions

    B. salmon

    C. beef

    D. pork

17. **What do the people of Argentina celebrate on August 17?**

   A. the death of General José de San Martin, who is known as the Liberator of Argentina, Chile, and Peru, from Spain

   B. the death of Simón Bolívar

   C. the independence of Argentina from Spain

   D. the independence of Argentina from Great Britain

18. **What is Argentina's national sport?**

   A. baseball

   B. soccer

   C. polo

   D. bullfighting

19. **What has El Salvador been nicknamed?**

   A. the land of eternal summer

   B. the land of eternal spring

   C. the soccer capital of Central America

   D. the sports capital of Central America

20. **In El Salvador, how is *canción popular* used?**

   A. Some musicians use *canción popular* to showcase mediocre poetry.

   B. Some musicians use *canción popular* to bring old folk songs back to popularity.

   C. Some musicians use *canción popular* to comment on current events in their turbulent nation.

   D. Some musicians use *canción popular* to entertain people at social gatherings.

21. **Into what three main groups are the people of Ecuador divided?**

   A. the *Serranos*, the *Costariqueños*, and the Native American groups from the Amazon region

   B. the *Serranos*, the *Costeños*, and the Native American groups from the Amazon region

   C. the Salvadorans, the *Costeños*, and the Native American groups from the Amazon region

   D. the *Serranos*, the *Costeños*, and the *Costariqueños*

22. **Spanish is Ecuador's official language, but what other language is commonly spoken?**

    A. Quechua

    B. Portuguese

    C. Achua

    D. English

23. **What is a popular national dish in Colombia?**

    A. *arroz con leche*, a kind of rice pudding

    B. *ají de gallina*, a spicy chicken sauce

    C. *papas a la huancaina*, potatoes with special cheese sauce

    D. *arroz con pollo*, chicken with rice

24. **Of what does Colombia's federal government consist?**

    A. a unicameral congress and a judiciary system

    B. a unicameral congress and a president

    C. a bicameral congress and a president

    D. a bicameral congress and a judiciary system

25. **Colombia borders which two bodies of water?**

    A. the Atlantic Ocean and the Caribbean Sea

    B. the Pacific Ocean and the Caribbean Sea

    C. the Pacific Ocean and the Atlantic Ocean

    D. the Atlantic Ocean and the Mediterranean Sea

Recipe: The Ultimate Salsa

- 1 gallon tomatoes, peeled and chopped
- 3 onions
- 6 mild green peppers
- 1 yellow pepper
- 4 green bell peppers
- 1 t cilantro
- 1 c white vinegar
- 1 t coriander
- 1/3 c sugar
- 1 t garlic powder

Directions   Mix all ingredients together in a very large pan. Cook 3-4 hours on simmer. Cool and eat or process for 10 minutes in pint bottles.

You have completed all the sections for

Module 2.3

and are now ready to take the module test. Before continuing, be sure you have learned the objectives for each activity in this module.

Module Test

INSTRUCTIONS Determine which verb is appropriate: *saber* or *conocer*. Check your answers on the "Grading Sheet" found on the last page of the book.

1. **He knew the phone number.**

   A. *saber*

   B. *conocer*

2. **Maria knew everyone.**

   A. *saber*

   B. *conocer*

3. **Because he had already seen the movie, he knew what happened.**

   A. *saber*

   B. *conocer*

4. **The student knows the answer.**

   A. *saber*

   B. *conocer*

5. **Pedro knows the city very well.**

   A. *saber*

   B. *conocer*

6. **Does Maria know Pedro?**

   A. *saber*

   B. *conocer*

7. **He knows Bach's music.**

   A. *saber*

   B. *conocer*

8. **Do you know who is singing?**

   A. *saber*

   B. *conocer*

9. **Do you know if John came?**

   A. *saber*

   B. *conocer*

10. **He knows his mom is right.**

    A. *saber*

    B. *conocer*

....

INSTRUCTIONS Determine whether or not the following phrases are grammatically correct.

11. **yo tengo**

    A. True

    B. False

12. **tú tienes**

    A. True

    B. False

13. **nosotros tenemos**

    A. True

    B. False

14. **él / ella tengan**

    A. True

    B. False

15. **ellos / ellas tiene**

    A. True

    B. False

16. **ustedes tienen**

    A. True

    B. False

17. *yo viene*

    A. True

    B. False

18. *ellos / ellas viene*

    A. True

    B. False

19. *nosotros venimos*

    A. True

    B. False

20. *él / ella viene*

    A. True

    B. False

INSTRUCTIONS   Choose the correct Spanish translation of the English sentence.

21. **Ana knows many things.**

    A. *Ella sabe mucho de ella.*

    B. *Ana sabe muchas cosas.*

    C. *Ana sabe que la princesa toma leche.*

    D. *Ana conoce a muchas reinas.*

22. **Ana knows many queens.**

    A. *Ana sabe muchas cosas.*

    B. *Ana conoce muchas reinas.*

    C. *Ana sabe que la princesa toma leche.*

    D. *Ella conoce bien a la princesa.*

23. **Ana knows that the princess drinks milk.**

    A. *Ella conoce bien a la princesa.*

    B. *Ana sabe muchas cosas.*

    C. *Ana conoce a muchas reinas.*

    D. *Ana sabe que la princesa toma leche.*

24. **She knows the princess well.**

   A. *Ella conoce bien a la princesa.*

   B. *Ella sabe mucho de ella.*

   C. *Ana sabe que la princesa toma leche.*

   D. *Ana conoce a muchas reinas.*

25. **She knows a lot about her.**

   A. *Ella conoce bien a la princesa.*

   B. *Ana sabe muchas cosas.*

   C. *Ella sabe mucho de ella.*

   D. *Ana conoce a muchas princesa.*

You have completed all the modules for

Semester 2

and are now ready to take the semester test for credit. Before continuing, be sure you have learned the objectives for each activity in this semester. Congratulations on completing the Power-Glide Spanish Ultimate Year 1 Course.

Semester Test for Credit

In order to provide as complete a foreign language experience as possible for our learners, Power-Glide enables learners to receive high school credit for their course work. For more information on how to receive credit, please visit our website at: <http://www.power-glide.com/credit>.

Appendix A
Answers

Answers to activity questions and exercises are provided for checking the student's own work. Answers to module tests and section quizzes are found on the last page of the book and are provided for grading purposes—the answer page may be removed if desired.

Activity Answers

Activity 2: Multiple-Choice Frames

A. *cuatro* (a); *dos* (b); *tres* (d)

B. *seis* (b); *cinco* (c); *cuatro* (d)

C. *cinco* (b); *dos* (d); *seis* (c)

D. *cuatro* (b); *tres* (c); *dos* (d)

E. *tres puntos y una línea* (b); *dos puntos* (a); *un punto y una línea* (d)

F. *dos puntos y un número* (c); *dos líneas y un número* (b); *dos puntos y una línea* (a)

G. *dos puntos y una línea* (d); *tres puntos y una línea* (c); *cuatro puntos* (a)

H. *dos números* (a); *dos puntos* (b); *dos líneas* (c)

I. *los números 1, 2, y 4* (b); *los números 1, 3, y 4* (d); *los números 1, 3, y 2* (c)

J. *seis números* (a); *cuatro números y cuatro puntos* (c); *tres líneas y cinco puntos* (d)

Activity 2: Listen and Draw

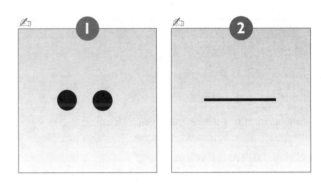

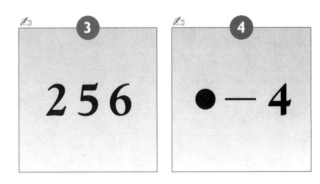

Activity 2: Read for Meaning

1. A line and the number one.

2. A point and the number five.

3. Two numbers, the numbers three and four.

4. Six points, three lines, and two numbers; the numbers three and one.

Activity 10: Word Breaks 1

1. Pablo y María.

2. Pablo es un muchacho.

3. María es una muchacha.

4. Pablo tiene dos hermanas.

5. María tiene tres hermanos.

6. Pablo es el hermano de María.

7. María es la hermana de Pablo.

8. Ella es una de las hermanas de Pablo.

9. La madre y el padre de Pablo y María.

10. Las hermanas y los hermanos de Pablo.

Activity 10: Translation 1

1. un padre

2. el padre

3. una madre

4. la madre

5. un hermano

6. el hermano

7. los hermanos

8. un muchacho

9. el muchacho

10. una muchacha

11. la muchacha

12. él tiene

13. ella tiene

14. una de (las hermanas)

15. una hermana

16. la hermana

17. las hermanas

18. de Pablo

19. de María

Activity 10: Word Breaks 2

1. Este muchacho es alto…muy alto.

2. El otro no es tan alto.

3. Este es rico; el tiene mucho dinero.

4. El otro no es rico; el no tiene dinero.

5. Esta hermana no es rica.

6. Pero ella es muy bonita.

7. Esa (la otra hermana) no es tan bonita.

8. Pero ella tiene más encanto.

Activity 10: Translation 2

1. esta muchacha

2. Ella es alta y rica.

3. Él es alto y rico.

4. el dinero de Pablo

5. ese muchacho

6. Él no es muy rico.

7. Ella no es tan alta.

8. Él tiene mucho dinero.

Activity 10: Word Breaks 3

1. Esta serpiente. Esa paloma.

2. Estas serpientes y esas palomas.

3. Una serpiente. La serpiente. La otra serpiente.

4. Unas serpientes. Las otras serpientes.

5. Las palomas. Unas otras palomas.

6. Unas serpientes duermen mucho.

7. Unas serpientes no duermen.

8. Esta paloma duerme; esa serpiente come.

9. Estas palomas duermen; esas serpientes comen.

10. Cuando las otras palomas duermen…

11. Una serpiente las ataca.

12. Si la serpiente duerme las palomas la atacan.

13. Pero si la paloma muere la serpiente vive.

14. La serpiente come la paloma.

15. Pero las palomas no comen la serpiente.

16. Las palomas la atacan pero no la comen.

17. *Las palomas las atacan pero no las comen.*

Activity 10: Verb Practice

1. *come*

2. *oye*

3. *ataca*

4. *no come*

5. *no oye*

6. *no ataca*

7. *comen*

8. *oyen*

9. *atacan*

10. *no comen*

11. *no oyen*

12. *no atacan*

13. *la oye*

14. *la ataca*

15. *no la oye*

16. *no la ataca*

Activity 11: Understanding Basic Sentences

1. The dove eats when the snake sleeps.

2. If the snakes eat, the doves sleep.

3. Those doves don't hear the snakes.

4. But these snakes see the doves and hear them, also.

5. Some doves sleep when the snakes eat.

6. If this dove doesn't hear, that snake doesn't see, either.

7. If the doves sleep, the snakes see (watch) them.

8. If these doves don't sleep, the snakes see (watch) the others.

9. Some snakes and some doves eat a lot, but these snakes and those doves don't eat much.

Activity 12: Sample Story Plot

1. *Una señora va a la tienda.*

2. *Ella compra una botella de limonada.*

3. *Ella lleva la botella a una maestra.*

4. *La maestra va a la farmacia.*

5. *Ella compra una botella de medicina.*

6. *Ella trae la medicina a la señora.*

7. *La medicina es buena.*

8. *La limonada no es buena.*

9. *La maestra lleva la botella de limonada a la tienda y dice, «La limonada no es buena.»*

10. *La señora en la tienda dice, «La botella es buena.»*

11. *La maestra dice, «No, la limonada no es buena. La botella es buena, pero la limonada en la botella no es buena.»*

12. *La señora de la tienda dice, «Okey, la limonada en la botella no es buena.»*

13. *La maestra dice, «Okey», y lleva una botella de naranjada.*

14. *Ella dice, «La naranjada es buena.»*

Activity 14: Rapid Oral Translation Exercise 1

1. *¿Quién es Pedro?*

2. *¿Y quién es Julio?*

3. *Entonces, ¿quién es Alberto?*

4. *Alberto es Juan.*

5. *¿Pero quién es Juan?*

6. *¿Quién es?*

7. *¿Es Jorge?*

8. *No, no es Jorge.*

9. *¿Es Manuel?*

10. *No es Manuel.*

11. *Es Amado, ¿verdad?*

12. *No, no es Amado.*

13. *Entonces ¿quién es?*

14. *Es Jaime.*

15. *¿Jaime?*

16. *Sí, Jaime.*

17. *O, Jaime.*

Activity 14: Rapid Oral Translation Exercise 2

1. *José es un amigo.*

2. *Él es un príncipe.*

3. *Josefina es una princesa, ¿verdad?*

4. *Sí, ella es una princesa y una amiga también.*

5. *¿Y Matilda?*

6. *Ella es una enemiga.*

7. *Pero ella es una princesa, ¿verdad?*

8. *Sí, ella es una princesa, pero también es una enemiga.*

9. *Una enemiga formidable.*

10. *Alfonzo es un príncipe, pero es un enemigo también.*

11. *Él es un príncipe terrible, pero un enemigo formidable.*

12. *Entonces, ¿quién es un bobo?*

13. *Usted es un bobo.*

14. *Él no es un príncipe, es un bobo.*

Activity 16: Self Quiz

1. *¿Usted habla español?*

2. *¿Usted habla inglés?*

3. *¿Cuánto?*

4. *¿Qué es esto?*

5. *Gracias.*

6. *No, gracias.*

7. *¿Entiende?*

8. *Sí.*

9. *¡Muy bien!*

10. *¿De dónde es usted?*

11. *De Cuba.*

12. *¿Adónde vamos?*

13. *Pase usted.*

14. *¿Dónde está la puerta?*

15. *¿Cuál (de las puertas)?*

16. *Ésta.*

17. *Entiendo.*

18. *¿Cómo se dice 'gimme a break' en español?*

19. *No sé.*

20. *Hasta la vista.*

21. *¿Por qué?*

22. *No sé por qué.*

23. *¿Quién?*

24. *No sé quién.*

25. (Spanish ditty from activity 8: *No sé cuándo,* etc.)

26. *¡Muy bien!*

Activity 17: Multiple-Choice Frames

A. *un punto pequeño* (a); *un número pequeño* (b); *un punto grande* (c); *un número grande* (d)

B. *el número 6 y un punto pequeño* (a); *una línea gruesa* (b); *un punto grande* (c); *una línea delgada* (d)

C. *una línea gruesa y dos líneas delgadas* (a); *una línea delgada y dos líneas gruesas* (b); *un punto pequeño y una línea gruesa* (c); *dos puntos grandes un punto pequeño* (d)

D. *el número dos* (a); *el número siete* (c); *dos líneas* (d)

E. *el número ocho* (b); *el número siete* (a); *el número cinco* (d)

F. *seis puntos* (c); *el número ocho* (b); *el número nueve* (a)

G. *diez* (d); *ocho* (c); *nueve* (a)

H. *ocho* (a); *once* (b); *nueve* (c)

I. *diez, ocho* (b); *nueve, diez* (d); *diez, nueve* (c)

J. *doce, once* (a); *doce, siete* (d); *doce, nueve* (c)

Activity 17: Listen and Draw

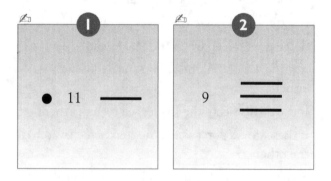

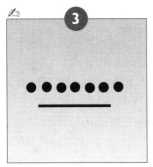

Activity 17: Reading For Meaning

1. Two lines: one thick and one thin.

2. Two plus two is four (2+2=4). Two points plus two points are four points.

3. Three lines plus two lines are five lines.

4. These lines are thick; these two lines are thin.

5. These are big points, and these are small points.

6. These two points are small, and these two are big. These are small points and big points.

7. These two lines are long, and these two are short.

Activity 18: Reading and Writing 1

1. *Este hombre es un rey.*

2. *Este hombre es este rey.*

3. *Este rey es un hombre.*

4. *Este servidor es un rey.*

5. *Este servidor es este rey.*

6. *Este rey es un servidor.*

7. *¿Quién es este rey?*

8. *Un hombre es un rey.*

9. *Un rey es un hombre.*

Activity 18: Reading and Writing 2

1. *¿Quién es una reina?*

2. *Aquella reina es una servidora.*

3. *Ella es una reina.*

4. *Aquella mujer es una reina.*

5. *Ella es esta mujer.*

6. *¿Quién es una servidora?*

7. *Ella es una servidora.*

8. *¿Quién es aquella mujer?*

9. *Una reina es una servidora.*

Activity 19: Rapid Oral Translation Exercise 1

1. *¿De dónde es José? ¿De México?*

2. *No, él es de Chile.*

3. *María es de Chile también.*

4. *¿Y es Matilda de Chile también?*

5. *No, ella es de España, de Sevilla.*

6. *¿Y quién es ésta?*

7. *Esta es mi madre.*

8. *¿Y éste?*

9. *Es mi padre.*

10. *¿De dónde es su padre?*

11. *De aquí.*

12. *Mi madre es de aquí también.*

13. *Su padre es de aquí, y su madre es de aquí, también.*

14. *Su padre es su amigo, y su madre es su amiga también.*

Activity 19: Rapid Oral Translation Exercise 2

1. *¿Quién es éste? Yo no sé quien es.*

2. *No sé si él es un amigo o un enemigo.*

3. *¿Es usted mi amigo?*

4. *Claro. ¿No es usted mi amiga?*

5. *[Yo] soy una amiga de Alberto. Yo también.*

6. *Pero no soy una amiga de Roberto. Yo tampoco.*

7. *¿Sabe usted si Pancho es un amigo de Anita?*

8. *Es cierto que él es un amigo de María, pero no sé si es un amigo de Anita también.*

9. *¿Quién es Francisco? No sé quién es.*

10. *Claro que no somos príncipes.*

11. *Pero es cierto que somos amigos.*

12. *Sé que usted es mi amigo, Carlos.*

13. *¿Sabe Ud. (standard abbreviation for usted) si Pancho es un amigo del príncipe?*

14. *No, no sé.*

Activity 22: Sample Story Plot

1. *Un vendedor vende dulces en el mercado.*
2. *Su amigo Manuel viene al (a + el) mercado.*
3. *Manuel pregunta si los dulces son buenos.*
4. *El vendedor responde que los dulces son muy buenos.*
5. *Él da un dulce a su amigo.*
6. *El amigo toma el dulce.*
7. *Él prueba el dulce y dice, «Mmm, sí, los dulces son muy buenos.»*
8. *El vendedor vende un kilo de dulces a su amigo.*
9. *Manuel lleva los dulces a un comedor.*
10. *Un amigo en el comedor prueba los dulces.*
11. *Él dice, «Mmm, muy dulce.»*
12. *Él prueba otro y dice: «¡Mmm, muy, muy dulce!»*
13. *Manuel da los dulces a su amigo.*
14. *El amigo come más dulces.*
15. *Él come más y más.*
16. *El come el kilo de dulces.*
17. *Manuel pregunta, «Muy dulce, ¿no?»*
18. *Su amigo no responde.*
19. *Manuel pregunta, «Muy dulce, ¿no?»*
20. *Su amigo responde, «No, los dulces no son buenos.»*
21. *Él amigo va al mercado y compra un kilo de dulces.*
22. *Él trae los dulces a Manuel.*
23. *Él da los dulces a Manuel.*
24. *Manuel toma los dulces.*
25. *Él prueba los dulces.*
26. *Él come los dulces.*
27. *Él dice, «Los dulces son muy buenos.»*

Activity 24: Self Quiz

1. *El rey canta o toca.*
2. *El rey está cantando o tocando.*
3. *El rey cantaba o tocaba.*
4. *El rey y la reina cantan.*
5. *Están cantando y tocando.*
6. *¿Cuál princesa llora?*

7. *El rey cantaba peor…peor que la reina.*
8. *La reina y la princesa cantaban mejor.*
9. *¿Cuál princesa lloraba?*
10. *Le gusta cantar en la torre.*
11. *Le gustaba cantar en el baño.*
12. *A la reina le gustaba cantar en el baño.*
13. *Al rey le gusta cantar en la torre.*
14. *¿Por qué canta? Porque le gusta cantar.*

Activity 27: Multiple-Choice Frames

A. *un punto y una línea vertical (a); un punto y una línea horizontal (c); un punto y una línea diagonal (d)*

B. *dos líneas diagonales (b); dos líneas horizontales (d); una línea vertical y una diagonal (a)*

C. *dos líneas largas y horizontales y una línea corta horizontal (a); cuatro líneas cortas diagonales y una línea vertical (d); cuatro líneas cortas diagonales y una línea horizontal (b)*

D. *un número grande, una línea vertical, y un número pequeño (d); un número grande, una línea horizontal, y un número pequeño (a)*

E. *un punto delante de una línea (c); un número delante de un punto (a); un punto delante de un número (d)*

F. *una línea horizontal delante de una línea diagonal (b); una línea vertical delante de una línea diagonal (c); una línea diagonal delante de una línea vertical (a)*

G. *el número doce delante de un punto (a); el número dos delante de una línea horizontal (d); el número dos delante de una línea diagonal (c)*

H. *un número pequeño delante de un punto grande (d); un número pequeño delante de un número grande (b); un número grande delante de un número pequeño (a)*

I. *un punto pequeño delante de un punto grande (a); un punto grande delante de un punto pequeño (b); un número pequeño delante de un punto pequeño (d)*

J. *una línea horizontal y una línea diagonal delante de un número grande (c); una línea horizontal y una línea diagonal delante de un número pequeño (d); una línea vertical delante de una línea diagonal delante de un punto grande (b)*

Activity 27: Listen and Draw

Activity 27: Read For Meaning

1. This is not a horizontal line, it's diagonal.

2. These are two vertical lines and two horizontal lines.

3. This is the number six in front of the long thick line.

4. And this is the number seven in front of the big dot.

5. This is a vertical line in front of a thick line and a small dot.

6. This is a vertical line and a diagonal line in front of a large (big) letter, the letter M.

7. This is a small dot and a big dot in front of a long and thin line.

Activity 34: Sample Beginning of a Mini-Story Plot

1. There are three people: a trombonist, a violinist, and a drummer.

2. The trombonist loves the violinist.

3. But the violinist doesn't love the trombonist.

4. She hates…detests the trombonist.

5. The violinist loves the drummer.

6. But the drummer doesn't love the violinist.

7. He loves an actress.

8. The drummer sings and dances with the actress.

9. He sends letters to the actress, and the actress sends letters to the drummer.

10. One day the trombonist sends a letter to the violinist.

11. The violinist receives the trombonist's letter.

12. The violinist attacks the trombonist.

Activity 35: Rapid Oral Translation Exercise 1

1. *Rolando era (un) príncipe y es (un) príncipe.*

2. *Ricardo no era (un) príncipe y no es (un) príncipe.*

3. *José es (un) amigo de Juanita, que es una princesa.*

4. *La amiga de Josefina no es una princesa.*

5. *El amigo de Pedro era un príncipe, sí.*

6. *Él era de España, y era amigo de su madre de Ud. María también, ¿no?*

7. *¿Quién es Juanita? Es la princesa que era amiga de José.*

8. *Usted era amigo de José, ¿no? Sí, yo era amigo del príncipe y de la princesa, pero no era amigo de Josefina.*

9. *¿Ella era enemiga? Sí, era.*

10. *Sí, somos enemigos. Ella era mi enemiga y todavía es mi enemiga.*

Activity 35: Rapid Oral Translation Exercise 2

1. *¿Dónde está el príncipe? ¿De dónde es?*

2. *¿Sabe Ud. si él es de España?*

3. *¿Sabe Ud. si él está en casa ahora?*

4. *¿Está el señor en la casa?*

5. *¿Estaba el señor en la casa?*

6. *¿Está el señor en casa?*

7. *¿Estaba el señor en casa?*

8. *¿Dónde está la señora? ¿Está en el jardín?*

9. *¿Dónde estaba la señora? ¿Estaba en el hospital?*

10. *La señorita que estaba aquí no es mi amiga.*

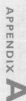

APPENDIX A

11. *Roberto es mi amigo, pero él no estaba aquí.*

12. *¿Quién estaba aquí y quién estaba allá?*

13. *¿Quién era su amigo y quién era su enemigo?*

Activity 39: Translation Exercise

1. *Comer es vivir.*

2. *Es imposible dormir allá.*

3. *Es imposible trabajar allá sin estar contento.*

4. *Comer mucho para dormir bien es estúpido.*

5. *Es imposible dormir sin reposar, pero es posible reposar sin dormir.*

6. *Es posible trabajar sin reposar, pero es estúpido.*

Activity 42: Self Quiz Part 1

1. E
2. B
3. N
4. F
5. I
6. C
7. D
8. J
9. A
10. K
11. M
12. L
13. O
14. F
15. N
16. C
17. E
18. A
19. J
20. B
21. L
22. D
23. M

Activity 46: Matching

1. E
2. B
3. N
4. F
5. I
6. C
7. D
8. J
9. A
10. K
11. M
12. L
13. O
14. F
15. N
16. C
17. E
18. A
19. J
20. B
21. L
22. D
23. M
24. I

Activity 46: Error Detection

1. Correct
2. Correct
3. Correct
4. Incorrect
5. Incorrect
6. Incorrect
7. Incorrect
8. Incorrect
9. Correct
10. Incorrect

11. Correct

12. Correct

13. Correct

14. Correct

15. Incorrect

16. Correct

17. Correct

18. Correct

19. Incorrect

20. Incorrect

21. Correct

22. Incorrect

23. Incorrect

24. Incorrect

25. Correct

26. Incorrect

27. Correct

Activity 46: Reading Comprehension

1. A

2. A

3. B

4. B

5. A

6. A

7. B

8. B

9. A

10. A

11. B

12. C

Activity 47: Multiple-Choice Frames

A. *una línea diagonal entre dos puntos* (a); *un número entre dos líneas diagonales* (d); *un punto entre dos líneas verticales* (b)

B. *una flecha negra apuntando hacia la izquierda* (b); *una flecha negra y una flecha blanca apuntando hacia la*

derecha (c); *una flecha blanca apuntando hacia la derecha* (a)

C. *dos flechas negras apuntando hacia la izquierda* (b); *dos flechas negras apuntando hacia la derecha* (c); *dos flechas negras apuntando hacia arriba* (d)

D. *un punto arriba de una línea horizontal* (a); *una línea horizontal debajo de un punto* (a); *una línea vertical debajo de un punto* (b)

E. *tres puntos entre dos líneas diagonales* (d); *tres puntos entre dos líneas verticales* (c); *tres puntos arriba de una línea horizontal* (b)

Activity 47: Listen and Draw

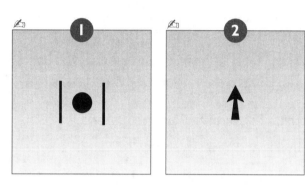

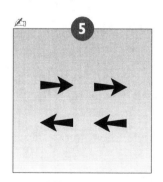

Activity 47: Read for Meaning

1. Two arrows: one pointing up and the other down.

2. A white arrow pointing toward a small point and a black arrow pointing to a large point.

3. A long horizontal line next to a short vertical line.

4. Two lines: A long, thick, horizontal line; and a short, thin, vertical line.

5. The horizontal line is next to the vertical line.

6. A number and a small point between two diagonal lines.

7. The number five and two large points between two vertical lines.

8. A white arrow pointing toward the right and a black arrow pointing toward the left.

9. The point is to the right side of the vertical line.

10. Two points are to the left side of the diagonal line.

Activity 58: Sample Plot

1. In this story there's a palace.

2. The king is in the palace.

3. The king has a treasure.

4. He has jewels.

5. He adores his jewels.

6. It's a secret where he keeps the jewels.

7. But the secretary knows the secret.

8. And the duke also knows where the king keeps the jewels.

9. In this story there's also a thief.

10. The thief also is in the palace.

11. He doesn't know where the jewels are.

12. But he thinks they are in the bathroom.

13. He enters the bathroom.

14. He searches and searches, but he finds nothing. He doesn't find the jewels.

15. He thinks that the jewels are in the tower.

16. He climbs up the tower.

17. He searches and searches, but doesn't find the jewels. He doesn't find anything.

18. He thinks that the jewels are in the chamber of the queen.

19. He enters the queen's chamber.

20. He searches and searches, and finally finds the jewels.

Activity 59: Self Quiz

Pictograph	English
	sit down
	stand up
	eat
	drink
	read
	write
	talk
	sing
	walk
	run

Activity 59: Multiple-Choice Frames

1. *¡Coma!* (a)

2. *¡Beba!* (b); *¡Coma!* (a); *¡Coma y beba!* (c)

3. *¡Beba y coma!* (a); *¡Coma y beba!* (b); *¡Siéntese!* (d)

4. *¡Siéntese y coma!* (d); *¡Siéntese y beba!* (b); *¡Póngase de pie!* (a)

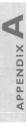

5. *¡Póngase de pie y beba!* (b); *¡Póngase de pie y siéntese!* (a); *¡Siéntese y póngase de pie!* (c)

6. *¡Lea!* (d); *¡Siéntese y lea!* (a); *¡Póngase de pie y lea!* (c)

7. *¡Beba y lea!* (c); *¡Siéntese y lea!* (b); *¡Póngase de pie y lea!* (a)

8. *¡Escriba!* (c); *¡Escriba y lea!* (a); *¡Coma y escriba!* (d)

9. *¡Lea y escriba!* (a); *¡Coma y beba!* (b); *¡Póngase de pie y escriba!* (c)

10. *¡Hable!* (b); *¡Siéntese y hable!* (c); *¡Beba y hable!* (a)

11. *¡Cante!* (a); *¡Cante y hable!* (c); *¡Póngase de pie y cante!* (d)

12. *¡Coma y hable!* (b); *¡Cante y hable!* (d); *¡Lea y escriba!* (a)

13. *¡Camine!* (c); *¡Póngase de pie y camine!* (a); *¡Camine y hable!* (d)

14. *¡Corra!* (b); *¡Camine y corra!* (a); *¡Póngase de pie y corra!* (d)

15. *¡Lea y escriba!* (a); *¡Camine y corra!* (b); *¡Cante y hable!* (d)

Activity 59: Listen and Anticipate the Response

1. *¿Qué hace este hombre? El come.*

2. *¿Qué hace esta mujer? Ella bebe.*

3. *¿Qué hacen estas personas? Ellos cantan.*

4. *¿Qué hacen estas personas? Ellos hablan. Los tres hablan.*

5. *¿Qué hacen estas personas? Uno se pone de pie, el otro se sienta.*

6. *¿Qué hacen estas personas? Una corre, y el otro camina.*

7. *¿Qué hacen estas personas? Dos escriben y dos leen.*

8. *¿Qué hace esta mujer? Ella come, bebe y canta.*

9. *¿Qué hacen estas personas? Una se pone de pie y corre, la otra se sienta y lee.*

10. *¿Qué hacen estas personas? Ellos comen, los dos comen.*

Activity 63: Multiple-Choice Frames

A. *un triángulo* (c); *un cuadrado* (d); *una estrella* (b)

B. *un triángulo al lado de un cuadrado* (a); *un triángulo arriba de un cuadrado* (d); *un triángulo debajo de un cuadrado* (c)

C. *un círculo al lado de otro círculo* (c); *un círculo arriba de otro círculo* (b); *un triángulo al lado de otro triángulo* (d)

D. *un cuadrado al lado de otro* (c); *dos figuras pequeñas* (b); *un círculo y una figura pequeña* (a)

E. *un cuadrado y una cruz arriba de una línea* (a); *una cruz y un triángulo debajo de una línea* (d); *una cruz y un triángulo arriba de una línea* (b)

Activity 63: Listen and Draw

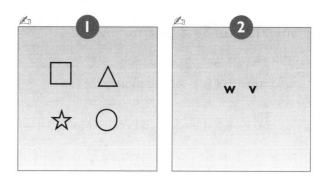

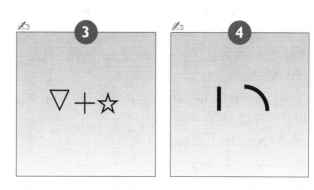

Activity 63: Read for Meaning

1. Which letter is this? Is it the letter D or the letter O? It's a D.

2. What type of figure is this? Is it a circle or a square?

3. All these triangles point up and all these arrows point down.

4. These two figures are between two vertical lines.

5. What type of figure precedes the letter F?

6. What type of figure follows the letter F?

7. Which letter follows the big triangle, and which precede the big circle?

8. Doesn't the letter B follow the big triangle?

Activity 71: Reading Activity

1. In this picture you can see a park.

2. And in the park you can see some tables and benches.

3. Also in the park there are soldiers from two countries.

4. This is a North American soldier.

5. The others are from Cuba.

6. These are the Cuban soldiers.

7. The park is situated in a town in a country of Central America.

8. What were the Cubans doing in the park, working or relaxing?

9. And what were the Yankees doing?

10. Working or playing?

11. Who is listening to music on the radio, the Yankees or the Cubans?

Activity 71: Comprehension Questions

	English	Spanish
1.	In Central America.	En Centro América.
2.	It's not known.	No se sabe.
3.	Cuban soldiers.	Soldados cubanos.
4.	They are playing baseball.	Están jugando béisbol.
5.	They are eating lunch and listening to music.	Están comiendo almuerzo y escuchando música.
6.	No, they are eating fruit and sandwiches.	No, están comiendo frutas y sandwiches.
7.	one of the Cubans.	uno de los cubanos.
8.	the Cuban	el cubano
9.	to the North Americans	a los norteamericanos.

Activity 81: Practice A

1. saber
2. conocer
3. saber
4. saber
5. conocer
6. conocer
7. saber
8. saber
9. conocer
10. saber

Activity 82: Sample Mini-Story Plot

There is a parrot. It is the parrot of the princess. The parrot always tells the truth. The princess never tells the truth. The parrot says that the king is coming. The princess says that the king isn't coming. In fact, the king is coming. He is coming with the queen. The princess hates the parrot because the parrot always tells the truth. The princess is in the kitchen with the cook. The cook is preparing tomato soup to give to the parrot. The secret agent 007 sees that the princess puts something in the soup. The princess gives a little of the soup to the parrot. Do you think the parrot drinks the soup? Do you think agent 007 comes?

Section Puzzle Answers

Section 1.1.3 Puzzle

1. cua**t**ro
2. pe**r**o
3. c**o**mpra
4. e no**t**ado
5. e**s**toy
6. bi**e**n
7. **s**istema

Section 1.2.3 Puzzle

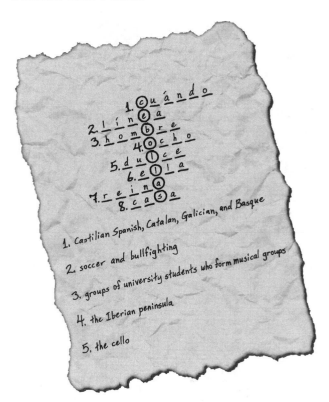

1. **c**uándo
2. lín**e**a
3. hom**b**re
4. **o**cho
5. du**l**ce
6. be**l**la
7. rein**a**
8. ca**s**a

1. Castilian Spanish, Catalan, Galician, and Basque
2. soccer and bullfighting
3. groups of university students who form musical groups
4. the Iberian peninsula
5. the cello

Section 1.3.3 Puzzle

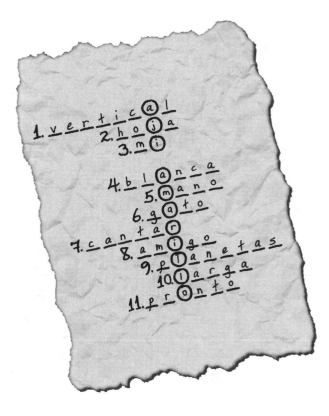

1. vertic**a**l
2. ho**j**a
3. m**i**
4. bl**a**nca
5. **m**ano
6. g**a**to
7. canta**r**
8. am**i**go
9. p**l**anetas
10. **l**arga
11. p**r**onto

Section 2.1.2 Puzzle

1. poco
2. siesta
3. más
4. también
5. mejor
6. entre
7. mentiras
8. Roma
9. está
10. llaves
11. puente
12. naranja
13. sábado
14. cerca
15. silla

y

16. cuál
17. viajar
18. leer
19. famoso
20. nombre
21. doscientos
22. recordaré
23. mucho

Section 2.2.2 Puzzle

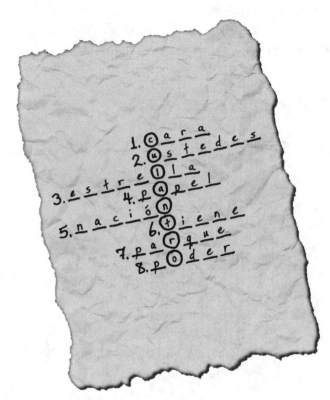

1. cara
2. ustedes
3. estrella
4. papel
5. nación
6. tiene
7. parque
8. poder

Section 2.2.1 Puzzle

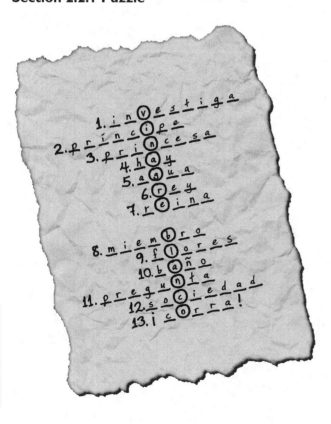

1. investiga
2. príncipe
3. princesa
4. hay
5. agua
6. rey
7. reina

8. miembro
9. flores
10. baño
11. pregunta
12. sociedad
13. ¡corra!

Section 2.3.1 Puzzle

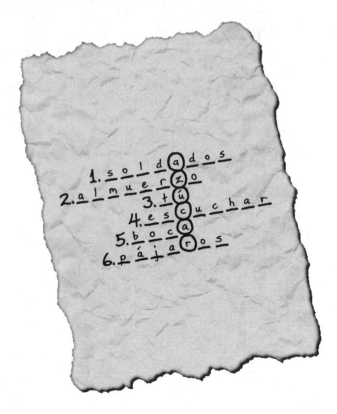

1. soldados
2. almuerzo
3. tú
4. escuchar
5. boca
6. pájaros

Section 2.3.2 Puzzle

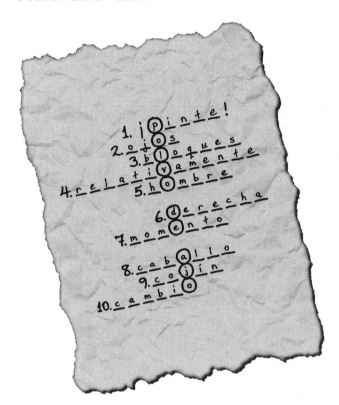

1. ¡**p**inte!
2. o**j**os
3. b**l**oques
4. relati**v**amente
5. h**o**mbre
6. **d**erecha
7. mom**e**nto
8. cab**a**llo
9. co**j**ín
10. camb**i**o

Appendix B
Scope and Sequence

Semester I Module I

Includes the following grammar and content:

Grammar	Content
Forming yes/no questions	Basic phrases
Conjunctions	Basic greetings
Articles	Simple questions
A few prepositions	Please & thank you
Spanish punctuation	Languages (*inglés, español, francés*)
Forming questions with interrogative words	Body parts
Forming simple negative sentences	Numbers 1-6, 10, 100, and 1000
Word breaks	Storytelling vocabulary
Declarative sentence construction	Spanish pronunciation guide
Basic subject-verb agreement	Select reading in Spanish
Basic noun-adjective agreement	Interrogative words
Third-person present tense verbs	Ditties
Forming plurals	Reading comprehension practice
Basic comparisons	Spanish forms of this/that
Some pronouns	Sentence translation activities
Simple adjectives	Sentence creation activity
Some first-person verbs	Pictographs
	DiglotWeave™ stories
	Culture information
	Self quizzes

Grammar *(cont.)*	Content
	Section quizzes
	Module test

Semester I Module 2

Includes previous module plus the following:

Grammar	Content
Additional declarative sentence structures	Location-related vocabulary
Uses of *ser*	Review of interrogative words
Exclamations	Geometry-related vocabulary
Expressing simple arithmetic in Spanish	Additional adjectives
Simple imperative verb forms	Listening comprehension activities
Additional third-person verbs	Additional translation activities
Third-person present tense uses of *gustar*	Additional pictographs
Additional prepositions	Reading and writing activities
Infinitive form verbs	Oral translation exercises
"likes to –"	The numbers 0, 7-9, and 11-19
Masculine and feminine words	Some colors
Gender agreement with articles	Classroom-related vocabulary
Past tense third person verbs	Shopping-related vocabulary
	Additional pictographs
	Additional culture information
	Self quizzes
	Section quizzes
	Module test

Semester I Module 3

Includes previous two modules plus the following:

Grammar	Content
Plural nouns, verbs, adjectives, and articles	Additional geometry-related vocabulary
Additional prepositions	Additional listening activities

Grammar *(cont.)*	Content
Additional questions	Additional reading activities
Some second-person informal verbs	Minidialogues
"here is—"	Leave-takings
Additional exclamations	Additional body parts
Different meanings and uses of *gustar*	Additional colors
Present perfect verb forms	Additional classroom-related vocabulary
Third person past tense of *ser*	Additional pictographs
"I believe—"	Additional adjectives
Additional imperative form verbs	Review activities
Additional adjectives	Sentence generation activities
"there is—" (more common phrase)	Storytelling activities
Additional infinitive form verbs	Additional translation activities
"one must—"	Explanations of the Spanish alphabet in Spanish
Spelling rules for cognate rules	Geography-related vocabulary
Additional conjunctions	Additional translation activities
"going to—"	Music-related vocabulary
	Additional culture information
	Self quizzes
	Section quizzes
	Module test

Semester 2 Module I

Includes previous semester plus the following:

Grammar	Content
First-person past tense verbs	Additional DiglotWeave™ stories
Use of *lo, la, los,* and *las* with conjugated verbs	Vocabulary practice
Use of *lo, la, los,* and *las* with infinitive verbs	Reading comprehension activities
Additional prepositions	Additional geometry-related vocabulary
Additional present tense and present perfect tense verbs	Additional location-related vocabulary

Grammar *(cont.)*	Content
Additional imperative form verbs	Listening comprehension activities
Future tense verbs	Reading comprehension activities
	Additional geography-related vocabulary
	Additional ditties
	Additional classroom-related vocabulary
	Verb practice chart
	Cognate words
	The numbers 100-900
	Telling a joke in Spanish
	Additional culture information
	Self quizzes
	Section quizzes
	Module test

Semester 2 Module 2

Includes previous module plus the following:

Grammar	Content
Past and present forms of *ser*	Pictographs practice
Hay and *había/habían*	Additional translation activities
Additional third-person verbs	Additional reading comprehension activities
Additional imperative form verbs	Additional sentence generation activities
Additional comparisons	Additional storytelling activities
Additional questions	Additional storytelling vocabulary
Conjugation rules for present tense –ar, -er, and –ir verbs	Additional pictographs
Present tense conjugations of *ser*	Multiple choice activities
Additional imperative form verbs	Additional listening comprehension activities

Grammar (cont.)	Content
Explanations of simple present, future, conditional, imperfective, preterite, familiar singular imperative, formal singular imperative, plural imperative, infinitive, present participle, past participle, present perfect, past perfect, future perfect, and conditional perfect verb forms	Additional geometry-related vocabulary
Additional infinitive form verbs	Additional classroom-related vocabulary
Expression possession	Familiar cognate words
	Animal-related vocabulary
	Additional DiglotWeave™ stories
	Additional geography-related vocabulary
	Additional culture information
	Self quizzes
	Section quizzes
	Module test

Semester 2 Module 3

Includes previous two modules plus the following:

Grammar	Content
Applications of previously explained verb forms	Additional DiglotWeave™ stories
Identification of previously explained verb forms	Additional storytelling activities
Additional comparisons	Additional reading activities
Additional imperative form verbs	Additional poems/ditties
Expressions using "can –"	Additional pictographs
Explanations of irregular verbs	Action activities
Additional questions	Question and answer activities
Additional pronouns	Additional verb practice activities
Saber vs. conocer	Additional classroom-related vocabulary
"want to—"	Additional geometry-related vocabulary
	Conversation activities
	Verb practice activities

Grammar (cont.)	Content
	Additional review activities
	Prepositions practice
	Additional vocabulary
	Questions and answers
	Additional ways of expressing location
	Additional culture information
	Self quizzes
	Section quizzes
	Module test

Semester I Objectives

Activity 1
→ Use words and phrases for introductions and greetings.

Activity 2
→ Use and say numbers 1-6.
→ Use geometrical shapes.

Activity 3
→ Use and say numbers 10, 100, and 1000.
→ Use geometrical shapes.

Activity 4
→ Learn what a DiglotWeave™ is and how it works.

Activity 5
→ Read a DiglotWeave™ story.

Activity 6
→ Pronounce Spanish vowels correctly.

Activity 7
→ Recognize words that are familiar to you as you read.

Activity 8
→ Use words and phrases to find out information.

Activity 9
→ Learn vocabulary through rhythm and cadence.

Activity 10
→ Identify word breaks in Spanish.

Activity 11
→ Use articles, plurals, and noun/adjective agreement with gender.

Activity 12
→ String together your own narratives.

Activity 13
→ Comprehend, understand, and act on instructions.

Activity 14
→ Develop speed and fluency in spontaneous speech.

Activity 15
→ Comprehend and understand the main idea when listening to a story or conversation.
→ Increase speaking skill.

Activity 16
→ Test your knowledge of basic expressions.

Activity 17
→ Increase usage of adjectives with nouns.

Activity 18
→ Think and communicate in Spanish using targeted vocabulary.

Activity 19
→ Recognize sentence patterns and build comprehension skills.
→ Increase fluency.

Activity 20
→ Learn numbers 0, 7-19 and how to use them alone, with hundreds, and with thousands.
→ Perform simple math functions in Spanish.

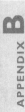

Activity 21
➜ Say nouns and adjectives in various types of sentences.

Activity 22
➜ String together your own narratives.

Activity 23
➜ Use pictographs to reinforce vocabulary and listening skills.

Activity 24
➜ Use identification, description, questions and answers, likes and dislikes, and tensing.

Activity 25
➜ Enhance skill with masculine and feminine nouns with various forms of articles.
➜ Use singular and plural article agreement.
➜ Use infinitive verbs.
➜ Express likes.
➜ Use passive voice.
➜ Understand Spanish translations.

Activity 26
➜ Turn statements into questions.

Activity 27
➜ Use geometrical shapes.

Activity 28
➜ Increase listening comprehension.
➜ Learn mini dialogues quickly.

Activity 29
➜ Read and comprehend the meaning of a text.
➜ Add body parts to your vocabulary base.

Activity 30
➜ String together narratives.

Activity 31
➜ Listen to and read a story.

Activity 32
➜ Use pictographs to reinforce vocabulary and listening skills.

Activity 33
➜ Recognize sentence patterns and structures.

Activity 34
➜ Re-tell stories using visuals.
➜ Use pictographs to master words and dialogues.

Activity 35
➜ Master new vocabulary and sentence patterns and increase translation skills.

Activity 36
➜ Master new vocabulary and sentence patterns and increase translation skills.

Activity 37
➜ Use geography vocabulary.

Activity 38
➜ Create your own sentences.
➜ Correct errors in writing.

Activity 39
➜ Express needs and opinions.

Activity 40
➜ Ask questions and understand answers.

Activity 41
➜ Increase speaking fluency.

Activity 42
➜ Use correct verb tenses.

Semester 2 Objectives

Activity 43
➜ Increase reading comprehension.

Activity 44
➜ Understand new vocabulary from context.

Activity 45
➜ Use pronouns in correct word order with infinitive verbs.

Activity 46
➜ Give and understand directions.

Activity 47
➜ Read for meaning.

Activity 48
➜ Learn new vocabulary from a story and then re-tell it.

Activity 49
➜ Increase vocabulary in geography.

Activity 50
➜ Retain vocabulary through songs and rhythm.

Activity 51
➜ Understand instructional order.
➜ Understand commands.
➜ Use past, present, and future tense.

Activity 52
→ Understand spelling cognates.

Activity 53
→ Say numbers 100-900 using plural form.

Activity 54
→ Understand a joke in Spanish.

Activity 55
→ Use demonstrative pronouns alone and with various tenses.

Activity 56
→ Use the various forms of the "to be" verbs.

Activity 57
→ Recognize how much you understand in Spanish.
→ Use explanations.

Activity 58
→ Create your own story using perception and plots.

Activity 59
→ Learn and retain action verbs.
→ Listen to a question and anticipate the correct response.

Activity 60
→ Understand the main points of a story.

Activity 61
→ Ask simple questions and understand the answer.

Activity 62
→ Use various verb conjugations.

Activity 63
→ Problem solve with geometrical shapes.

Activity 64
→ Expand listening and reading comprehension.

Activity 65
→ Build fluency using imperatives.
→ Use pronouns as objects in a sentence.

Activity 66
→ Improve spelling.

Activity 67
→ Understand a conversation without pictographs.

Activity 68
→ Read a DiglotWeave™ and comprehend the information.

Activity 69
→ Increase verb structures.

Activity 70
→ Understand a Spanish geography lesson and master the vocabulary related to Europe.

Activity 71
→ Comprehend a Spanish story and re-tell it in your own words.
→ Read and answer questions in Spanish.

Activity 72
→ Learn new vocabulary through Spanish poems and jingles.

Activity 73
→ Learn new vocabulary through Spanish poems and jingles.

Activity 74
→ Learn new action verbs.
→ Act out what you've read.
→ Compose new sentences orally and in writing.

Activity 75
→ Compare and contrast different objects.

Activity 76
→ Comprehend new vocabulary in context.

Activity 77
→ Understand irregular verbs.

Activity 78
→ Expand listening and reading comprehension.

Activity 79
→ Use weights and measurements.

Activity 80
→ Use a verb phrase as a description.

Activity 81
→ Understand the different nuances between *saber* and *conocer.*

Activity 82
→ Create your own mini-story.

Activity 83
→ Use placement terms.

Activity 84
→ Build fluency in past tense.

Activity 85
→ Ask and answer useful questions.

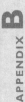

Appendix C
Index of Marginalia

Introduction

Culture facts and other interesting information can be found in the margins throughout the course. While not part of your course curriculum, these marginalia provide a fun and educational view into the many exciting facets of Spanish and Spanish-speaking countries. Sign up for the Power-Glide Multilingual E-*correo* newsletter for more interesting facts and explorations at <http://www.power-glide.com/newsletter>.

Index

Hispanic Culture Overview, page 14.

Facts and Figures on Spanish Speakers of the World, page 17.

Study Spanish: Millions of Spanish Speakers, page 18.

Study Spanish: Traveling Throughout the World, page 23.

Study Spanish: A People Rich in Culture and Tradition, page 26.

Study Spanish: Increase Your Opportunities, page 29.

Spanish Names, page 31.

Spanish Girls' Names, page 38.

Spanish Boys' Names, page 39.

Spanish Family Names: *Los Apellidos,* page 40.

Origins of Spanish, page 42.

Spanish-Speaking Families, page 43.

Hispanic Concepts of Time, page 47.

La Quinceañera, page 50.

Personal Space in Hispanic Cultures, page 51.

The *Abrazo* as a Greeting, page 65.

Mediodía, page 67.

Work, page 68.

Industries in Hispanic Countries, page 72.

Meals, page 75.

Family, page 76.

Spain Culture Overview, page 79.

Facts and Figures on Spain, page 95.

Traditions in Spain, page 98.

El Flamenco, page 116.

La Semana Santa, page 121.

La Navidad, page 126.

Día de los Reyes, page 127.

The Iberian Peninsula, page 137.

Northern Spain, page 142.

Central Spain, page 147.

Southern Spain, page 153.

Mexico Culture Overview, page 171.

Facts and Figures on Mexico, page 178.

Our Southern Neighbor, page 180.

Mexico's Other Neighbors, page 183.

Mexico's Mountains, Forests, and Bodies of Water, page 187.

The Volcanoes of Mexico, page 194.

Mexico's Plateau Region, page 199.

The People and Culture of Mexico, page 202.

Mexican Families, page 212.

Meals in Mexico, page 217.

Mexican Hospitality, page 219.

Mexican Holidays, page 227.

Details on Five Popular Holidays, page 231.

Mexico's Two Independence Days, page 235.

Guatemala Culture Overview, page 237.

Facts and Figures on Guatemala, page 241.

Argentina Culture Overview, page 262.

Facts and Figures on Argentina, page 269.

Greetings in Argentina, page 272.

Argentine Spanish, page 283.

Family Life in Argentina, page 291.

Argentina's Cultural Background, page 295.

Eating in Argentina, page 298.

Argentina's Holidays, page 307.

El Salvador Culture Overview, page 321.

Facts and Figures on El Salvador, page 325.

Rebuilding El Salvador, page 329.

Accident-Prone San Salvador, page 335.

A Brief History of El Salvador, page 343.

Poetry and Song in El Salvador, page 350.

Geography of El Salvador, page 353.

Ecuador Culture Overview, page 358.

Facts and Figures on Ecuador, page 361.

Ecuador's Population, page 364.

Foods of Ecuador, page 365.

Sites to See in Quito, page 369.

Colombia Culture Overview, page 388.

Facts and Figures on Colombia, page 396.

Colombian Arts, page 405.

Colombian Food, page 418.

Troubles in Colombia, page 427.

Colombian Geography, page 431.

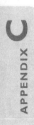

APPENDIX **C**

Power-Glide Spanish Ultimate Year 1 Grading Sheet

Module Test Answers

1.1	1.2	1.3	2.1	2.2	2.3
1. B	1. B	1. A	1. B	1. A	1. A
2. C	2. C	2. B	2. A	2. A	2. B
3. A	3. B	3. B	3. B	3. B	3. A
4. D	4. A	4. B	4. B	4. A	4. A
5. D	5. B	5. B	5. B	5. A	5. B
6. B	6. D	6. B	6. A	6. A	6. B
7. A	7. B	7. A	7. B	7. B	7. B
8. C	8. C	8. B	8. B	8. A	8. B
9. A	9. A	9. A	9. B	9. B	9. A
10. A	10. C	10. B	10. A	10. B	10. A
11. B	11. A	11. B	11. B	11. A	11. A
12. D	12. D	12. B	12. A	12. A	12. A
13. A	13. C	13. C	13. A	13. B	13. A
14. C	14. A	14. D	14. B	14. A	14. B
15. D	15. B	15. A	15. A	15. B	15. B
16. B	16. B	16. A	16. B	16. A	16. A
17. C	17. A	17. B	17. A	17. B	17. B
18. B	18. A	18. C	18. D	18. A	18. B
19. D	19. B	19. D	19. A	19. A	19. A
20. C	20. A	20. D	20. B	20. B	20. A
21. A	21. A	21. C	21. C	21. A	21. B
22. D	22. A	22. A	22. C	22. A	22. B
23. C	23. B	23. D	23. C	23. B	23. D
24. B	24. A	24. A	24. B	24. A	24. A
25. B	25. B	25. B	25. C	25. A	25. C

Power-Glide Spanish Ultimate Year 1 Grading Sheet

Section Quiz Answers

1.1.1	1.1.2	1.1.3	1.2.1	1.2.2	1.2.3	1.3.1	1.3.2	1.3.3	2.1.1	2.1.2	2.2.1	2.2.2	2.3.1	2.3.2	2.3.3
1. B	1. B	1. B	1. C	1. B	1. B	1. A	1. B	1. C	1. B	1. A	1. A	1. D	1. B	1. B	1. B
2. B	2. B	2. A	2. A	2. C	2. C	2. C	2. B	2. D	2. C	2. A	2. B	2. B	2. B	2. D	2. D
3. A	3. A	3. D	3. D	3. A	3. D	3. D	3. C	3. D	3. B	3. A	3. C	3. C	3. C	3. A	3. C
4. C	4. D	4. C	4. B	4. D	4. C	4. C	4. D	4. C	4. B	4. B	4. A	4. A	4. A	4. B	4. A
5. C	5. C	5. B	5. A	5. B	5. A	5. D	5. D	5. B	5. A	5. D	5. C	5. A	5. B	5. C	5. C
6. A	6. B	6. C	6. D	6. A	6. D	6. D	6. A	6. A	6. D	6. C	6. B	6. B	6. B	6. C	6. D
7. D	7. B	7. C	7. B	7. D	7. C	7. B	7. C	7. C	7. A	7. C	7. D	7. C	7. C	7. B	7. A
8. C	8. D	8. A	8. C	8. C	8. C	8. D	8. A	8. B	8. B	8. D	8. A	8. B	8. C	8. D	8. B
9. B	9. C	9. D	9. B	9. C	9. A	9. A	9. B	9. C	9. D	9. C	9. C	9. A	9. A	9. A	9. A
10. C	10. C	10. B	10. D	10. B	10. B	10. B	10. D	10. A	10. C	10. A	10. B	10. D	10. C	10. A	10. D
					11. C										11. B
					12. C										12. C
					13. D										13. D
					14. C										14. B
					15. A										15. A
					16. B										16. C
					17. D										17. A
					18. A										18. B
					19. B										19. D
					20. B										20. C
															21. B
															22. A
															23. D
															24. C
															25. B